Transatlantic Relations since 1945

Transatlantic Relations since 1945 offers a comprehensive account of transatlantic relations in the second half of the twentieth century (extending to the present day).

The transatlantic relationship has been the bedrock of international relations since the end of World War II. This new textbook focuses on the period since the defeat of Nazi Germany, when the multitude of links between the United States and Western Europe were created, extended and multiplied. Written in an accessible style, it emphasizes transatlantic interactions, avoiding the temptation to focus on either US 'domination' or European attempts to 'resist' an American effort to subjugate the old continent. That influence has travelled across the Atlantic in both directions is one of the starting points of this text.

Structured chronologically, the book is built around three key themes:

- Security: from the Cold War to the War on Terror
- Economics: integration and competition
- 'Soft power' and transatlantic relations.

This book will be of great interest to students of transatlantic relations, NATO, US Foreign Policy, Cold War history, European history and IR International history.

Jussi M. Hanhimäki is Professor of International History and Politics at The Graduate Institute of International Studies (GIIS), Geneva. He is author/co-author of six books and won the 2002 Bernath Prize from the Society for Historians of American Foreign Relations.

Benedikt Schoenborn is a Senior Research Fellow at the University of Tampere, Finland, and a former Fellow of the Norwegian Nobel Institute. He is the author of various articles on Western Europe in the Cold War and of the prize-winning book *La mésentente apprivoisée: De Gaulle et les Allemands*.

Barbara Zanchetta is a Researcher at the Finnish Institute of International Affairs in Helsinki, focusing on US foreign policy, transatlantic relations and 'out of area' issues.

Transatlantic Relations since 1945

An introduction

**Jussi M. Hanhimäki,
Benedikt Schoenborn and
Barbara Zanchetta**

Routledge
Taylor & Francis Group

LONDON AND NEW YORK

First published 2012
by Routledge
2 Park Square, Milton Park, Abingdon, Oxon OX14 4RN

Simultaneously published in the USA and Canada
by Routledge
711 Third Avenue, New York, NY 10017

Routledge is an imprint of the Taylor & Francis Group, an informa business

British Library Cataloguing in Publication Data
A catalogue record for this book is available from the British Library

Library of Congress Cataloging-in-Publication Data
Hanhimäki, Jussi M., 1965–
Transatlantic relations since 1945 : an introduction / Jussi M. Hanhimaki,
Barbara Zanchetta and Benedikt Schoenborn.
  p. cm.
  Includes bibliographical references and index.
  1. Europe--Foreign relations--United States--Textbooks. 2. United States--Foreign
  relations--Europe--Textbooks. 3. Europe--Foreign relations--1945---Textbooks.
  4. United States--Foreign relations--1945-1989--Textbooks. 5. United States--
  Foreign relations--1989---Textbooks. I. Zanchetta, Barbara, 1976- II. Schoenborn,
  Benedikt. III. Title.
  D1065.U5H26 2012   327.7304--dc23
  2011042694

ISBN13: 978-0-415-48697-2 (hbk)
ISBN13: 978-0-415-48698-9 (pbk)
ISBN13: 978-0-203-12139-9 (ebk)

Typeset in Times New Roman
by Bookcraft Ltd, Stroud, Gloucestershire

Contents

Figures, tables and boxes

Figures

Tables

Boxes

Notes on authors

Jussi M. Hanhimäki is Professor of International History at The Graduate Institute of International and Development Studies in Geneva, Switzerland, and Finland Distinguished Professor (Academy of Finland). His publications include *The Handbook of Transatlantic Security* (2010), *The United Nations: A Very Short Introduction* (2008) and *The Flawed Architect: Henry Kissinger and American Foreign Policy* (2004).

Benedikt Schoenborn is a Senior Research Fellow at the University of Tampere, Finland, and a former Fellow of the Norwegian Nobel Institute. He is the author of various articles on Western Europe in the Cold War and of the prize-winning book *La mésentente apprivoisée: De Gaulle et les Allemands* (2007). He is currently preparing a monograph on Willy Brandt and the German Question.

Barbara Zanchetta is a Researcher at the Finnish Institute of International Affairs in Helsinki. She has published widely on US foreign policy, transatlantic relations and 'out of area' issues. She is completing a book titled *From Dominance to Leadership: The Transformation of American Power in the 1970s*.

Acknowledgements

Although only one of the authors is Finnish, this work was conceived and mostly written in Finland. The idea for this book emerged when the three of us were collaborating on a research project entitled 'Conflict and Community: Transatlantic Relations in the "Long" Twentieth Century', hosted by Tampere University and funded by the Academy of Finland. We are grateful for the financial and institutional support of these institutions, as well as to the colleagues and staff at our other institutional 'homes': the Graduate Institute of International and Development Studies in Geneva, and the Finnish Institute of International Affairs in Helsinki. In particular, we would like to acknowledge the unfortunate students who endured our joint or individual teaching of transatlantic relations at the Graduate Institute and at the universities of Tampere and Helsinki. It is their curiosity that ultimately motivated us to complete this book alongside many other duties.

The History Department at Tampere University was, ultimately, the 'home' of this project. We are especially grateful for the opportunity to share our ideas in the many sessions of 'Ollin klubi', a series of seminars organized by our project. Moreover, we are thankful for the support in the organization of the international conference 'Conflict and Community: Transatlantic Relations during the Cold War', held in Tampere in May 2008, during which many of the issues covered in this book were heatedly debated among scholars. We would like to particularly acknowledge the many colleagues and friends who cheered us on, in one way or another, during our respective stays at 'Pinni B': Touko Berry, Pertti Haapala, Risto Heiskala, Marjatta Hietala, Miia Ijas, Christian Krötzl, Risto Kunnari, Sari Pasto, Katri Sieberg and Olli Vehviläinen (whose name our seminar respectfully borrowed). A special thanks to Virginia Mattila for help with editing several of the chapters.

Another international conference, organized at the Graduate Institute in Geneva in April 2009, also stimulated our thinking about the issues discussed in this book. Many of the papers presented during 'Transatlantic Security Issues from the Cold War to the 21st Century' – including those of the three authors of the present work – have since been published as chapters in *The Routledge Handbook of Transatlantic Security* (2010). None of it would have been possible without the generous support from the Pierre du Bois Foundation and its founder, Irina du Bois. Our warmest thanks to her and to Bernhard Blumenau at the Graduate Institute, who played a major role in organizing that conference with Jussi Hanhimäki.

We would also like to acknowledge the support of the Finnish Institute of International Affairs for the organization of various seminars and events on transatlantic relations. In particular, thanks to the former and current directors of the Institute – Raimo Väyrynen and Teija Tiilikainen – for embracing the idea that history does matter for a better understanding of current affairs. Thanks also to Matti Nojonen and Mika Aaltola for their unrelenting support. A special thank you to Juho Hynynen for helping us in the design of the cover.

At Routledge our greatest debt goes to Andrew Humphrys, who took this project under his wing and tolerated our many delays with more cheer than we deserved. We would also like to thank the rest of the Routledge production team, in particular Annabelle Harris, for their expert attention during the process that led to the publication of this work.

If we have unwittingly omitted mentioning someone please accept our collective apologies.

Last, we would like to acknowledge each other. In part because we were not working under the same 'roof', the completion of this book took longer than we had planned. Yet we seem to have found ways of tolerating each other's delays and idiosyncrasies with great humour. We can only hope that those using this book will find that our efforts were not completely in vain.

Abbreviations

ACE	Allied Command Europe
CDU	Christian Democratic Union (Germany)
CFSP	Common Foreign and Security Policy (of the European Union)
CIA	Central Intelligence Agency
CIS	Commonwealth of Independent States
COMECON	Council for Mutual Economic Assistance (orig. in Russian)
CPSU	Communist Party of the Soviet Union
CSCE	Conference on Security and Cooperation in Europe
DM	Deutschmark (German currency)
EC	European Communities
ECA	European Cooperation Administration
ECB	European Central Bank
ECSC	European Coal and Steel Community
ECU	European currency unit
EDC	European Defence Community
EEC	European Economic Community
EFTA	European Free Trade Association
EMS	European Monetary System
EMU	economic and monetary union
EP	European Parliament
ERP	European Recovery Program
ERW	enhanced radiation warhead ('neutron bomb')
ESDI	European Security and Defence Identity
ESDP	European Security and Defence Policy
EU	European Union
EURATOM	European Atomic Energy Community
FDI	foreign direct investment
FDP	Free Democratic Party (Germany)
FRG	Federal Republic of Germany
GATT	General Agreement on Tariffs and Trade
GDP	gross domestic product
GDR	German Democratic Republic (East Germany)
GWT	Global War on Terror
IAE	International Energy Agency
ICBM	inter-continental ballistic missile
ICC	International Criminal Court

IFOR	Implementation Force (Bosnia)
IMF	International Monetary Fund
INF	intermediate-range nuclear forces
IRBM	intermediate-range ballistic missile
ISAF	International Security Assistance Force (Afghanistan)
ISG	Iraq Study Group
JFK	John F. Kennedy
JHA	Justice and Home Affairs (of the European Union)
KFOR	Kosovo Force
KLA	Kosovo Liberation Army
MAD	mutually assured destruction
MLF	multi-lateral force
NACC	North Atlantic Cooperation Council
NAFTA	North American Free Trade Agreement
NATO	North Atlantic Treaty Organization
NSC	National Security Council (US)
NTA	New Transatlantic Agenda
OECD	Organisation for Economic Co-operation and Development
OPEC	Organization of Petroleum Exporting Countries
OSCE	Organization for Security and Co-operation in Europe
PfP	Partnership for Peace
PLO	Palestine Liberation Organization
SACEUR	Supreme Allied Commander Europe
SACLANT	Supreme Allied Commander Atlantic
SALT	Strategic Arms Limitation Talks
SDI	Strategic Defense Initiative
SEATO	South East Asia Treaty Organization
SHAPE	Supreme Headquarters Allied Powers Europe
START	Strategic Arms Reduction Talks
TEU	Treaty of European Union
UN	United Nations
UNCED	UN Conference on Environment and Development
UNFCCC	UN Framework Convention on Climate Change
UNMOVIC	UN Monitoring, Verification and Inspection Commission (Iraq)
UNSCOM	UN Special Commission (Iraq)
US	United States
USSR	Union of Soviet Socialist Republics
WEU	Western European Union
WMD	weapon of mass destruction
WTO	World Trade Organization

Introduction

The transatlantic relationship has been one of the central features of international relations since the end of World War II. Even before the formation of the North Atlantic Treaty Organization (NATO), the United States and major European countries (France and Great Britain in particular) formed a partnership in the shadow of the emerging East–West confrontation. Over the next four decades the transatlantic relationship deepened and formed an integral part of the international system. Since the early 1990s, the ties – military, economic, and cultural – developed in earlier years were expanded to include an ever-larger community of nations. In 1949, for example, NATO had 12 member states. Sixty years later this roster had more than doubled to 28. Judged on this basis alone, the transatlantic relationship has been a uniquely successful one since the end of World War II, complemented by the simultaneous success of European integration. While most other parts of the world have seen endless conflict and tremendous human suffering, Europe and North America appear to have experienced a 'Pax Transatlantica'.

Judged from political rhetoric and the writings of historians, political scientists and other commentators, however, the last six decades have seen but an endless series of transatlantic crises and conflicts. The evolution of NATO, the transfer of European colonies to independence, changing perceptions of the Soviet threat and the emergence of anti-American sentiment in Europe are among the issues that caused periods of 'unprecedented' transatlantic rows. At various times different observers declared these to be major breaking points in the transatlantic relationship. For example, in 2003 the American writer Robert Kagan tersely noted that 'it was time for Americans and Europeans to stop pretending that they share the same world view, or even occupy the same planet'.

However, despite the never-ending supply of confrontations and crises, the transatlantic relationship has endured, even blossomed. This textbook will provide an analysis of this apparently contradictory tale of a partnership that, while constantly in trouble, remains extraordinarily close. In essence, it will grapple with a basic question: which has been the more 'normal' (or commonplace) state of transatlantic relations since 1945 – tension or unity, conflict or community?

Although this book focuses on the period after World War II, the transatlantic relationship has deep roots in history. From the 'discovery' of America in 1492 through the various waves of migration and colonization in the centuries that followed, Europe and the Americas were linked together. The American Revolution in the late 18th century may have been directed against British colonial rule, but it was inspired by European ideas and supported by France. The subsequent expansion of the United States was intertwined with the imperial struggles of European powers; struggles that were eventually joined by the United States in the late

19th century. By that point American economic power had surpassed its former imperial masters. This newfound power was on display in the closing stages of World War I, when American troops, for the first time in history, engaged in a European war. At the end of the Great War, American economic power placed it in a powerful position to shape post-war Europe. To an extent, the US President Woodrow Wilson did exactly that, championing the ideas of national self-determination and collective security. Yet, in the 1920s and 1930s, America retreated from Europe: the United States did not join the League of Nations, while the onset of the Great Depression strengthened isolationist sentiments. In Europe, difficult economic conditions allowed extreme political movements to gather strength while democracies were under siege. Ultimately, Nazi Germany's attack on Poland in September 1939 plunged the continent into the most devastating war in human history.

World War II had two important consequences for the transatlantic relationship: it weakened Europeans and made the United States into a European power. After Germany overran Poland, Denmark, Norway, the Benelux countries and France in 1939–1940, American assistance helped keep the British afloat. The Anglo-American cooperation that emerged – what Winston Churchill dubbed the 'special relationship' – grew increasingly important even before the United States officially entered the war following the Japanese attack on Pearl Harbour in December 1941. But no matter how many stirring speeches Churchill gave, it was clear that Americans were the senior partner in that relationship. Indeed, it was the massive American materiel and human resources that ultimately turned the tables in the Allies' favour. By 1944 American, British and other forces landed in France. On 8 May 1945 Germany surrendered.

Unlike after World War I, Americans would stay deeply involved in European affairs after 1945. They did so in large part because of a shared belief on both sides of the Atlantic that the defeat of Germany had not produced a long-term solution for Western Europe's security. The Soviet Union – a partner in the war against Germany – quickly emerged as an aggressive nemesis. For the most part, Europeans, confronted with shattered national economies and an uncertain future, welcomed American economic aid and security guarantees. For reasons of economic profit, ideology and security, Americans ultimately opted to link their future closely with that of post-war (Western) Europe. Consequently, World War II was a significant watershed in the evolution of transatlantic relations.

The period since the defeat of Nazi Germany is the era when the multitude of links between United States and Western Europe were created, extended, multiplied and repeatedly challenged. Given the devastation of most of Europe during World War II and the spectre of potential Soviet expansionism, the United States exercised a particularly preponderant influence in reconstructing and reshaping post-war Western Europe. The Marshall Plan, NATO and other transatlantic initiatives also contributed to the emergence of European integration in its various forms. Yet, while post-war Europe may have been to some extent an 'American' creation, the second half of the Cold War saw a growing set of European challenges to United States predominance. Since the collapse of the Soviet Union, the deepening and widening of the European Union (EU) has in some ways reversed the situation that existed six decades ago. As early as the 1990s, the EU had a higher GDP (if not per capita income) than the US and boasted a larger population; due to the enlargements of 1995, 2004 and 2007 these gaps have continued to grow. Recognizing and documenting the impact of this development – a historical irony of sorts – seems crucial for our understanding of the post-war history of transatlantic relations, as well as for comprehending their present state and possible future direction.

Within this context it is important to note that the close transatlantic links created during the Cold War extended far beyond security policy or economic development. In some ways, more influential than anything else was the rapid spread of American popular and consumer culture to Western Europe. Not, of course, without resistance from certain quarters. 'We want neither Coca-Cola nor vodka', one French newspaper declared in 1949. In reality, however, most French people and other Europeans easily preferred Coca-Cola and the American way of life to the alternative.

The post-1945 era also spelled the end of a 'European' globe. As a result of rapid decolonization, by the 1970s the empires of France, Great Britain, the Netherlands and Belgium – as well as the remaining colonial possessions of the Spanish and the Portuguese – had all passed into history. Although overshadowed by the Cold War, decolonization clearly altered the respective global outlooks of Americans and Europeans alike. To simplify the situation in caricature form, the end result was that Europeans turned inwards while Americans pioneered globalization. Europeans took offence when former Secretary of State Henry Kissinger in 1973 pronounced that the old continent's interests were 'regional' (in contrast to America's 'global' ones). But in some ways his words still resonate almost 40 years later. They reflect the continued imbalance between America's military abilities, which allow the country to project its power abroad, and Europe's relative impotence when it comes down to exercising coercive power. This imbalance – whether one views it in a positive or negative light – is, of course, not a new development but a product and legacy of the Cold War.

The two major themes of this book reflect the preoccupations of most policymakers on both sides of the Atlantic since the end of World War II: security and economics. To these we should add a third: what is today referred to as 'soft power'. A brief explanation of each is in order.

In security terms, the American role in Europe during the second half of the twentieth century seems to have experienced a virtually linear course. Since the end of World War II, Americans retained a strong presence as the dominant member of NATO throughout the Cold War. Former enemies, such as Germany, became close allies, while even countries that often criticized the United States were reluctant to break completely with Washington. France's dramatic exit from NATO's integrated military structure in 1966 did not amount to a withdrawal. Nor has this pattern of security cooperation changed dramatically since the end of the Cold War. NATO expansion has, in fact, extended US influence, while the American role in such conflicts following the break-up of the former Yugoslavia illustrates the relative incapacity of Europeans when faced with the need to take decisive military action.

But security issues – cooperation and conflict – extend far beyond the immediate transatlantic region. The 2002–2003 crisis over the invasion of Iraq was but the latest in a string of debates between the United States and its allies across the Atlantic over events outside the actual geopolitical space of the transatlantic community. Indeed, such differences go back to the late 19th century, when the United States acquired its own empire after defeating Spain in a brief war and taking over the Philippines. Yet, from the very start, Americans distinguished between European colonialism and their own 'imperialism' by maintaining that the United States was, in fact, engaged in a 'democracy enlargement' exercise. This explanation has ever since accompanied American military engagements and occupations, be it in the Caribbean region before World War II, in Vietnam during the Cold War, or in Iraq and Afghanistan in the 21st century. Many Europeans have found the argument less than convincing, at best.

The economic side of transatlantic relations has been dominated by the evolution of European integration. By most measures, this has been a remarkable success story. During the Cold War, integration transformed one half of the continent from a region traditionally marred by constant strife and violent national ambitions into a community of nations that had effectively managed to eradicate war as a means to political ends. No doubt this development was made all the more remarkable by the successful integration of the western half of Germany into the European Economic Community (EEC) and the continued, if increasingly ambivalent, American support for European integration. Moreover, as events in the 1990s and the early 21st century have shown, European integration – even with nagging doubts about the direction of the EU – was to prosper even further after the collapse of the Cold War order in Europe.

From the perspective of transatlantic relations, however, European integration has been a complicated phenomenon. Early American support – traceable at least as far back as the Marshall Plan – became increasingly ambivalent as European economic recovery translated into the relative decline of the US dominance in transatlantic economic relations. Frequent trade and tariff disputes created tension across the Atlantic. European challenges – perhaps most prominently that spearheaded by France under Charles de Gaulle – raised concerns over the growing political independence of Europe, which was, in part, related to the increased collective economic power of the EEC (and later the EU). Today, almost six decades since the launching of the Marshall Plan, many Americans tend to consider the EU as a competitor rather than a partner. In the meantime, many Europeans tend to view the EU as a necessary counterbalance to American (or Anglo-American) dominance.

The third, least comprehensively covered, theme concerns the 'softer side' of transatlantic relations. The Americanization of Europe, and European resistance to it, has been a persistent theme in American studies, cultural history and Cold War scholarship. More recently, studies have also pointed to the (admittedly more limited) Europeanization of American culture. The title of one book (by Richard Pells) summed up the impact of the spread of American culture in its various forms on post-1945 Europe: *Not Like Us*. Indeed, since the 1990s it has become fashionable to talk about the globalization – rather than Americanization – of culture, and to emphasize that in today's world cultural trends do not simply flow from one nation or region to another. While acknowledging the impact of culture, this textbook will also make reference to the impact that popular perceptions have had on policymaking; how, for example, the positive or negative images of an American president (e.g. John F. Kennedy or George W. Bush) have had an impact on the transatlantic relationship. In short, our work is interested more in the role of so-called 'soft power' in transatlantic relations than in the appeal of, say, blue jeans or rock music (or their roles as cultural metaphors).

The book is divided chronologically into nine chapters.

Chapter 1 focuses on the origins of the transatlantic relationship. The common perception in Western Europe and the United States of the Soviet threat was the central element shaping the transatlantic partnership. While initially envisioning a disengagement from European affairs, America instead gradually undertook the leadership of the Western camp with such policies as the Truman doctrine and the Marshall Plan. Then, as the Cold War became a concrete reality, the North Atlantic Treaty permanently linked the security of the United States to that of Western Europe, therefore complementing the political and economic relationship with a military alliance. Chapter 2 assesses the evolution of the transatlantic relationship through the creation of institutional frameworks to sustain and guide its future development. The institutionalization of NATO and the first steps of

European integration – which led to the creation of the EEC – are central aspects of the chapter, which also assesses the shifting dynamics of the Cold War – with its stabilization in Europe and the emergence of the first 'out of area' issues. While Europe proceeded on the path of economic integration, for its security and defence it continued to predominantly rely on the United States. Chapter 3 analyses the emergence of the first tensions between the United States and Europe, a consequence of the sense of vulnerability caused by the Soviet launch of Sputnik. The impact of the process of decolonization, Kennedy's grand design for the Western Alliance and the repercussions of the Berlin crisis are also crucial focal points of the chapter.

Chapter 4 describes the emerging European challenges to American hegemony between 1961 and 1972. In the context of a booming Common Market in Western Europe, super-power entente on the European status quo and America's controversial war in Vietnam, French President Charles de Gaulle and West German Chancellor Willy Brandt introduced new levels of European initiative into the Atlantic framework. The premises of transat-lantic cooperation persisted throughout the years 1973–1983, albeit characterized by an increased distance between the Atlantic partners (Chapter 5). The Western Europeans and the Americans now prioritized their own concerns over Atlantic unity, and after 1979 disa-greed over strategies to confront the Soviet Union in the 'Second Cold War'. Chapter 5 ends with the final culmination of East–West tensions in late 1983. Chapter 6 covers the increas-ingly fast transformation of the Cold War antagonism, from Reagan's political turnaround in early 1984 and Gorbachev's subsequent accession to power in the Soviet Union until the fall of the Berlin Wall in November 1989. In the course of events, transatlantic differences over East–West and security issues lost much of their substance. Rather, the transformations of 1989 raised the question of whether the traditional Atlantic framework still made sense in the face of a fundamentally new situation.

The end of the Cold War and the collapse of the Soviet Union opened a new era in trans-atlantic relations. Yet, while questions were raised about the durability of NATO and the potential for increased transatlantic competition in the wake of the founding of the EU, the post-Cold War era actually resulted in a strengthened American role in Europe. As discussed in Chapter 7, the series of conflicts that raged in the former Yugoslavia in the first half of the 1990s confirmed the importance of the United States for Europe's security. After 1995, this role was further emphasized as the Clinton administration trumpeted 'enlargement' as a key theme of its foreign policy (Chapter 8). Within the context of transatlantic relations, the first NATO enlargement in 1999 essentially meant that the Cold War American–West European relationship was no more. Not only had former Soviet bloc countries become 'insiders', but transatlantic relations were under some strain from both the EU's drive for deeper and wider integration, as well as the persistent forces of economic globalization.

In surveying the evolution of transatlantic relations during the decade following 11 September 2001, Chapter 9 describes the tensions that grew from America's pursuit of the Global War on Terror (GWT), which resulted in a dramatic increase of transatlantic tension, particularly in the context of the Iraq War. But the chapter also evaluates the continued enlargement of NATO and the progress of European integration in the early 21st century. By 2011, despite gloomy predictions, the transatlantic relationship had been reinvigorated by several factors: the ascendancy of Barack Obama to the US presidency, the threat posed to the transatlantic economic space by the global financial crisis of 2007–2008, and the need to cooperate in the face of events collectively dubbed the 'Arab Spring' of 2011. Furthermore, with the rise of 'the rest' (China, India, Brazil and other rapidly developing economies), the United States and Europe find themselves, yet again, facing a common set of challenges.

It needs to be emphasized that this is not the 'full' story of the evolution of transatlantic relations since 1945. As the title of this book indicates, ours is but an 'introduction', aimed at those who wish to begin making sense of one of the bedrocks of contemporary international relations. To help readers identify certain key issues and points in the evolution of transatlantic relations, we have included a number of graphs, maps, tables and information boxes throughout the book. To assist those (hopefully numerous) readers who wish to explore certain aspects of the transatlantic relationship further, we have included suggestions for supplementary readings.

1 American commitment to Europe, 1945–1949

Europe in ruins

As the Soviet troops advanced into Germany at the end of World War II, the German dictator wrote – in what would become known as *The Testament of Adolf Hitler* – these famously prophetic words:

> With the defeat of the Reich and pending the emergence of the Asiatic, the African, and perhaps the South American nationalisms, there will remain in the world only two Great Powers capable of confronting each other – the United States and Soviet Russia. The laws of both history and geography will compel these two Powers to a trial of strength, either military or in the fields of economics and ideology. These same laws make it inevitable that both Powers should become enemies of Europe. And it is equally certain that both these Powers will sooner or later find it desirable to seek support of the sole surviving great nation in Europe, the German people.[1]

Europe's weakened condition after the war, and the collapse of the German economic and political power did, indeed, clear the way for the preponderant emergence on the world scene of the United States and the Soviet Union. It was the beginning of the bipolar era. Much of the history of the post-war years, in fact, revolves around the European attempt to recapture the centrality lost in 1945. The trial of strength between the United States and the Soviet Union predicted by the German dictator did ensue. However, the new superpowers would not become enemies *of* Europe, but rather enemies *in* Europe. And Germany was to be, at least initially, the battleground of the rivalry.

World War II had destroyed much of Europe. After the war, the assessments on the conditions of the European economy and possibilities of reconstruction were not encouraging. Most of the continent had been devastated by the military operations. In particular, the countries of Central and Eastern Europe – through which the front line had passed – had suffered enormous damages. Poland had lost almost 20 per cent of its population, Yugoslavia around 10 per cent, and the casualties for the Soviet Union are estimated to have been between 15 and 20 million. Germany lay in ruins. Not only its industrial capacity, but also its administrative and political structure had totally disintegrated after the collapse of the Nazi regime. And any future prospect was hindered by the military occupation and division of the country. While the Western European countries had suffered fewer human casualties, the material damages were catastrophic. France, weakened by the Nazi occupation and its internal divisions, suffered damages that were estimated as triple the annual pre-war internal growth rate, while the industrial sector was working at only 35 per cent of its overall capacity. Italy's agricultural production – the most important sector for the country's economy – was 60 per cent less in 1945 than in 1938, while the industrial sector lost around 20 per cent of its capacity. Both France's and Italy's transport infrastructure – roads and railways in particular – had suffered huge damages. In contrast, Great Britain's structural losses were comparatively less, although the German air bombings had inflicted severe damages in the cities. But it was mainly in economic terms that World War II was a hollow victory for the British. The second largest creditor nation in 1939, Britain became the largest debtor as a result of the war, which had cost an estimated quarter of the country's overall wealth. Exports were reduced to 60 per cent of the pre-war total, while expenditures had increased fivefold.

Considering the situation in Europe, the emergence of the United States and of the Soviet Union on the world scene was, perhaps, inevitable. The United States was the only country untouched by the devastation of the war. It was the rising economic power, already expanding during the interwar years, despite the negative impact of the Great Depression. The Soviet Union, while having paid an overwhelmingly high price for the war, was the only power that maintained a direct and preponderant military presence on half of the European continent. Europe lay in-between, divided by a front line that did not match any political, ethnic or historical criteria. The military occupation created a geographic division, which would then evolve into opposing political and ideological entities. The end of the war there-fore also marked the abrupt emergence of an East–West division that would last for four decades. The Western European countries turned to the United States for both economic relief and protection against Soviet expansionism. For its part, Washington pursued its own strategic objectives and the expansion of its influence over Western Europe. The Cold War transatlantic relationship was at its inception.

American idealism versus European realism

Roosevelt's grand design

When the Allied leaders met at the Yalta conference in February 1945 they were aware that the end of the war in Europe had become only a matter of time. The 'big three' – Franklin Roosevelt, Winston Churchill and Joseph Stalin – therefore looked to the future. While the wartime alliance was still perceived as solid, different visions of the post-war European order were clearly emerging. For the United States, the war had been necessary in order to counter the threat posed by Hitler's regime. But as the objective of defeating Nazi Germany was being achieved, Roosevelt looked towards creating a new international world order, one that would avoid the devastations of another world war.

The key element of the American president's 'grand design' was the creation of inter-national organizations, such as the United Nations, to maintain peace and security, and financial institutions to regulate economic relationships and coordinate the reconstruction. Roosevelt's ideas derived from America's traditional aversion towards defining perma-nent spheres of influence and from the Wilsonian idealism that, in the interwar years, had inspired the League of Nations. At the same time, Roosevelt's vision was coherent with promoting American interests. In 1945, these were *not* identified with the maintenance of a presence in Europe. Before the coming of the Cold War, the US objective was to assure for itself the pivotal role in the economic relationship with Europe, while delegating security aspects to the newly founded United Nations.

Churchill's and Stalin's realpolitik

The American plans for the post-war international order raised questions and reservations for Great Britain and the Soviet Union. Churchill's and Stalin's visions were inspired by more traditionally realistic security concerns. Both wanted to create and defend their respective spheres of influence in Europe, and thus pursued the type of policies that Roosevelt's grand design sought to overcome. Despite their radically different ideologies, the two European leaders in fact shared a common approach, which had clearly surfaced in the so-called 'percentage agreement' of 1944. As Soviet troops moved to liberate Romania and Bulgaria in the fall of 1944, Churchill decided to deter further Soviet expansion by reaching an agreement with the Soviet dictator. At a meeting in October 1944, the two agreed that the Soviet Union would have 90 per cent control over affairs in Romania and 75 per cent influence in Bulgaria. With the Red Army already in control of both countries, Churchill felt he was not sacrificing much. Both sides would have equal influence over Yugoslavia and Hungary. In return, the British leader obtained 90 per cent Western influence over Greece. While Churchill would later undermine the importance of this agreement, for the Soviet leader it would remain a reference point in his dealings with the West and the basis for justifying his subsequent demands.

Spheres of influence emerge

Since the early stages of World War II, Washington had acknowledged Stalin's desire to create a 'security belt' around the perimeter of the Soviet Union, composed of governments friendly to Moscow. Roosevelt himself realized that a future predominant role of the Soviet Union in Eastern European affairs was inevitable. However, during the Allies' various war conferences little was done to actually define the extent of Stalin's requests and their concrete political significance. Moreover, the unfolding of the war operations seemed to prompt the emergence of different spheres of influence, as the Western powers moved towards Germany from Italy and France, while the Soviet troops advanced from the East. The principle – outlined by Stalin – that the occupying military power would impose its control over the liberated territory was gradually emerging.

However, the surfacing of spheres of influence, perhaps a consequence of ill-conceived wartime strategies, did not necessarily entail the political and ideological confrontation of the Cold War. This resulted, on the one hand, from the American refusal to accept the imposition of a strictly enforced communist rule on the countries of Eastern Europe and, on the other, from the Soviet Union's insecurity and 'capitalist encirclement' complex, which induced Stalin to pursue those policies. The European countries themselves, weakened by the war, were unable to effectively counter these two positions. Ultimately, each European country would turn to one or the other of the superpowers (either by choice or by imposition) for its reconstruction and development. Consequently, Europe as a continent and collective unity would come to accept its division.

America's economic policy

Initially, America's policy towards Europe seemed to have a long-term vision only in terms of economic policy. According to US policymakers, such as Cordell Hull and Hans Morgenthau, the political crisis in Europe, which had led to the emergence of Nazism, had been caused by the repercussions of the Great Depression. The collapse of the world's economy had led to the creation of closed economic spaces through the erection of tariffs and trade barriers. This had in turn contributed to fuel the potent nationalist forces which triggered World War II. If economic protectionism had – directly or indirectly – led to the tensions that developed into war, then the precondition for assuring peace and security was the lifting of barriers and the creation of an open market.

This was a revolutionary development. For decades, in fact, Washington had adopted rigorous protectionist policies in order to protect the US economy from European competition. The war changed this framework. The United States emerged as the unquestionable leader and driving force of the world's economy, producing half of the world's industrial goods in 1945. Consequently, Washington had to adopt policies that would both promote international development and ensure America's predominant position.

These notions constituted the basis of the Bretton Woods agreements, which established a set of rules and regulations for commercial and financial relations, thus creating a new system for the post-war international economic order. The central aspect of the agreements was the decision to link each country's currency to a reserve currency that would guarantee the stability of exchange rates. The only currency that could play this role was the US dollar. The American currency therefore became the reserve currency and, to bolster confidence in the dollar, Washington agreed to link it to gold for the price of 35 dollars per ounce. At this rate, dollars could be exchanged for gold. This created a system for international payments in which all currencies were defined in relation to the dollar, itself convertible into gold. Another important aspect of the Bretton Woods accords was the decision to create two new financial institutions: the International Monetary Fund (IMF) and the International Bank for Reconstruction and Development (later called the World Bank). The IMF was designed as the keeper of the rules of the new system, while the World Bank's purpose was to lend money to countries in need of capital.

The decisions adopted at Bretton Woods put the United States in a position of absolute centrality in the world's future economic system. This marked the beginning of a profound evolution in America's relationship with the rest of the world, and with Europe in particular. It signalled the overcoming of America's traditional economic and political isolationism. Washington realized that an assumption of responsibility on its part was needed in order to foster the reconstruction and development of Europe. The United States therefore prepared itself for this role, novel to its history. And with the assumption of responsibility came also a series of advantages, as the US gradually emerged as the leader of the Western camp.

The wartime alliance starts to crack

In the weeks following the Yalta conference, the relationship between the United States and the Soviet Union became progressively more strained. The key controversy related to Stalin's policy towards Eastern Europe. At Yalta, the Soviet leader had agreed to issue the Declaration on Liberated Europe, according to which the Allied powers had to consult during the transition in order to aid the creation of governments responsive to the will of the people. However, Stalin, strengthened by his army's presence in Eastern Europe and reassured by Churchill's tacit approval expressed in the 'percentage agreement', did not abide by the Declaration (the Soviet dictator cited as a justification the so-called 'Italian precedent' by which the Allies had *not* consulted with him on the future government of Italy). In fact, a few months after the Declaration, the Soviet Union imposed a 'friendly' government in Romania. Afterwards, the main point of contention would focus on the future of Poland.

Truman enters the White House

In the United States, the stiffening of the stance towards the Soviet Union coincided with the death of President Roosevelt (on 12 April 1945). The arrival of Harry Truman at the White House brought about a reassessment of US policies, which resulted in a more rigid and intransigent attitude towards Moscow. The incoming president was convinced that Roosevelt had been too forthcoming towards Stalin and had, particularly at Yalta, made too many concessions. Consequently, Truman corrected the US line of action. In a meeting with Soviet foreign minister Molotov in April 1945, the new American president forcefully protested against Moscow's inobservance of the Yalta agreements on Poland. The US leadership had by then realized that the Soviet occupation of Eastern Europe was translating into tight political control. This triggered an even greater preoccupation in Washington: that the Soviet Union would seek to expand its political and ideological sphere of influence to the countries of Western Europe that had been most weakened by the war. The idea of setting a clear limit to the expansion of Soviet influence was therefore emerging.

The US and the major Western European countries

Concurrently, the United States moved to tighten its relationship with the key Western European countries. Within the framework of America's new economic policy, already in late 1945 Washington decided on a series of loans – to Great Britain, France and Italy in particular. The most substantial aid programme was given to the UK, for both economic and political reasons. Despite the acknowledgement of the inevitable decline of British power after the war, the relationship with London remained central to the pursuit of American objectives. Great Britain still maintained a strong political and military position compared with the other European countries. Moreover, it had strong and long-standing cultural ties with the United States, which both sides sought to deepen after the war. In short, it was a 'special relationship', which would have a deep impact both on British domestic policies and on the shaping of the post-war world order, as Washington stepped in to undertake the global role previously held by London. The special character of the relationship did not, however, eliminate the causes of tension. It was only reluctantly, in fact, that the British accepted (as the precondition to the aid programmes) to ratify the Bretton Woods agreements and to gradually abolish restrictions on its trade policies. London's defence of its economic interests within the Commonwealth contradicted Washington's view of promoting free trade and open access to resources. This dichotomy would continue to be a cause of friction between the two countries, particularly throughout the 1950s.

The American policy vis-à-vis France was geared towards restoring its pre-war international standing. The American attitude was influenced by the British vision, according to which a strong France was important to both deter Soviet influence and to balance a resurgent Germany. The potential power and future influence of France was therefore considered more important than its actual position in the aftermath of the war. This resulted in a series of policies that greatly benefited the French, such as the decision to assign to France a permanent seat in the Security Council of the United Nations and its participation with a separate force in the occupation of Germany.

Since the armistice agreement of 1943, the US position towards Italy aimed at re-establishing positive relations. Washington therefore recognized the new Italian interim government as early as the autumn of 1944. Later, the US favoured Italy's participation in the United Nations and the maintenance of its territorial integrity, rebuking the aspirations of France and Yugoslavia on portions of Italian territory. However, American interests in Italy remained relatively marginal until the Cold War greatly elevated the strategic significance of the entire Mediterranean region. At that point, the domestic developments in Italy – and the future political orientation of the country – became a priority for Washington.

Despite the importance of strengthened ties with various Western European countries, in late 1945 it was a different attitude towards Germany that revealed the change of priorities for Washington. During the war, the prevailing vision – energetically set forth by French General Charles de Gaulle and in part shared by the US leadership – was that there could be no permanent future peace in Europe unless Germany was completely deprived of its potential to resurge. This meant keeping the country politically divided and maintaining its economy at a rural and primitive state so as to eliminate its industrial capacity. However, as the war moved to an end and the prospect that Germany might become the battleground of East–West confrontation clearly surfaced, the American stance gradually shifted. The turning point was marked by decisions made at the Potsdam conference (held in late July and early August 1945).

The Potsdam conference

In fact, at the last inter-Allied war conference (which took place after the end of the fighting in Europe), the US objective was to avoid excessively punitive measures that would weaken the German state to the point of pushing it into the Soviet sphere of influence. Two issues dominated the conversations at Potsdam: the decision on the Polish borders and the question of demanding reparations from Germany. The final outcome reflected the tension that was emerging between East and West. On Poland, the Anglo-Americans could only accept the de facto shift of its Western border to the line marked by the rivers Oder and Neisse, decided by Stalin. In this way, the resource-rich territory of Silesia passed from Germany to Poland, which was, despite the declarations, already under heavy Soviet influence. At the same time, the Soviet Union definitely annexed the Polish territories controlled since 1939, thus unilaterally tracing the eastern border of Poland. The passage of Silesia to Poland rendered the issue of extracting reparations from Germany all the more sensitive. Had the Soviet Union succeeded in obtaining the dismantling of the entire German industrial capacity, it would have been difficult for the West to ensure the survival of the political and economic entity of the German state. Therefore, the Americans insisted that reparations could be extracted only from each country's respective occupation zones and only to a degree that would not jeopardize the future standard of living of the German people. Formally, Germany was to survive as a single administrative unit to be governed by an Inter-Allied Control Council. In reality, however, the decisions taken at Potsdam would eventually contribute to the division of Germany.

America's more intransigent position at Potsdam was sustained by its monopoly of the atomic bomb (tested while the conference was ongoing). After the end of the war, the US decision *not* to share the secrets of the atomic bomb contributed to the deterioration of the relationship with Moscow. The American nuclear monopoly, which lasted until 1949, enabled Washington to compensate for the inferiority of its conventional forces in Europe when compared with Moscow's. Later, the monopoly of the atomic bomb would greatly improve the credibility of America's commitments towards Western Europe, while deepening the Western European countries' military dependence on the United States.

The Iron Curtain descends

By early 1946 the signs of the coming of the Cold War became unequivocal. The beginning of the works of the UN General Assembly and Security Council in London revealed the Soviet Union's intransigence on issues relating to the Middle East, Iran and Asia. According to Western representatives, the Soviet attitude indicated that Moscow had no intention of taking part in collective and cooperative security structures. Moreover, in February 1946, Stalin gave a speech – meant for Soviet domestic purposes – in which his theory on the inevitability of conflict between the communist and capitalist systems resurfaced. In the United States and in Western Europe this speech was associated with Soviet policies in Eastern Europe, triggering a reflection on the actual objectives of Moscow's foreign policy. Around the same time, Winston Churchill – a private citizen after his defeat in the British elections of July 1945 – delivered a speech at a graduation ceremony in Fulton, Missouri, which became emblematic of the widespread sentiments of the West. The former British prime minister stated:

> From Stettin in the Baltic to Trieste in the Adriatic an iron curtain has descended across the Continent. Behind that line lie all the capitals of the ancient states of Central and Eastern Europe. Warsaw, Berlin, Prague, Vienna, Budapest, Belgrade, Bucharest and Sofia; all these famous cities and the populations around them lie in what I must call the Soviet sphere, and all are subject, in one form or another, not only to Soviet influence but to a very high and in some cases increasing measure of control from Moscow.[2]

While Churchill was not in a position to actually influence American policy, similar prescriptions were contained in a document that reached Washington in February 1946. This 'long telegram', sent from the American embassy in Moscow and written by senior official George F. Kennan, was to profoundly influence the making of US policy. According to Kennan, Soviet conduct was motivated by the traditional Russian sense of insecurity, which was likely to translate into the expansion of Soviet-style communism in the areas of Eastern Europe where the Red Army was still stationed. A compromise was no longer possible. The United States had to react to Moscow's pressure and, by forming a Western bloc, contain the further expansion of the Soviet Union's influence. The US strategy of containment – which was to shape Washington's Cold War posture for decades – and a sharp shift in America's stance towards Europe were therefore in the making. The change started to surface publicly in relation to Germany.

The German question

The decisions taken at Potsdam on administering Germany as one entity entailed cooperation between the four occupying powers. This soon proved to be impossible. After one year of occupation, Germany consisted of four small economic units with almost no free exchange of commodities, people and ideas. The common economic infrastructure called for at Potsdam had not been established. The French adamantly opposed the idea of a unified German entity and pressed for the internationalization of the industrially rich region of the Ruhr. The Soviet Union had started to nationalize the industries in its zone, while extracting raw materials and machineries as reparations. To counter this reality, in the summer of 1946, US Secretary of State James Byrnes proposed a 25-year, four-power agreement to reunite Germany, and guarantee its neutrality and complete disarmament. This was the last attempt at seeking cooperation with the Soviet Union.

While this proposal was formally issued to appease French fears of a resurgent Germany, Byrnes's proposal nevertheless entailed a long-term American commitment to European affairs. This anticipated the stance taken by the United States in the official Restatement of Policy on Germany, better known as Secretary Byrnes's Stuttgart speech of September 1946. According to Byrnes, the time had come for the Germans, 'under proper safeguards', to assume the primary responsibility for the running of their own affairs. War industries had to be removed and eliminated, but the other industrial capacities had to be restored. Germany had to be allowed to maintain 'average European living standards'. The American people, continued the US secretary of state, 'want to help the German people to win their way back to an honourable place among the free and peace-loving nations of the world'. The economic conditions of Germany were desperate and necessitated urgent intervention. And, unless measures were taken to aid the recovery of the German economy, the overall reconstruction of Europe would be delayed.

Byrnes's words were also directed to the Soviet Union: 'It is not in the interest of the German people or in the interest of world peace that Germany should become a pawn or partner in a military struggle for power between East and West.' Hence, the turning point for US policy:

> Security forces will probably have to remain in Germany for a long period. I want no misunderstanding. We will not shirk our duty. We are not withdrawing. We are staying here. As long as there is an occupation army in Germany, American armed forces will be part of that occupation army.[3]

In this way, the US leadership linked the recovery of Germany to the reconstruction of Europe, therefore definitely setting aside the punitive plans that surfaced during the war (the so-called Morgenthau Plan, which advocated the annihilation of Germany). Moreover, Byrnes's speech anticipated the future presence of American troops in Europe in the absence of war and for an indefinite period of time.

The reaction to the Stuttgart speech was mixed. The British approved wholeheartedly and moved towards the economic unification of the British and American occupation zones. This was agreed upon in December 1946 and the 'bi-zone' became effective in January 1947. The French, however, were outraged. Only one year after the end of the war, they still opposed the concept of a unified Germany, despite the American guarantees. For the time being the Soviets remained silent. Understandably, the most enthusiastic were the Germans, who saw the possibility of being able to rebuild their country and reshape their destiny. However, as the Western zones moved towards a merger (France would eventually overcome its reservations), the Soviet zone remained separated and increasingly isolated. From 1947 onwards, the division of Germany in two opposing entities would become a concrete reality. And it would soon come to symbolize the Cold War division of Europe.

The Truman doctrine

The shift in Washington's policy towards Europe was the consequence of the realization that the security of the United States and the defence of American interests were linked to maintaining the political balance of power in Europe. For decades, the British had played a crucial role in both guaranteeing the equilibrium in European affairs and in ensuring a positive relationship between the two sides of the Atlantic. However, World War II definitely compromised Britain's capacity to act as a transatlantic power. The United States would, in fact, step in, assuming the leadership of the nascent transatlantic partnership.

The British had intervened in the Greek civil war, started immediately after the end of World War II, by actively supporting the internationally recognized Greek government (elected in 1946) against the leftist factions sponsored by the Communist Party. But London's enduring financial difficulties led the British government to announce – on 21 February 1947 – that it could no longer maintain troops in Greece. The British also added that, without outside aid, the Greek government would be unable to counter the communist forces. And should Greece fall to communism, there would be severe repercussions for the entire eastern Mediterranean region. The combination of Britain's financial crisis and the situation caused by the civil war in Greece created the conditions for the emergence of America's new role.

The bilateral Anglo-American relationship had already significantly changed (in favour of the United States) after the decision of the British government to accept the conditions of a massive US loan, meant to stabilize London's finances. Approved by the US Senate in May 1946, it subordinated the American aid to the commitment to convert the British pound into dollars in the entire Commonwealth area. In this way, the underlying principle of the Bretton Woods agreements – promoting free exchanges in absence of barriers – would be respected and, as a result, international trade relations would be boosted. At the same time, the US obtained that a large part of the world's commercial relations would take place in dollars. London's acceptance of these conditions marked the transition from its previous position of dominance on the global economic scene to one of subordination to Washington.

This transition in the economic–commercial domain anticipated America's political assumption of responsibility, made public in what came to be known as the Truman doctrine. On 12 March 1947 the American president asked the US Congress for authorization to dispatch economic and military aid (a mounting to about 400 million dollars) to Greece and Turkey. In the context of the Greek civil war, and after the British decision to withdraw its aid, the United States had to provide assistance to the Greek army in order for it to be able to regain control of the country. The Greek government, stated Truman:

> is unable to cope with the situation. The Greek army is small and poorly equipped. It needs supplies and equipment if it is to restore the authority of the government throughout Greek territory. Greece must have assistance if it is to become a self-supporting and self-respecting democracy.

It was up to the United States to grant such assistance because there was no other country to which a 'democratic Greece' could turn. While the situation in Turkey was considerably different (the country had been spared the disasters afflicting Greece), it needed support 'for the purpose of effecting that modernization necessary for the maintenance of its national integrity. 'That integrity is essential to the preservation of order in the Middle East', stated the president (thus demanding to allocate about a quarter of the total amount requested to Turkey).[4]

In his speech, President Truman called for an American intervention in defence of liberty and democracy. The notion of the division of the world in two opposing camps clearly surfaced, as the US president referred to the choice between two alternative 'ways of life' – the Western democratic way versus the communist system – a choice that, too often, was not a free one. The United States had to put the countries in question in a condition to be able to choose freely. The president's message was clear: the United States had the responsibility to guide the transition towards democracy for all the peoples who requested help. While Roosevelt's interventionism had foreseen a US role within a nascent collective international system, Truman – though referring to the Charter of the United Nations – gave priority to the leadership exercised by Washington in the defence of the 'free world'.

The American Congress approved Truman's request for aid to Greece and Turkey on 22 May 1947. The text of the law explicitly stated that the territorial integrity and survival of these nations was important for the security of the United States and of all peace-loving nations. This introduced the then-revolutionary concept that American national interests extended to the protection of the eastern Mediterranean and Middle Eastern region. In other words, the United States formally sanctioned the extension of its international role. This contrasted with America's traditional aversion towards long-term involvement in European affairs and contradicted the wartime assumption that the US would rapidly disengage from Europe after the end of the hostilities. The relative lack of domestic opposition encountered by Truman demonstrated a shift in America's public opinion, which, it seems, had come to realize that Washington's leadership after the victory over Germany and Japan was inevitable. Moreover, the deeply ingrained anti-communism – momentarily set aside during the war – resurfaced as a consequence of Soviet policies in Eastern Europe. This added an ideological component to the geopolitical competition with the Soviet Union, making the emerging bipolar conflict more explicable to the US public, not used to engagement in great power politics.

Europe's recovery stagnates

In the two years following the end of the war, the economic conditions of Europe remained precarious. The Western European countries seemed far from being able to initiate a stable recovery. The United States had dispatched millions of dollars in loans and aid programmes for the European countries, but more to counter the critical contingency than to finance long-term recovery programmes. Moreover, the American aid was not immediately producing beneficial results. The British financial situation had not significantly improved, despite the US loan. In February 1947, for example, *The Times* defined the economic conditions of the country – made public by a governmental report – as most worrisome. In July 1947, in order to fulfil the obligations undertaken with the United States, the British government declared the convertibility of the pound. But this had to be suspended a month later due to the massive requests to convert pounds into dollars. The conditions on continental Europe were not more encouraging. In 1947, the industrial production in Italy and Austria, for example, was still only two-thirds of the pre-war level and less than one-third in the Western zones of Germany. Worker productivity was hampered by malnutrition and inefficient organization. The economic recovery was made more difficult by the rigid winter of 1946–1947, which negatively impacted on the agricultural production all over Europe.

In addition, the political developments in Europe rendered the unfavourable economic situation all the more troublesome. In Great Britain, the landslide victory of the Labour Party in July 1945 had enabled the government to rapidly implement a widespread social welfare programme, destined to profoundly change the structure of British society. These reforms, however, further burdened the fragile British economy, worsening an already critical situation. The restructuring of British society thus prompted a foreign policy of disengagement. In addition to Greece, London announced its withdrawal from Palestine (whose administration passed to the United Nations) and India (anticipating the independence granted in 1948).

From the American point of view, the political developments in France and Italy were more worrisome, and complicated the already difficult economic recovery of the two countries. After General de Gaulle's decision to withdraw from political life, the French governments were formed by socialists (Félix Gouin in January to June 1946 and Léon Blum in December 1946 to January 1947) and Christian Democrats (Georges Bidault in June to November 1946). In Italy, the transitional governments were formed by an anti-fascist coalition led by Christian Democrat Alcide De Gasperi. The June 1946 elections (curiously held on the same day in both countries) created constitutional assemblies to rewrite the constitutions. Both in France and Italy, the Communist Party emerged as greatly strengthened and was thus able, through the action of various worker unions, to influence the action of the governments. This created tension with the moderate political forces and, ultimately, paralysed the economic revival. This situation not only impacted on the overall recovery of Europe, but could also have led the two largest communist parties of the West to power. Such prospects inevitably alarmed the American leadership (it is important to note that George Kennan's analysis – which shaped the US strategy of containment – had pointed to the potential rise of the Western communist parties as the most serious threat to the security and stability of Western Europe). Consequently, the internal situation in France and Italy came to be linked to the evolution of the Cold War and the consolidation of the democratic form of government in these countries became an essential element of America's policy towards Europe.

The Marshall Plan

The large-scale economic aid programme of the United States – officially called the European Recovery Program (ERP), but generally referred to as the Marshall Plan (after US Secretary of State George Marshall) – emerged in response to various inter-related factors. The first was the stalemate on the German question. In March 1947, the foreign ministers of the four occupying countries met again to discuss the future of Germany, but their positions were very distant. The United States and Great Britain favoured the creation of a federal state, decentralizing power in the hands of the various 'Länder'. The French clearly opposed any possibility of creating a strong Germany while, conversely, the Soviet Union sponsored a centralized state. The debate was thus inconclusive and the future prospects remained dim. In this context, the American leadership understood that, in order to address the French concerns, the economic and political reconstruction of Germany had to be part of a larger European design.

The second factor that triggered the Marshall Plan was the overall state of the European economy. The shortage of capital, the slow industrial recovery, the severe deficit in the balance of payments (creating conditions of dependency on the United States) and the widespread inflation produced a recipe for chronic economic dissatisfaction. The presence of the Soviets in Eastern Europe added urgency to the sense of crisis in the West. An outside stimulus was seen as the only remedy. The American decision to exercise its leadership within the Western 'free world' would be the decisive factor.

On 5 June 1947, in an address to the graduating class of Harvard University, US Secretary of State George Marshall outlined the major points of the American offer to promote European reconstruction. Marshall underlined the political and economic problems of Europe, and their negative repercussions on the US economy. There were two major aspects of the speech. First, the offer was general: 'Our policy is not directed against any country,' stated Marshall, 'but against hunger, poverty, desperation and chaos. Any government that is willing to assist in recovery will find full cooperation on the part of the USA.'[5] This was an allusion to the Soviet Union, which the American leadership did not want to formally exclude (although it was more than evident at that point that Stalin would not accept a US offer). There were no details and no numbers in the speech. It was more a proposal than a plan. The second important aspect was its call for common European action: it was up to the Europeans to conceive and coordinate a plan, which the United States would then finance.

The British and French immediately reacted to Marshall's speech and rapidly coordinated a European response to, and acceptance of, the American offer. Sixteen nations met in Paris in July 1947 to determine the amount and type of aid to request from the United States (a Soviet delegation attended the conference but left, rejecting the plan). The negotiations were long and complex, hampered by the different positions of the European countries. As France insisted on demanding guarantees against a resurgent Germany, the Benelux countries, for example, underlined that their economy greatly depended upon the revival of Germany. For its part, the UK demanded a special status, wary that if it were treated equally with the devastated continental powers it would receive virtually no aid. The American delegation – concerned about the need for congressional approval of the plan – insisted on mechanisms which would create incentives to boost European productivity, while not relying uniquely on the American aid. Agreement was eventually reached and the Europeans requested around 22 billion dollars from the United States. In return, they agreed to favour the convertibility of their currencies, to create a customs union, and to initiate the first steps of the European integration process. Moreover, the need to insert the reconstruction of Germany within the European context was accepted in principle as an essential element for the rebirth of Europe.

President Truman signed the European Cooperation Act (the official name for the Marshall Plan) into law on 3 April 1948. It created the European Cooperation Administration (ECA) to administer the ERP. The participating countries then signed an accord establishing an aid coordination agency, the Organisation for European Economic Co-operation (later called the Organisation for Economic Co-operation and Development, or OECD).

Table 1.1 Marshall Plan aid to Western Europe

Country	1950 population (thousands)	Total Marshall Plan assistance (millions of dollars)
Austria	6935	677.8
Belgium and Luxembourg	8935	559.3
Denmark	4271	273.0
France	41,829	2713.6
Germany, West	49,986	1390.6
Greece	7566	706.7
Iceland	143	29.3
Ireland	2963	147.5
Italy	47,105	1508.8
Netherlands	10,114	1083.5
Norway	3265	255.3
Portugal	8443	51.2
Sweden	7014	107.3
United Kingdom	50,127	3189.8

Source: http://learningtogive.org/lessons/unit231/lesson3.html

The approval of this massive aid programme for Europe had encountered some opposition within the American Congress. The Republican right advocated a more isolationist policy, while the criticism from the left focused on the effects of the plan, destined to further polarize the division between East and West. However, after the February 1948 Soviet-backed overthrow of the democratic government in Czechoslovakia (which caused a generalized shock in the West), the opposition in the United States subsided and Truman was able to insert the approval of the ECA into the overall American policies aimed at containing the further spread of Soviet influence (ultimately the US aid programme amounted to almost 13 billion dollars, thus less than the European request, for the 4-year duration of the plan).

The Marshall Plan made a decisive contribution to the reconstruction of Western Europe and was successful in achieving its objectives, which were not exclusively economic. The ERP was in fact accompanied by an intense propaganda aimed at spreading American values and ideals, and, in general, favouring private entrepreneurial initiatives, typical of the capitalist economic system. While Marshall's original offer had been, in theory, open for all, the conditions attached to the US aid in reality made it acceptable only to systems compatible with the American one. Moreover, because of the Soviet Union's pressure on the countries of Eastern Europe (mainly Czechoslovakia and Poland) not to accept the American offers, the Marshall Plan ultimately led to the consolidation of the East–West divide.

Box 1.1 Not only economic purposes: the broader significance of the Marshall Plan

The Marshall Plan made a substantial contribution in aiding the reconstruction of the European economies. During the years of the plan, the European countries recovered from the post-war crisis and initiated stable and – in some cases – unprecedented growth rates. However, beyond the undisputed economic importance of the US aid programme, the Marshall Plan also had other related purposes.

By stimulating the recovery of the European economies, America wanted to create a group of countries that shared the values and objectives of the United States. The Plan was therefore accompanied by an intense propaganda in favour of liberal entrepreneurship, economic efficiency, free markets and competitiveness – the elements that characterized the capitalist economic system. These were summarized in the concept of productivity, not only as an economic objective but also as the indirect means of alleviating social tensions and raising individual standards of living. This was therefore in clear contraposition to the class struggle socialist model advocated by the Soviet Union. In this sense the Marshall Plan contributed to dividing the European continent: the countries accepting the plan implicitly accepted the US conception of the economic system and way of life, while those that refused the American aid programme (either voluntarily or by imposition) repudiated that system and its values.

Another goal of the Marshall Plan was to encourage the European countries to search for means of cooperation and to resolve their disputes without resorting to armed conflict. The American stimulus had to aid the overcoming of Europe's traditional divisions in order to build a Western bloc free of internal rivalries – which, in the vision of the US policymakers, would only aid the expansion of the Soviet Union's influence. For this reason, in the immediate post-war years the United States clearly supported the European integration process.

For both its economic impact and, perhaps most importantly, because of the related community of values and interests that it created, the Marshall Plan is considered one of the central building blocks of the transatlantic relationship.

The first steps of European integration

The American call for unity and coordination linked to the Marshall Plan emerged in parallel with the first initiatives towards European integration. The Western European countries, in fact, sought to consolidate their recovery by overcoming their traditional antagonism and divisions (seen as having led to the two world wars). The European drive for unity was motivated by a dual apprehension: the first related to the Soviet advance on the continent, while the second, inter-related fear was that the United States – which had concentrated its resources mainly on economic aid – would not (or could not) provide the Europeans with an effective defence against the Soviet Union. Consequently, some Western European countries moved to sign the first political and military agreements for their defence. These were the initial steps in the creation of a Western European front that would enable France to overcome its fears of a resurgent Germany, while at the same time preparing Europe to respond to the threat posed by the looming Cold War.

The Treaty of Brussels

In March 1947, France and the United Kingdom signed the Treaty of Dunkirk, a treaty of alliance and mutual assistance against a potential attack from Germany. But it was the political – rather than the military – aspect that was most significant. A few months later, after the creation of the Cominform (the organization of the European communist parties) and the increasing influence of the Italian and French communist parties, the British foreign minister Ernest Bevin denounced the Soviet Union's policies and called for a collective response to Stalin's manoeuvres. The democratic countries of Western Europe had to negotiate agreements similar to the Dunkirk Treaty, and thus collectively address the issue of their security and defence. This initiated the negotiations that led to the signing of the Treaty of Brussels in March 1948 between the United Kingdom, France, Belgium, the Netherlands and Luxembourg. The treaty committed its members to collective self-defence against any armed attack for the next fifty years. It was an extension of the previous year's treaty between France and the UK, and formally provided a further guarantee against the potential of a resurgent Germany (the Soviet Union was therefore still not explicitly mentioned). The implicit meaning of the treaty was to demonstrate the willingness of the European countries to enhance their security cooperation. At the same time, this initiative signalled to the United States that while the drive towards European integration was autonomous and independent, it fitted well within the scheme of enhanced European–American collaboration called for by Washington as a consequence of the Cold War.

The Council of Europe

The initiatives on a governmental level came to be intertwined with those of the International Committee of the Movements for European Unity – an organization presided over by Winston Churchill (no longer the British prime minister), and composed of the various movements across Europe that advocated greater unity and integration. In May 1948, the International Committee hosted the Hague Congress, which brought together over 800 delegates from all over Europe, including politicians, writers, academics, trade union leaders and others. Under Churchill's auspices, the event focused on the development of European political cooperation and called for the creation of a political, economic and monetary union for Europe. It was attended by notable personalities, such as Konrad Adenauer, Harold

Macmillan, François Mitterrand, Paul Henri Spaak, Alcide De Gasperi, Albert Coppé, Bertrand Russell and Altiero Spinelli. While the European governments proved reluctant to proceed on the path of political integration (the 'United States of Europe' called for by Winston Churchill in a famous speech in Zurich in 1946), the Hague Congress led to the creation of the Council of Europe – an international organization for greater European integration, with a special focus on harmonizing legal standards, promoting human rights and cultural cooperation. The Council of Europe was founded by the Treaty of London in May 1949, and was originally composed of 10 states: Belgium, Denmark, France, Ireland, Italy, Luxembourg, the Netherlands, Norway, Sweden and the United Kingdom.

The Berlin blockade

By mid-1947 the ideological division of Europe into two rival camps was almost complete, except in Germany (and the two divided cities of Vienna and Berlin), where the United Kingdom, France, the United States and the Soviet Union still maintained the façade of cooperation. The crisis was, however, in the making. In late 1947, the Council of Foreign Ministers of the four occupying powers met in London and ended in sharp disagreement over the issues of reparations, the authority over the industries of the Ruhr and the future unity of Germany. After the failure of this meeting, the three Western powers decided to move towards the unification of their zones. In February 1948, representatives from the UK, France, Belgium, the Netherlands and Luxembourg, along with the United States, met again in London to plan for a future West German entity. News of this conference reached the Soviets who, at the routine meeting of the Allied Control Council a month later, demanded that the Western powers disclose the content of their agreements. Faced with their refusal, the Soviets walked out of the Council, de facto ending the quadripartite collaboration in Germany. Afterwards, the three Western powers accelerated the plans to integrate their zones in order to create a new West German state. At the same time, they decided that the area of the Ruhr would be administered by an international authority, that the Western 'tri-zone' had to gradually move towards independence and that the ERP would be extended to this new German entity. These decisions were at the origins of the Berlin blockade, generally considered the first major crisis of the Cold War.

The decisions taken at the Potsdam conference, which had divided Germany into four, had also divided the city of Berlin into four occupied zones. Agreements on access to Berlin, which was deep within the Soviet occupation zone, were subsequently formalized (in September 1945), and the four nations concurred on which road and rail lines would be used in supplying areas of the city occupied by the Western Allies. Air corridors across the Soviet zone between Berlin and the Western sectors of Germany were also established. For three years there was free movement along the accepted routes of access to Berlin.

However, in the spring of 1948, the tensions between the Soviets and the Western powers had repercussions on the precarious status of Berlin. The Soviets started to restrict access to the city. Controls were placed, for example, on traffic through the autobahn between Berlin and the British sector in the west, and the bridge over the Elbe at Hohenwarte, the only other road-crossing point, was closed. Other measures followed, as the Western powers moved towards the creation of their tri-zone. The point of rupture came after the West's decision to reform the German monetary system by introducing a new currency (the Deutschmark, to replace the devalued Reichsmark). This was needed to create greater monetary stability, a precondition to the extension of the Marshall Plan to the Western zones. The Soviet Union opposed the plans for reform and thus refused to circulate the new currency in Berlin.

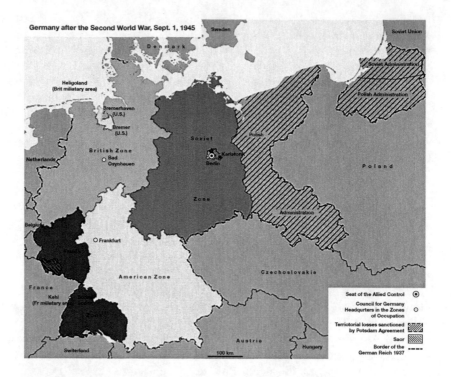

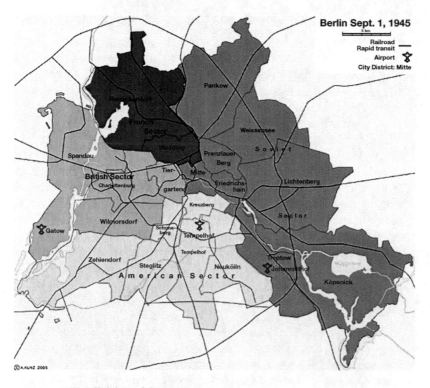

Figure 1.1 The division of Germany and of Berlin

Instead, it proposed another currency (the Ostmark) to be used in all sectors of the city. Following the West's refusal to accept the Soviet conditions and the arrival in Berlin of the new marks – which quickly became the standard currency – in June 1948, Moscow severed all communication and access routes between the non-Soviet zones and Berlin.

The Western powers responded by bypassing the ground blockade with an airlift to supply the Western zones of Berlin. This decision put the Soviets on the defensive. The cargo airplanes could not be stopped unless Moscow decided to escalate the crisis from political to military (i.e. by shooting down unarmed aircraft). The airlift – which lasted from June 1948 to May 1949 – demonstrated the West's ability to constantly supply the city via air alone. In the end, the Soviets yielded to the pressure and signalled their willingness to lift the blockade in exchange for discussions on the future of Germany. In early 1949, the four powers initiated negotiations and, on 12 May, the Soviet Union ended the blockade. The only political price paid by the West was the concession not to fully include West Berlin into the newly formed West German state (its representatives would take part in the Bundestag, but without voting power). Moreover, the occupying powers would maintain a presence in Berlin that the Western powers eventually limited to the minimum, but which, nonetheless, would be a constant reminder of the volatile status of the divided city. Ultimately, however, the Soviet Union was unable to prevent the unification of the Western zones and the creation of the Federal Republic of Germany (proclaimed by the new federal parliament on 7 September 1949). A month later, the Eastern zone of Germany formally became the German Democratic Republic.

The North Atlantic Treaty

The consequences of the Berlin blockade on the evolution of the Cold War and of the trans-atlantic relationship were far-reaching. The beginning of the crisis came only months after the overthrow of the democratic government in Czechoslovakia, deepening the Western preoccupations regarding Soviet policies. The events in Prague and Berlin increased the European countries' determination to enhance their collective security by signing agreements similar to the Brussels Treaty. At the same time, the Europeans sought a greater and formalized commitment of America to defending Europe.

In the United States, the events in Berlin were viewed as a confirmation of the aggressiveness and brutality of Soviet policies, thus intensifying the anti-communist sentiments which were already pervasive. In June 1948 (i.e. as the Berlin blockade started), the US Senate passed a resolution calling for the United States to enter into 'regional and other collective agreements' for the defence of vital American national security interests. Lobbied strongly by Republican Senator Arthur H. Vandenberg, who sought congressional support for Truman's Cold War policies, the Vandenberg resolution marked a historic turning point for American foreign policy. Since George Washington's farewell address, in which he had warned against entering 'entangling alliances', the United States had constantly opposed and avoided permanent military alliances. This traditional and long-standing principle was set aside by the US Senate, which passed the resolution by 64 to 4 votes, therefore demonstrating ample bipartisanship. This cleared the way for the signing (and eventual ratification) of the North Atlantic Treaty a year later.

As the Berlin crisis unfolded, in fact, the European nations and the United States had entered negotiations on a military alliance that would defend Western Europe from the Soviet Union. This was the result of the convergence between the policies pursued by the signatories of the Brussels Treaty and the United States. The major debate focused on

Germany, since the United States firmly advocated including the future West German entity in the Western European collective security system. This issue could not be immediately addressed – considering the ongoing crisis in Berlin – but would remain a major concern in Washington. Another point of contention revolved around which countries to include in the alliance. The extension of the treaty to Italy, for example, had particular significance since its inclusion completed the geographic defensive perimeter along the Iron Curtain, while expanding the North Atlantic dimension of the alliance to include the Mediterranean. After months of negotiations, the North Atlantic Treaty was signed on 4 April 1949 between 12 nations: United States, Canada, United Kingdom, France, Italy, Portugal, Norway, Denmark, Iceland, Belgium, the Netherlands and Luxembourg. The most significant element of the Treaty was (and is) Article V, which created a collective defence mechanism.

Henceforth, the defence of Europe came to be profoundly linked to (and for many decades dependent on) the United States of America. The transatlantic relationship, which until then had developed on the basis of an economic and political partnership, came to include a military dimension – which was to become all the more important as the Cold War escalated in Europe and beyond.

Conclusion

The end of World War II marked the demise of Europe's centrality in the international system, with the emergence of the United States and the Soviet Union as the predominant

---

Box 1.2 Document extract: The North Atlantic Treaty (4 April 1949)

The Treaty had 14 articles and came into force on 24 August 1949 after the deposition of the ratifications of all signatory states.

The Parties to this Treaty reaffirm their faith in the purposes and principles of the Charter of the United Nations and their desire to live in peace with all peoples and all governments. They are determined to safeguard the freedom, common heritage and civilisation of their peoples, founded on the principles of democracy, individual liberty and the rule of law. They seek to promote stability and well-being in the North Atlantic area. They are resolved to unite their efforts for collective defence and for the preservation of peace and security. They therefore agree to this North Atlantic Treaty:

Article V
The Parties agree that an armed attack against one or more of them in Europe or North America shall be considered an attack against them all and consequently they agree that, if such an armed attack occurs, each of them, in exercise of the right of individual or collective self-defence recognized by Article 51 of the Charter of the United Nations, will assist the Party or Parties so attacked by taking forthwith, individually and in concert with the other Parties, such action as it deems necessary, including the use of armed force, to restore and maintain the security of the North Atlantic area.

Any such armed attack and all measures taken as a result thereof shall immediately be reported to the Security Council. Such measures shall be terminated when the Security Council has taken the measures necessary to restore and maintain international peace and security.

world powers. The common perception in Western Europe and America of the threat of Soviet expansionism was the central element in the shaping of the transatlantic partnership. The relationship was initially based on economic policies – in the form of American loans to various European countries – and, subsequently, on political statements such as the Truman doctrine, through which the United States took on the leadership of the emerging Western camp. As the Cold War became a tangible reality, the American policies became more systemic – with the Marshall Plan – and, concurrently, the Western European countries moved to overcome their divisions by initiating their integration process, called for and encouraged by the United States.

By 1949 the economic and political relationship seemed no longer sufficient to provide both sides of the Atlantic with the security and defence needed in the face of their common enemy. Therefore, by signing the North Atlantic Treaty, the transatlantic relationship was enhanced and strengthened by a military alliance that formally linked the security of Western Europe to that of the United States (and vice versa). For the European countries, the American nuclear monopoly compensated for the Soviet superiority in conventional forces

---

Box 1.3 Empire by invitation?

The motives behind America's commitment to Europe in the immediate post-war years have been debated by historians for decades. Traditionalist views – which coincide with the first scholarship on the origins of the Cold War – have pointed to America's and Western Europe's need for protection and security in face of the threat from the Soviet Union. In this view, the American policies were for the most part 'defensive', in line with the notion of containment and of preventing the expansion of Soviet influence in Western Europe. Revisionists – a second generation of scholarship – have instead reversed the argument and pointed to more 'aggressive' motivations behind America's policy, which, in their view, was geared towards establishing hegemony over Western Europe. These scholars highlight in particular the economic motivations of the US capitalist system and its inherent need to expand its market, thus sponsoring economies compatible with the American model.

A third group of scholars have instead reassessed America's policies on the basis of less Manichaean approaches, considering such factors as the simple need and desire for the United States, the emerging Great Power on the world scene at the time, to expand its influence abroad. According to this viewpoint, the United States gradually moved to establish its 'empire' around the world, for a combination of economic, political, military and security reasons. Norwegian historian Geir Lundestad has added an interpretative layer to these arguments by famously setting forth the notion of an American empire 'by invitation'. While the United States indisputably had its own motivations in deepening the links with Western Europe, the particularity – when compared to other parts of the world where the US progressively engaged – was that Washington was 'invited in' by the countries subject to its influence. According to Lundestad, the Western European countries – devastated by the war and vulnerable to Soviet expansion – encouraged and invited America's economic and military role in Europe. The Western European countries, in other words, called for a much-needed American leadership.

This particular pattern of 'invitation' is only convincing for the immediate post-war years – Lundestad himself states that after the 1970s the dynamics of the transatlantic relationship necessarily changed, as Western Europe gained economic strength and political vitality. However, it is perhaps because of the uniqueness of this feature that the transatlantic relationship developed, expanded and endured many crises throughout the decades.

deployed in Europe, providing a strong security guarantee. Consequently, the European fear of American disengagement from European affairs subsided. It would, however, repeatedly resurface throughout the 1950s (and later) and become a characteristic element of the transatlantic relationship.

Suggested further reading

Gaddis, John Lewis (2000) *The United States and the Origins of the Cold War, 1941–1947*. New York: Columbia University Press.

Hanhimäki, Jussi M. and Odd Arne Westad (eds) (2003) *The Cold War: A History in Documents and Eyewitness Accounts*. Oxford: Oxford University Press.

Leffler, Melvyn P. (1992) *A Preponderance of Power: National Security, the Truman Administration, and the Cold War*. Palo Alto, CA: Stanford University Press.

Lundestad, Geir (1998) *'Empire' by Integration: The United States and European Integration, 1945–1997*. Oxford: Oxford University Press.

Lundestad, Geir (2003) *The United States and Western Europe since 1945: From 'Empire' by Invitation to Transatlantic Drift*. Oxford: Oxford University Press.

Mastny, Vojtech (1996) *The Cold War and Soviet Insecurity: The Stalin Years*. New York: Oxford University Press.

Milward, Alan S. (1984) *The Reconstruction of Western Europe, 1945–1951*. London: Methuen.

Shain, Martin (ed.) (2001) *The Marshall Plan: Fifty Years After*. New York: Palgrave.

2   Institutional frameworks, 1949–1957

The Cold War escalates

In 1949 the United States suffered two serious foreign policy setbacks. On 29 August 1949, the Soviet Union exploded its first atomic bomb. Since 1945, the US leadership had guarded the atomic secret, thus maintaining the nuclear monopoly, and had not expected the Soviet Union to develop the know-how to build the nuclear weapon so soon. Only a month later, on 1 October 1949, the leader of the Chinese Communist Party Chairman Mao Tse-tung declared the birth of the People's Republic of China, marking the victory of the Communist Party over the Chinese Nationalist Party (the latter supported by Washington). The fall to communism of the most populous nation in the world and its subsequent alignment with the Soviet Union caused profound shock and alarm in the United States.

The combination of these two events triggered a general review of American policy, resulting in a reassertion of US power and strength in order to counter what was perceived in Washington as a Soviet bid for world domination. In early 1950, President Truman asked his secretaries of state and defence to undertake a study of US objectives and the effect of these on strategic planning. The resulting document (NSC-68) underlined the gravity of the situation and advocated, with alarmist tones, the need to react to Soviet policies. Since the threat to the United States had escalated, Washington needed to respond by restructuring its economy and reorient it to sustain the long-term battle with the Soviet Union. Initially, the document was received with scepticism, viewed as calling for an unnecessary escalation of the Cold War (Truman himself hesitated in adopting its prescriptions). But after the outbreak of the Korean War in June 1950 it took on a greater importance. The arguments contained in the NSC-68 report seemed to be validated by the Soviet stance in Korea. Consequently, the US State Department and White House stirred congressional and public opinion in support of rearmament, comprehensive containment of the Soviets and an overall militarization of the Cold War. This new and more assertive US posture had important repercussions on the transatlantic relationship.

The European countries sought a greater and deeper commitment on America's part to counter the escalation of the Soviet threat. Therefore, there was a convergence between the European need for greater protection and the US review of its general Cold War posture. The United States agreed to a stable military presence in Europe and the North Atlantic Treaty evolved into a permanent organization, thus institutionalizing the transatlantic bond. In parallel, the United States pressured the European allies to accept the rearmament of West Germany and to include it in the emerging Western security structure (the analogy between the situation in Korea and the division of Germany was, in fact, particularly pervasive).

At the same time, various European countries initiated the integration process, a process that would lead to the creation of the European Economic Community. The European countries' striving for greater cooperation coincided with the deepening of European–American ties. The making of a European system had to include the countries most exposed to the Soviet threat, the Federal Republic of Germany above all. Concurrently, the internal developments in France and Italy – where the communist parties had been excluded from the governments since 1948 – contributed to the creation of a compact Western European camp, strongly linked to the United States of America.

The development of NATO

The outbreak of the Korean War was interpreted in the West as confirmation that the Cold War had, indeed, become a 'real war'. The East–West divide, until then a political confrontation, had escalated into open war. The United States reacted by implementing the recommendations of NSC-68, thus initiating a massive rearmament programme that would quadruple the American military budget in three years (1950–1953). The Korean War aroused deep preoccupations also in Europe. Only months after the shock of the Soviet nuclear test, the Europeans feared that the United States would divert resources from Europe to focus on the developments in Asia. The immediate reaction in the single European countries – Great Britain, France and Italy, for example – was to also increase their defence efforts.

The European countries were, however, soon to redivert resources away from defence spending, while continuing to rely on the United States for their security. The longer-term consequence of the developments of late 1949 on the transatlantic relationship was the decision taken on both sides of the Atlantic to strengthen the structure of the North Atlantic Treaty. While the twelve founding members ('the Alliance') had committed to collectively defend each other in April 1949, they were not technically equipped to carry out such a task. They lacked in number of troops potentially deployable and had no command structure to overlook the defence of Western Europe. Therefore, in early 1950 the nations forming the Alliance decided to create an integrated military command structure. The first step was to nominate the commander of NATO forces in Europe. In December 1950, the North Atlantic Council appointed US Army General Dwight D. Eisenhower, who had led allied forces in Europe during World War II, to be the first Supreme Allied Commander in Europe (SACEUR).

Eisenhower and a small multinational planning group started working in early 1951 on the structure of the new integrated command, the Allied Command Europe (ACE), and its headquarters, the Supreme Headquarters Allied Powers Europe (SHAPE). This planning group worked in temporary headquarters located in the Hotel Astoria in central Paris, while construction of a permanent facility began in the Parisian suburb of Rocquencourt. The SHAPE planners benefited from the existing plans and personnel of the embryonic military organization created under the Brussels Treaty, which was later incorporated into ACE. By mid-1951, both ACE and its headquarters became fully operational. The following year, the North Atlantic Council meeting held in Lisbon recognized the structure of the Alliance, which from that moment onwards became a permanent organization. It also decided on the nomination of a NATO Secretary General to coordinate all civilian agencies and to represent the organization as a whole (Lord Hastings Ismay was later chosen to serve as the first Secretary General). At the same time, Greece and Turkey both entered NATO, therefore greatly strengthening the Alliance's southern flank. A few months later, in April 1952, the headquarters of the second NATO supreme commander, the Supreme Allied Commander

---

Box 2.1 Anti-communist hysteria, McCarthyism and the militarization of the Cold War

The series of foreign policy setbacks suffered by the United States in the late 1940s and early 1950s generated a heightened sense of threat of Soviet communism. This fear penetrated American civil society and developed into a widespread cultural phenomenon following the activities of Republican Senator Joseph McCarthy. In February 1950, McCarthy publicly denounced the existence of a list containing the names of members of the American Communist Party – allegedly 205 individuals – working at the US State Department, and thus in a position to influence the making of American foreign policy. This speech resulted in massive media attention, initiating the path that made McCarthy one of the most well-known politicians in the United States. Allegations that Soviet or 'Red' spies had penetrated the highest levels of government agencies were used to explain the foreign policy setbacks suffered by the United States.

Publicized cases such as those of State Department official Alger Hiss (convicted of perjury and found guilty of espionage) and Julius and Ethel Rosenberg (arrested in 1950 and executed three years later for having passed atomic secrets to the Soviet Union) initiated the widespread anti-communist 'witch-hunt' that became known as McCarthyism. During this era, thousands of Americans were accused of being communists, or communist sympathizers, becoming targets of aggressive investigations and questioning. Suspicions were often given credit despite inconclusive or questionable evidence, and the level of threat posed by the individual's real or supposed leftist associations was often greatly exaggerated. Famous examples include investigations and hearings of McCarthy himself, and various anti-communist activities of the Federal Bureau of Investigation (FBI) under J. Edgar Hoover.

In the later part of the 1950s McCarthyism declined, as public sentiments shifted and a series of Supreme Court decisions reversed the conviction of communist sympathizers. During the early 1950s, it nevertheless demonstrated the widespread anti-communist hysteria that spread throughout America. It was against this background that the US leadership decided to massively invest in defence spending, following through with the recommendations of NSC-68 and progressively militarizing the Cold War.

Atlantic (SACLANT), located in Norfolk, Virginia, became operational, thus completing the institutional organization of the Alliance.

The first steps of European integration

The perception of an increased Soviet threat had obvious repercussions also on the most pressing issue left unresolved by World War II: the question of Germany. After the West German state was formally established in May 1949, two contradictory elements had to be addressed: on the one side, the Germans desired to achieve equal status with their neighbouring countries; on the other, there was the desire – expressed mainly by the French – to contain Germany and prevent its nationalistic resurgence. These issues had to be related in turn to the overriding concern in the West: the necessity to contain the expansion of the Soviet Union. In this context, the European integration process emerged as a means of incorporating Germany into a strong Western European system, considered the best way to effectively counter the looming Soviet threat.

The United States insisted that the restrictions on Germany had to be modified and eventually lifted in order for the West German state to become fully independent. At the same time, Washington adamantly opposed any neutrality option for the Federal Republic: West Germany had to be firmly linked to the emerging European–American framework. For this to be possible it was necessary to promote French–German reconciliation. And this could only take place within a wider European context. Therefore, the US leadership encouraged the European countries to cooperate with each other and favoured initiatives which would lead towards their greater integration.

In Europe, however, no single country seemed willing to take the lead in triggering the process. The British – who in Washington were seen as the natural leaders – had both economic and political reservations. Economically, for London the relationship with the continent had to be balanced with the relationship – still considered crucial – with the Commonwealth. In political terms, the British Labour government led by Clement Attlee (the prime minister from 1945 to 1951) had different objectives from the conservative governments of the key continental powers. More generally, the British did not share the overall crisis of nationalist sentiment that was pervasive in Europe. The war experience had, in fact, been profoundly different. While in continental Europe it led to the crisis of nationalism and the search for alternative models, the British remained proud of their nation's contribution to the defeat of Nazism. Consequently, London opposed any integration process that limited, even if only partially, national sovereignty. In addition, the British considered it essential to maintain and strengthen the ties with the United States and viewed European integration as a means of weakening the Atlantic link. In other words, London feared that the US pressure to find forms of European unification anticipated a return to traditional American isolationism, once Europe had become strong enough to protect itself.

The Schuman declaration

The United States constantly encouraged European integration. But, contrary to London's assessment, the Truman and Eisenhower administrations saw this as a means to strengthen, rather than weaken, the transatlantic bond. Since London was unwilling to take the initiative, and considering the deeply rooted reservations about Germany of the French, Paris seemed to be the only alternative. Washington thus welcomed the declaration of French Foreign Minister Robert Schuman on 9 May 1950, in which he proposed to place the coal and steel production of France and Germany under a common High Authority, within the framework of an organization open to the participation of other countries. At the time, coal and steel were the essential raw materials for the war industry. Therefore, the project aimed at abolishing the main source of tension between the two countries by substituting elements of dominance or subordination with the concept of supranationality.

The European Coal and Steel Community

German Chancellor Konrad Adenauer reacted positively to Schuman's proposal and the negotiations began for the creation of the first European community. The Treaty of Paris, establishing the European Coal and Steel Community (ECSC), was signed on 18 April 1951 between France, the Federal Republic of Germany, Italy, Belgium, Luxembourg and the Netherlands. It was the first international organization based on supranational principles and which aimed at the creation of a common market for coal and steel. Through the integration of this sector of the members' economy, the ECSC intended to progressively rationalize the distribution of production, while promoting stability and increasing employment. The common market for coal started to operate in February 1953 and for steel in May 1953.

The United States was the first non-member country to recognize the ECSC and to establish a delegation in Brussels. The first president of the ECSC's High Authority was French European integration activist Jean Monnet.

The rise and fall of the European Defence Community

The Schuman declaration and the creation of the ECSC were important steps towards integrating West Germany into a wider European context. However, the main issue – the rearmament of the FRG – remained unaddressed. On this point Washington was unequivocal: West Germany would have to gradually rearm in order to provide an effective barrier against Soviet expansionism. In fact, as the developments on the international scene conveyed the perception of a greater and more imminent threat, the US responded by increasing its military presence in Europe and by agreeing to an integrated force under its command. But America's greater commitment was subordinated to the acceptance of the rearmament of Germany and to the participation of German units in the newly created European–American system. Initially, the most logical solution seemed to insert German rearmament within the framework of NATO.

The Pleven plan

However, French acceptance of German rearmament remained extremely problematic. In order to overcome the problem, in late 1950 the French Prime Minister René Pleven tried to bypass the issue by proposing the creation of a European Defence Community (EDC). Just a few years after the end of the war, a European supranational army, which deprived Germany of control over its military contingents, seemed to be the only acceptable solution for France. This pan-European military would then be closely linked to the United States, thereby satisfying the American call for German rearmament within a European–American framework.

The British reaction to the Pleven plan was not enthusiastic. London remained committed to strengthening the Atlantic link and to integrate West Germany into a European–American force. Moreover, the British government was opposed to the limitation of sovereignty implicit in the idea of the EDC. Nevertheless, it agreed to stipulate accords of mutual assistance and support between Great Britain and the prospected European Defence Community.

In the United States, the incoming Eisenhower administration acknowledged that the solution to the issue of German rearmament had to be found among Europeans. The US thus accepted the Pleven plan, provided mechanisms were created to link the European system to the Atlantic one (i.e. to NATO). Therefore, despite the resentment of Germany (which was clearly being discriminated against), the negotiations on the European Defence Community started in February 1951. The treaty establishing the EDC was signed between the Federal Republic of Germany, France, Italy, Belgium, the Netherlands and Luxembourg – the same six founding members of the ECSC – in May 1952. It created a multinational army in which the various national contingents were integrated under a unified European command.

The French vote against the EDC

After the signing of the treaty, however, the new community entered a problematic phase. In order for the treaty to enter into force, it had to be ratified by the signatories' respective national parliaments. Despite the proposal having been set forth by French Prime Minister

Pleven, there was strong criticism against the EDC within the French parliament. The concept of supranationality was opposed by the Gaullists, who advocated the defence of French national sovereignty and the independence of the French armed forces. The EDU was also criticized, albeit for other reasons, by the socialist and communist parties. After a long impasse, the French parliament voted against the treaty in August 1954. By then, the death of Stalin (in 1953) and the end of the Korean War had created an entirely different context, diminishing the overall sense of crisis of the early 1950s. This further discouraged the already sceptical French parliament on the need to establish the European Defence Community.

In fact, by 1953 the change in the leadership of the two superpowers had obvious repercussions on both the dynamics of the Cold War and on the evolution of the transatlantic relationship. The death of Stalin – which triggered a power struggle in the Kremlin until the emergence of Nikita Khrushchev in 1955 – opened the possibility of a tentative dialogue with the West. The Soviet leadership seemed to be moving away from the theory of the inevitability of conflict between communism and capitalism, while gradually signalling the possibility of coexistence between the two systems. In the United States, the victory of the Republican Party brought General Eisenhower to the White House. The incoming president – and his Secretary of State John Foster Dulles – had expressed the intention of continuing Truman's policy towards Europe, provided that the other members of the Atlantic Alliance would tangibly demonstrate their determination to strengthen their defences and cooperate closely with NATO. From the new administration's point of view, a tentative dialogue with the Soviets could only be initiated if the West was perceived as strong and unified. Considering the EDC as a means to solidify infra-European cooperation (including French–German rapprochement), Eisenhower and Dulles went as far as threatening the revision of US policy towards Europe – an 'agonizing reappraisal' in the words of Secretary Dulles – should the French parliament reject the plans on a European army.

Ultimately, America's policy towards Europe did not undergo any reappraisal as a consequence of the fall of the EDC. The French vote did, however, cause a crisis in the relationship between France and the United States. Until 1954, the French had always participated in the decisions concerning Germany. But this would no longer be the case after the outcome of the EDC vote. The episode therefore anticipated the far deeper breach between France and the United States of the mid-1960s. Another consequence of the crisis of the EDC was the further strengthening of the special relationship between the US and Great Britain. More generally, the failure to create a European army in the early 1950s and the refusal to conceive ways of autonomously integrating the European defences would come to entail an ever-stronger reliance of the European countries on the United States on matters of security and defence. This element would remain a characteristic feature of the transatlantic relationship, constantly unbalanced on security issues due to the much stronger military power of the United States.

West Germany enters NATO

After the French rejection of the EDC, the British took the initiative to both maintain the unity of the transatlantic relationship and to address the issue of German rearmament. The British Conservative government (Winston Churchill returned to power in 1951 and was succeeded by Anthony Eden in 1955) proposed to extend the Brussels Treaty, stipulated in March 1948 between France, Britain and the Benelux countries, to include Italy and West Germany. The new alliance, called the Western European Union (WEU), would recognize full sovereignty to the Federal Republic of Germany, which would then enter NATO. Acknowledging its isolation, and under pressure from the United States, France was forced to accept this solution. The British, as the promoters of the initiative and as formal signatories of the WEU, became more strongly linked to the security structure of continental Europe. The member countries reached agreement at the Paris Conference in October 1954 and the WEU formally entered into force in May 1955. This concluded the process, started in 1948, geared towards creating an integrated Western European defensive system. The European countries proved determined to strengthen their inter-relationship, while firmly recognizing the close alliance with the United States.

This also concluded the thorny issue of German rearmament. The West German entry into NATO definitely confirmed the division of the country and excluded – for the time being – any possibility for German unification. At the same time, the solution chosen by the Europeans marked the end of the search for an autonomous defensive structure and of any form of supranationality on matters of security. However, even in the absence of formal integration, the European countries started to deeply cooperate with each other, therefore overcoming their traditional rivalries. Western Europe as a whole became more tied and dependent on the United States for its security and defence. This was the reality of the new bipolar world order that emerged from World War II – a reality which, from the start, France only reluctantly came to accept.

The year 1955 marked the definitive stabilization of the division of Europe into two opposing camps. The Soviet Union reacted to the developments in the West first by denouncing pre-existing treaties of friendship with France and Britain, and then by initiating negotiations on a military alliance between Moscow and the major Eastern European countries. In May 1955 (as West Germany formally entered NATO), the Warsaw Treaty (commonly referred to as the Warsaw Pact) was signed between the Soviet Union, Albania, Bulgaria, Czechoslovakia, Hungary, Poland, Romania and the German Democratic Republic (East Germany). It was a treaty of friendship, cooperation and mutual assistance. In essence it established a collective defence mechanism similar to NATO's. A system led by the Soviet Union was thus created in contra-position to one led by the United States. The Cold War division of Europe in two opposing blocs – with the exception of a few neutral countries – was therefore completed.

A tentative dialogue?

By the mid-1950s, the two Cold War blocs were still perceived as antagonistic and hostile. But the emphasis had gradually shifted on the necessity of conceiving forms of coexistence. In the Soviet Union, Georgi Malenkov emerged as the leading figure after Stalin's death. He became premier and leader of the Communist Party for a brief period, until he was ousted by Nikita Khrushchev in 1955. Malenkov initiated the first internal reforms in the USSR and appeared to loosen the iron-fist dictatorship established by Stalin. While continuing to put emphasis on Soviet strength and superiority (ordering, for example, the testing of the hydrogen nuclear bomb), at the same time he opened a cautious dialogue with the West.

The Geneva conference of 1954

Evidence of a first tentative form of détente between the superpowers came from the convening of the Geneva conference in 1954, with the dual scope of addressing the Korean question and of restoring peace to Indochina (the population of the French colonies

Source: adapted from Reynolds (1994)

Figure 2.1 The Cold War in Europe

– particularly in present-day North Vietnam – had been fighting against French authority since 1946). Representatives from the United States, the Soviet Union, France, the United Kingdom and the People's Republic of China (together with other nations which had partici-pated with the UN force in Korea) met in Geneva from April to July 1954. The discus-sions on Korea focused on the modality of possible elections to be held in North and South Korea. No agreement was found and no declaration was issued. On Indochina, instead, the conference produced a set of documents called the Geneva Accords, which supported the territorial integrity and sovereignty of Indochina, thereby granting it its independence from France (see Chapter 3). In order to facilitate the end of the hostilities, a line was drawn between northern and southern zones into which the Vietnamese forces and the forces that had supported the French had to withdraw. Unification would have to take place under inter-nationally supervised free elections scheduled for 1956.

The Austrian State Treaty

The different climate between the superpowers, which had at least initiated a dialogue even in the absence of concrete agreements, enabled the conclusion of the Austrian State Treaty in May 1955. Formally not a peace treaty, because Austria had been the first victim of Nazi Germany, the agreement re-established Austria as an independent sovereign state. It was signed by the four occupying powers (US, UK, France and USSR) and the Austrian government. In addition to recognizing the Austrian state, the treaty outlawed the Anschluss (the political union between Germany and Austria) and prohibited Nazi or Fascist organizations. An important part of the agreement was the declaration on permanent neutrality made by the Austrian government upon ratification of the treaty, therefore ensuring Moscow that Austria would not join NATO after the Soviet withdrawal. As a consequence of the treaty, the occupying powers withdrew from Austria in October 1955. This was the first case in which the Soviet Union voluntarily withdrew from a formally occupied European country. On the other hand, by recognizing Austrian neutrality, the West accepted breaking the territorial continuity of the Western front.

The Geneva summit of 1955

A second summit in Geneva, held in July 1955, further signalled the tentative relaxation of Cold War tensions. The four formerly allied countries (France, UK, US and USSR) met to discuss East–West trade agreements, international security and disarmament, and the future of Germany. In this context, President Eisenhower set forth the so-called 'open skies' proposal, which called for the US and the Soviet Union to exchange maps indicating the location of their military installations. With these maps, each side would be authorized to conduct aerial surveillance of the installations to ensure compliance with any future potential arms control agreement. While the British and the French expressed interest in the proposal, the Soviets predictably rejected it. On Germany, the Soviets stated that they were willing to accept its unification, provided that the new united Germany would remain neutral. This statement was de facto deprived of significance, considering the Federal Republic's entry into NATO only a few months earlier. Although the Geneva summit ended with no agreements, it nevertheless re-established the pattern of high-level meetings and marked a new era of cautious optimism in Cold War relations.

Adenauer in Moscow

In the aftermath of the Geneva summit, another signal of a tentative new course for the Cold War came from West German Chancellor Adenauer's visit to Moscow in September 1955. Only a few years earlier, it would have been unforeseeable for the leader of the Federal Republic – which was being integrated into the Western European security structure – to visit the Soviet Union (Moscow had issued the invitation to Adenauer in June 1955, only days after the ratification of the treaties creating the Western European Union). The scope of the Soviet invitation was to pressure Adenauer into opening a dialogue with East Germany (the GDR).

This proposal challenged the so-called Hallstein doctrine – named after Adenauer's close adviser and senior civil servant Walter Hallstein – according to which the Federal Republic would not establish or maintain diplomatic relations with any state that recognized the GDR. Predictably, the conversations in Moscow were not friendly, and no concrete agreement could be reached on the topic of German unification. However, in contradiction to the Hallstein doctrine, Adenauer did establish diplomatic relations with Moscow and, in exchange, obtained the liberation of German prisoners of war detained in the Soviet Union (a concession which was deemed very important in Germany and for which the chancellor was willing to pay the price of partial incoherence). While Moscow failed to break the unity of the Western camp, Adenauer demonstrated some freedom of action and confirmed the unrelenting importance of Germany within the architecture of the Western security structure.

The stability of the Cold War in Europe

De-Stalinization

As some rules of coexistence were emerging between the two blocs, a major crisis unfolded in Hungary, one of the member countries of the Warsaw Pact. In 1956, Nikita Khrushchev – by then the new leader of the Soviet Union – shocked the 20th Congress of the Communist Party by denouncing Stalin's 'cult of personality' and his numerous crimes. In foreign policy, Khrushchev underscored coexistence with the capitalist West and stated that war between the two systems was no longer inevitable. In his view, the socialist system would eventually prevail because of its inherent superiority. Other forms of transition to socialism – different from the rigid Stalinist model – were recognized as means of strengthening the socialist camp. Khrushchev's approach – which came to be known as de-Stalinization – was pursued cautiously, but it nevertheless created a crisis of legitimacy in the Eastern European countries dominated by the Soviet Union.

The most serious crises occurred in Poland and Hungary, two countries where the communist parties had very limited popular support and where the Catholic Church represented a strong unifying force for the opposition. In June 1956, the workers in the Polish city of Poznan demonstrated, demanding reforms. The riots and strikes were suppressed by the authorities, but reformist Communist leader Wladyslaw Gomulka emerged as a leader capable of addressing popular discontent, while remaining strongly linked and loyal to the Soviet Union.

The Hungarian crisis

In October 1956 the Hungarians followed the Polish example by testing the limits of de-Stalinization. Protesters rallied around reformist premier Imre Nagy and violent demonstrations erupted after he was ousted from power. Soviet troops entered the scene but could not disperse the insurgents. On 24 October, Nagy was reappointed prime minister and, seeking to address the demands of the protesters, constituted a new government that included non-communists. He also ended the one-party state system, promised freedom of speech and declared that Hungary would withdraw from the Warsaw Pact. The Soviet Union reacted and launched a major offensive against Budapest. The reform movement was violently repressed, and a new Soviet-aligned government was reinstituted. Nagy and other leaders of the insurgency were executed in June 1958.

The Hungarian crisis constituted the greatest crisis within the Soviet bloc before the Warsaw Pact invasion of Czechoslovakia in August 1968. To the Western European countries and to the United States it demonstrated that, despite Khrushchev's new course, the Soviet system was kept together only by force. This had an impact on some members of the communist parties of the Western countries, which started to gradually distance themselves from the Soviet Union. While these defections did not have a serious impact on the dimension and cohesion of the communist parties, they did signal a rupture from the Soviet leadership, which would fully emerge after 1968.

Most significantly, the Hungarian episode confirmed that in Europe the bipolar competition between the Soviet Union and the United States had entered the phase of so-called peaceful coexistence. While Hungary's fate hung in balance, the Western powers watched without intervening in support of Imre Nagy's decision to challenge Moscow and exit the Soviet sphere of influence. Both in Europe and in the United States, the Hungarian quest for more freedom was deemed an affair internal to the Soviet empire, by then implicitly recognized by the West. Challenging the boundaries of the Soviet sphere and forcing a Soviet withdrawal was no longer in the interests of the Western powers.

The American objectives

No 'roll back'

During the American presidential campaign of 1952, Eisenhower had criticized the Truman administration's policy of containment as a weak and passive policy. Instead, the future US president had advocated a more dynamic stance: America would have to pressure the Soviet Union into liberating Eastern Europe. Containment had to be substituted by what was labelled as 'roll back' (i.e. the Soviet Union would have to withdraw, or roll back from Eastern Europe, thus freeing the oppressed people of the countries under heavy Soviet influence). But when Eisenhower became president, the roll back policy proved to have been purely rhetorical. Two concrete opportunities had unfolded in which the United States could have intervened in order to push the Soviets 'back' – in Poland and, all the more dramatically, in Hungary. Instead, Washington remained idle in face of the Soviet consolidation of its sphere of influence. Despite the more aggressive tones, the Eisenhower administration chose not to challenge the stability of the Cold War order that had emerged in Europe.

The doctrine of 'massive retaliation'

In the mid-1950s, Washington wanted to strengthen its leadership within the Atlantic Alliance. The priority was to enhance the credibility of the American commitment to the defence of Europe by providing adequate military guarantees. However, the US leadership also sought to diminish the financial burden of sustaining, or of having to increase, its conventional forces in Europe.

These contradictory objectives were addressed in two ways. First, Washington called upon its European allies to increase their contribution to the transatlantic security system. Second, the US leadership elaborated a new strategic doctrine, which came to be known as the doctrine of 'massive retaliation'. The term was first used by Secretary of State John Foster Dulles in a speech at the Council of Foreign Relations in January 1954. Dulles stated that Washington would respond to military provocation 'at places and with means of our own choosing. Local defence must be reinforced by the further deterrent of massive retaliatory power.' In essence, this meant that America would back up its conventional forces with a massive nuclear retaliatory capability.

The aim of this strategy was to deter any potential Soviet attack in Europe. It was meant to counter the increasing preoccupations in the West regarding the imbalance of power between NATO and Warsaw Pact conventional forces. By relying on America's nuclear arsenal, the US leadership believed that the imbalance of conventional forces would be rendered insignificant. In fact, conventional forces could even be reduced, thus alleviating the financial burden of maintaining American troops in Europe. The Western bloc would be protected by a large US nuclear umbrella.

The development of this new American strategic posture had important consequences for the transatlantic relationship. Both the issue of diminishing the financial burden carried predominantly by the United States and the implications of the doctrine of massive retaliation would create the first serious ruptures between America and its Western European allies. While Washington willingly undertook and continued to sustain the leadership of the Alliance, it started to call for greater 'burden-sharing' on the part of Europe. This issue would emerge fully during the 1960s and would remain a constant feature of the military aspect of the transatlantic partnership throughout the Cold War, and beyond.

Moreover, the doctrine of massive retaliation had, from the beginning, some problematic aspects. A threat of a massive retaliatory strike was, in fact, difficult to make credible and it diminished the foreign policy options available to Washington. In addition, it was based on the premise that the Soviet Union would be in condition to suffer a massive nuclear strike without any possibility to react. But as the Soviets rapidly developed their nuclear forces, the US doctrine would gradually lose its significance. Ultimately (as will emerge in Chapter 3), instead of improving the credibility of the US guarantee, the massive retaliation doctrine would weaken it, causing a crisis of confidence in Europe regarding America's willingness to provide an effective defence.

The first 'out of area' challenge? The Suez Canal crisis

By the mid-1950s, the priority for both the Soviet Union and the United States was to strengthen and consolidate their respective spheres of influence which had emerged in Europe as a consequence of World War II. Neither superpower seemed willing to challenge the order in Europe. Within the transatlantic relationship, Washington underscored its leadership, particularly regarding the military and security aspects of the partnership. At the same time, as the rules of coexistence emerged in Europe, the United States focused on developing anti-Soviet alliances in other parts of the world. In September 1954, eight states – Australia, New Zealand, Pakistan, the Philippines, Thailand, France, the UK and the US – signed the Southeast Asia Collective Defence Treaty, creating the Southeast Asia Treaty Organization (SEATO). This treaty was modelled on NATO and extended the concept of anti-communist collective defence to Southeast Asia. In 1955, the United States focused on the Middle East and supported the creation of the Baghdad Pact, an alliance between Iraq, Turkey, Pakistan, Iran and the UK geared towards excluding the Soviet influence on the Middle East. Clearly, the Cold War was moving outside of Europe.

A year later, the unfolding of the Suez Canal crisis demonstrated the increased strategic importance of the Middle East as a potential future battleground of the Cold War. The crisis had an important impact on the transatlantic relationship because, for the first time, it broke the unity of the Western camp (with a rupture between the Anglo-French and the Americans). Moreover, the events in Suez marked the definitive end of any residual colonial-style influence of the Europeans in the Middle East.

The lead-up to the crisis

In the immediate post-war years, the British still considered the region to be under their predominant political and military influence. For its part, Washington had, during the inter-war years, already increased its economic presence by investing in the region's oil companies. By the mid-1950s, however, regional developments, particularly in Egypt, complicated the scenario. After the overthrow of the monarchy in 1952, the new Egyptian leader Gamal Abdel Nasser was determined to eliminate British influence from the country. According to a 1936 treaty, British troops were still stationed along the Suez Canal, but, in October 1954 London and Cairo agreed on a complete British withdrawal within two years.

The American policy towards the region rotated around the dual necessity of maintaining positive relations with the oil-producing countries, without undermining America's support for Israel. This led Washington to privilege relations with other Arab countries – such as Saudi Arabia – rather than with Egypt, because of Nasser's more open anti-Israeli stance. In 1955, the Egyptian leader attended the Bandung conference that created the movement of the non-aligned countries, therefore choosing an allegedly neutral stance in the bipolar conflict. However, he still sought to strengthen Egyptian forces in case of a conflict with Israel. He thus turned to the United States for arms agreements, but in the face of Washington's refusal he signed an arms agreement with Czechoslovakia in September 1955. Given Prague's close relationship with Moscow, the agreement potentially opened the way for Soviet advancement into the region, a prospect clearly unwelcomed by the American leadership.

In order to prevent the advance of Soviet influence, while at the same time seeking to deter any potential anti-Israeli war plans, US Secretary of State Dulles proposed to Nasser that the United States (together with the UK and the World Bank) would finance the construction of the Aswan Dam – a project that would allow better utilization of the River Nile's water for irrigation. But because of America's continued delays (due to internal resistance in Washington) and the absence of any aid from the Soviet Union, in July 1956 Nasser nationalized the Suez Canal Company, which controlled the passage through the Canal, and was jointly owned by the British and the French. The Egyptian leader declared that from that moment onwards the Canal would be controlled by Egypt and that the income gained by the navigation tariffs would be used for the construction of the Aswan Dam. This decision initiated an intense crisis, which climaxed with the war of France, Great Britain and Israel against Egypt in October and November 1956.

The Anglo-French intervention

Refusing to accept the loss of influence implicit in the nationalization, France and Britain signed a secret agreement with Israel, which would initially attack Egypt and would then be supported by a joint Anglo-French force. Accordingly, on 29 October 1956 Israeli troops invaded Egypt and, two days later, British and French military forces entered the Canal Zone. The Soviet Union reacted and threatened to intervene on Egypt's behalf. US President Eisenhower, fearing that Moscow would use the crisis as a means of gaining influence in the Middle East, pressured Britain, France and Israel into agreeing to a ceasefire, and an eventual withdrawal from Egypt in November 1956.

The rupture between the United States and its European allies could not have been more evident. In order to bypass the French and British veto at the UN Security Council, Washington proposed a General Assembly vote along the same lines as the scheme that had allowed the UN to pass the Uniting for Peace resolution in 1950, paving the way for the entry of UN forces in Korea. The American proposal was overwhelmingly approved. The United Nations therefore enforced a ceasefire and the withdrawal of outside forces within the armistice line. Britain and France were forced to back down, UN forces entered the area to maintain the ceasefire and, in March 1957, the control of the canal returned to Egypt (which, in turn, committed to its open and free navigation).

The Suez crisis had a huge impact on the interests and aspirations of the French and the British. France's loss of influence had repercussions both domestically and in the context of the Algerian war (Paris would encounter increasing difficulties in building consensus on its policy towards Algeria, a situation which would be resolved only after the return to political life of General Charles de Gaulle in 1959 – see Chapter 3). Having already agreed to withdraw from Egypt, the consequences for the British were less demoralizing. The rapport between London and Washington remained tense for some time, but when Harold Macmillan replaced Anthony Eden as prime minister in January 1957, the special relationship was restored. The British did, however, have to concede the role of key player to the United States also in the Middle East.

For both the French and the British, the Suez episode confirmed the difficulties of undertaking military operations without US approval and support. At the same time, this realization strengthened the factions which advocated more autonomous policies: both the British objective of an independent nuclear deterrent and the French project on the 'force de frappe' would find justification and further incentive from the Suez debacle (see Chapter 3). Also, the notion of a Europe as a third force between the United States and the Soviet Union started to surface soon after Suez, in a speech delivered by French Prime Minister Guy Mollet to the French Parliament in January 1957.

The American position

Throughout the crisis the Americans had sought to protect their interests in the region and had thus distanced themselves from the Anglo-French action. The US, in fact, had pursued a dual objective: first, it wanted to avoid the perception that the attack against Egypt was an action of the West against the Arab world; second, it wanted to prevent the Soviets from expanding their influence in the area as a consequence of the crisis. Therefore, during the conflict Dulles and Eisenhower never interrupted their contacts with Egypt, and they tried to mediate between Nasser and the Anglo-French. Then, in a speech to Congress in January 1957, President Eisenhower outlined the main points of America's future policy towards the Middle East. The president asked Congress to 'authorize the United States to cooperate with and assist any nation or group of nations in the general area of the Middle East in the development of economic strength dedicated to the maintenance of national independence'. Such aid could extend to 'military assistance and cooperation' and 'include the employment of the armed forces of the United States to secure and protect the territorial integrity and political independence' of nations threatened by international communism.[1]

With this statement – which became known as the Eisenhower doctrine – the president in essence extended the US strategy of containment to the entire Middle Eastern region. The American stance during and after the Suez crisis demonstrated that, for Washington, the containment of the Soviet Union had priority over the solidarity with its European allies, particularly in areas of crucial strategic importance. As will more fully emerge in the next chapters, such areas would increasingly be located outside the North Atlantic territory. In decades to come 'out of area' issues emerged, and would repeatedly cause ruptures and crises between the United States and the European countries.

The development of European integration

The stabilization of the Cold War in Europe forced East and West to coexist and accept the division of the continent along the lines marked by the Iron Curtain. Consequently, both sides had to adapt to the new order, which, for the time being, went unchallenged. In Western Europe, the post-war reconstruction had given way to dynamic economic growth rates. In the Federal Republic of Germany, the growth rate had reached 7 per cent of the GDP; in Italy, the 1950s marked the beginning of the so-called 'economic miracle', with an average growth rate of 6 per cent, but with peaks of up to 10 per cent; France and Britain, though to a lesser degree, also underwent a period of prosperity. From an economic point of view, therefore, the conditions for Western Europe to regain a central position in the world's economic system were being created. The limitations, however, were inherent in the fragmentation of the European market. This reduced free trade among the various (small) national entities, thus hindering further growth rates, while at the same time perpetuating traditional intra-European rivalries.

Economic integration

The failure of the European Defence Community had demonstrated the difficulty for the European countries to conceive supranational entities that would enable them to overcome specific national differences. In the mid-1950s, however, a few key personalities – such as Jean Monnet, then the president of ECSC, and the foreign ministers of the Benelux countries – relaunched the European integration initiative by shifting away from the political and military aspects, while focusing exclusively on economic integration.

As early as May 1954, in a speech at the common assembly of the European Coal and Steel Community, Jean Monnet stressed the positive repercussions of the creation of the ECSC for the six member states' economies. He therefore called for further economic integration of Europe. Jean Monnet then discussed how to pursue deeper integration of Europe with the representatives of the six's governments. The objectives he proposed were twofold: the extension of the competence of the ECSC to other sectors, such as transportation and energy (thus implicitly calling for further integration by sectors, along the model of the ECSC); and the creation of a separate European community to govern the peaceful uses of nuclear energy.

Box 2.2 Document extract: Speech by Mr Jean Monnet, president of the High Authority (Strasbourg, 12 May 1954)

Everyone can now see that our experiment has produced results. The way to make Europe, I want to repeat here, is to pool resources, create common institutions by transferring sovereignty to them and granting them the power of decision and to set up common rules which apply equally to all, and a common ideal of freedom and social progress. In the final analysis, this beginning of Europe has been less difficult than a good many people believed it would be ... Surrounded by the United States which alone account for half of the world production, a Russia in progress and Asia on the move, how could Europe possibly hope to escape from the necessity to change?

... At a moment when the peoples of Europe are looking to their future with a feeling of uncertainty and concern, the High Authority asks your Assembly to give them the message that the unity of Europe, with all the hopes that it brings with it, is possible and that it is being achieved.

The British reaction to these proposals was not enthusiastic. The Conservative government led by Prime Minister Anthony Eden (who had succeeded Churchill's second government in April 1955) favoured strengthened links between the six ECSC countries, but these did not have to be extended to include the UK. The British were far from foreseeing membership in a European integrated system. Their foreign policy rotated around three priorities: the Commonwealth, a positive relationship with Europe and the special relationship with the United States. No one aspect was to overshadow the others. Therefore, the integrationist views concerning Europe were, for the time being, limited to continental Europe, although positive external support from London would obviously constitute an asset.

At the same time, Monnet's initiative could not be seen as a French proposal. After the fall of the EDC, France – struggling with instability domestically, and challenged internationally by the war in Indochina and the revolutions in Africa – was no longer in a credible position to take the lead on European integration. The initiative was instead taken by the Benelux countries. In April 1955, Belgian foreign minister Paul-Henri Spaak officially endorsed Jean Monnet's ideas. The Federal Republic of Germany, France and Italy reacted cautiously, while both Luxembourg's foreign minister Joseph Bech and Dutch foreign minister Johann Willem Beyen supported the initiative wholeheartedly. Beyen went a step further: he criticized the idea of sector integration, and proposed a general economic integration of Europe to take place in phases. His plan set forth an idea of economic integration that differed from the kind of sector-based integration achieved by the six countries in the ECSC framework. Beyen's proposal was that the six should open, on a resolutely supranational basis, a general common market with neither customs duties nor import quotas. The first step would be the establishment of a customs union designed to lead towards economic union, or a common European market.

The Messina conference

The three Benelux countries rapidly defined a common position and, combining their initiative with Monnet's, invited the French, German and Italian governments to discuss these ideas at an international conference. The six countries were already scheduled to meet in Messina in May 1955 to designate Monnet's successor at the ECSC, and agreed to also discuss how to proceed with further integration. The three Benelux countries decided to propose to their European partners a sector approach for transport and energy, especially nuclear energy, and the parallel establishment of a general common market.

The Messina conference ended with a generic commitment to pursue the unification of Europe through the creation of common institutions, the gradual integration of national economies, the creation of a common market, and the gradual harmonization of each country's economic and social policies. These pledges were made more concrete by specifying that on the one side the six would create a European community for the peaceful uses of nuclear energy – to be called Euratom – and, on the other, that the objective of their common action was the establishment, in phases, of a common market. In order to achieve these goals, an intergovernmental committee – chaired by Paul-Henri Spaak – was tasked with organizing follow-up conferences and compiling a final report with concrete recommendations. The follow-up conferences took place in the second half of 1955 and early 1956, and the Spaak report was presented to the Council of Foreign Ministers of the six ECSC countries held in Venice in May 1956.

The European Economic Community

The negotiations leading to the Spaak report had been long and complex, influenced by the domestic situation in France (the Fourth Republic of 1946–1958 was characterized by high domestic instability with successive changes of governments, sometimes in the brief time span of a few months), as well as the Hungarian and Suez crises. Nevertheless, the delegations that had worked on the Spaak report were able to produce a concrete action plan, which was submitted to the six governments as a basis for the negotiations on the treaties founding the European Economic Community and the Euratom. The report was approved by the six countries at the Venice conference, and thereafter the work on the actual texts of the treaties started. The treaties establishing the European Economic Community (EEC) and the European Atomic Energy Community (Euratom) were signed less than a year later, in Rome, on 25 March 1957, by the representatives of the six member states of the European Coal and Steel Community (ECSC) – the Federal Republic of Germany, France, Italy, Belgium, the Netherlands and Luxembourg. The treaties were then debated and ratified by the national parliaments of the six signatory countries between May and December 1957. They entered into force on 1 January 1958.

The United States welcomed the creation of the European Economic Community, a project viewed as an important first step towards the political unification of Western Europe, a longer-term objective that the US leadership clearly supported. During the negotiations leading to the treaties, the American government had remained relatively detached, fearing that active involvement in support of the initiative might be counterproductive (as had happened with the EDC). Therefore, American Europeanists and the US government more openly endorsed the Euratom project, considered politically and militarily extremely significant, the negotiations of which – dealing with only one sector – proceeded more rapidly and smoothly than those for the EEC. In February 1957, President Eisenhower declared US support for the Euratom and, subsequently, approved a technical and financial assistance programme for the new community. Accordingly, the following year, the United States and Euratom signed a treaty of cooperation.

The British position towards the EEC was ambivalent. As had been the case with the ECSC and the EDC, London had stated – since the Messina conference – that it was not willing to be directly involved in the new, and more ambitious, European integration projects. The British policy remained subordinated to the links with the Commonwealth; it was contrary to the concept of supranationality and loyal to the role of mediator between the United States and Europe.

However, as the initiatives of the six countries proceeded towards concrete realization, the positive attitude of external support initially expressed by the British gradually shifted to a position that anticipated future antagonism. In July 1956, London proposed to link the project on the European Common Market to the creation of a free trade area – a proposal that was to lead to the creation of the European Free Trade Association (EFTA) in May 1960 (the founding members were Austria, Denmark, Norway, Portugal, Sweden, Switzerland and the United Kingdom). The main difference between the two projects was the absence of a common external tariff for the members of the free trade area. Each country could thus maintain its own tariff towards third countries (i.e. the countries outside the zone). In this way, the British would maintain their privileged position towards the Commonwealth states. While the British proposal was not seen as contrary to the scope and objectives of the EEC as such, London's insistence on negotiating a free trade area before entering discussions on the common market was perceived negatively by the six EEC countries. The British position did not prevent the successful conclusion and ratification of the EEC treaty. However, intra-European rivalries related to the EEC and EFTA would soon surface, complicating both the evolution of the newly born European Economic Community and the development of the transatlantic relationship.

Conclusion

The early to mid-1950s witnessed the creation of durable structures and frameworks to sustain and guide the future development of the transatlantic relationship. The institutionalization of NATO permanently linked the security of the United States to the security of Western Europe, and was (and would remain) the strongest tangible demonstration of the importance of the European–American partnership. Economically and politically, amid many difficulties, Western Europe was gradually strengthening itself. Not only was a distinct European identity emerging, within the context of the alliance with the United States, but also a new political and institutional autonomy had been created, first with the ECSC and later with the EEC.

After overcoming the post-war crisis and the efforts dedicated to its reconstruction, Europe was acquiring awareness of the possibilities and opportunities, as well as of the inherent limitations, of its actions. This led to the development of European economic integration, while continuing to heavily rely on the United States for security and defence. Concurrently, as the Cold War order had stabilized in Europe and the bipolar conflict increasingly moved outside the European theatre, the dilemmas on how to manage 'out of area' issues started to surface within the transatlantic alliance, challenging its unity and coherence.

Suggested further reading

Grosser, Alfred (1980) *The Western Alliance: European–American Relations since 1945*. New York: Continuum.

Hitchcock, William I. (2004) *The Struggle for Europe: The Turbulent History of a Divided Continent, 1945 to the Present*. New York: Anchor Books.

Kaplan, Lawrence S. (1984) *NATO: The Formative Years*. Lexington, KY: University Press of Kentucky.

Lundestad, Geir (1998) *'Empire' by Integration: The United States and European Integration, 1945–1997*. Oxford: Oxford University Press.

Lundestad, Geir (2003) *The United States and Western Europe since 1945: From 'Empire' by Invitation to Transatlantic Drift*. Oxford: Oxford University Press.

Mastny, Vojtech and Malcolm Byrne (eds) (2005) *A Cardboard Castle? An Inside History of the Warsaw Pact, 1955–1991*. New York: Central European University Press.

Moravcsik, Andrew (1999) *The Choice for Europe: Social Purpose and State Power from Messina to Maastricht*. London: UCL Press.

Powaski, Ronald E. (1994) *The Entangling Alliance: The United States and European Security, 1950–1993*. Westport, CT: Greenwood.

Schmidt, Gustav (ed.) (2001) *A History of NATO: The First Fifty Years*. Basingstoke, UK: Palgrave.

3 Tension and coexistence, 1957–1961

The process of decolonization

After World War II, the process of decolonization further accelerated the loss of global influence of the European powers. The diminished power and resources of the major colonizing powers were insufficient to maintain control over their colonies. Faced with the rise of nationalist movements, the European powers (Britain and France mainly, and later Portugal, the Netherlands and Belgium) no longer possessed the means or the political support domestically to repress the demands – and sometimes violent protests – of the independence movements. This process coincided with the emergence on the global scene of the two superpowers, which both advocated – albeit in different forms – a transition to independence (the United States relinquished its only colony, the Philippines, in 1946; the Soviet Union had never had any colonies).

The end of the British Empire

For centuries the British had administered a huge empire, consisting of dominions, colonies, protectorates and mandates (starting in the late 16th century, Britain had ruled over vast portions of the Americas and Africa, and then later also over India and other parts of Asia). At its peak, it was said that 'the sun never sets on the British Empire'. But from 1947, with the independence of India, the empire began to crumble and, within 20 years, it ceased to exist. Over 500 million people were given independent self-government in this relatively short period of time. The British financial situation after World War II, combined with the rise of anti-colonial movements, rendered the upholding of the empire impossible.

One of the most pressing questions facing London in 1945 was the issue of Indian independence. India's two independence movements had been campaigning for independence since the end of World War I, but disagreed on the best form of government for their future state. The Indian National Congress favoured a unified secular state (with a Hindu majority), while the Muslim League advocated a separate Islamic state for the regions with a Muslim majority. Increased popular unrest (including the mutiny of the Royal Indian Navy during 1946) and the prospect of civil war convinced the British government to grant independence in August 1947. British India was partitioned into the newly independent states of India and Pakistan, with millions of Muslims crossing from India into Pakistan, and Hindus in the reverse direction (violence between the two communities cost thousands of lives and mutual tension, which endures to the present day). Former British colonies of Burma and Ceylon were granted independence in 1948.

The British government faced a situation similar to India in the British mandate over Palestine, where an Arab majority lived alongside a Jewish minority. In 1947, London declared its withdrawal from Palestine, passing the issue to the newly created United Nations (which subsequently voted for the partition of Palestine into a Jewish and Arab state; but this resolution was never implemented, with only Israel declaring its statehood in 1948). In the 1950s, Britain was forced to completely withdraw from Egypt (following the Suez Canal crisis; see Chapter 2), but did maintain a limited presence in the Middle East (in Aden and Bahrain) until the late 1960s. Between the 1950s and the 1960s, Britain also completely withdrew from Africa.

The end of the French Empire

In the 19th and 20th centuries, the French colonial empire (which dated back to the 17th century) was second in size only to the British Empire. It extended over vast portions of Africa and Asia (the French had lost most of their territories in the Americas and India in the 18th century). Also the French Empire started to vacillate during World War II, when various parts of it were occupied by other powers (Japan occupied Indochina; Britain occupied Syria and Lebanon; the US and Britain occupied Morocco and Algeria). However, control was re-established by General de Gaulle and in 1946 the colonial empire was included in the new French Union. While France was also immediately confronted with the revendications of the decolonization movements, it held on to its possessions until the late 1950s, waging costly wars against the independence movements in Algeria and Indochina (while granting independence to Tunisia and Morocco in 1956).

The British and French retreats from their colonial possessions represented a turning point in world affairs. While the process was gradual (but relatively rapid compared with the decades of colonial rule), the European powers only reluctantly accepted their loss of power and global influence, as various episodes demonstrate (such as the Suez Canal crisis). The American policy towards the decolonization process was one of detachment from the European powers. This was motivated by the concern that a close identification with the former colonial powers would hamper future US policies towards the newly independent countries. As the decolonization process came to be intertwined with the unfolding of the Cold War, Washington's policy emerged as one meant to fill the 'vacuum' of power left by the retreating European powers in order to prevent the potential advancement of Soviet/ Marxist influence. The cases of Iran (after the 1953 coup, which restored the Shah back in power) and Indochina (where the United States took on the role previously retained by the French) are emblematic of the shift in power in favour of the United States, as Washington stepped in to substitute the British and the French.

While the British generally adopted a policy of peaceful disengagement from the colonies, and managed to retain informal ties and links by expanding the organization of the Commonwealth, the French (and later the Belgian and Portuguese) decolonization process was more traumatic. For France, the case of Algeria was particularly problematic because of the large number of European settlers living in the African country (the oldest of the French colonies, which had been under French rule for over a century). The war of independence broke out in 1954 and turned into a prolonged crisis, resolved only after General de Gaulle's return to power in 1958. Algeria was eventually granted independence in 1962.

The second problematic case of French decolonization with longer-term and more global repercussions was Indochina. The war between the Vietminh (the League for the Independence of Vietnam) and the French Union's forces (which fought together

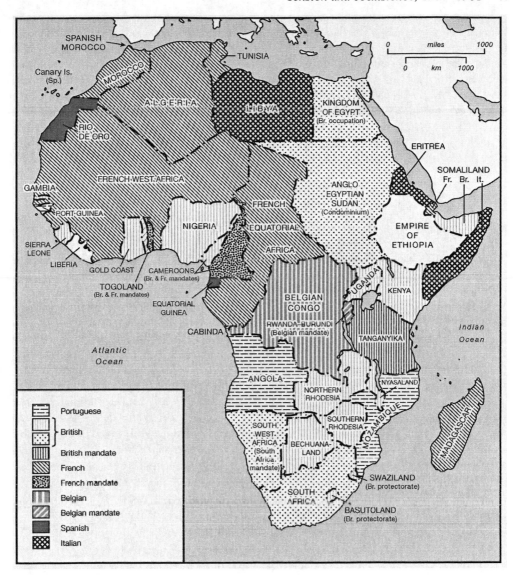

Source: adapted from Holland (1985)

Figure 3.1 Map of European colonies in Africa before 1945

with the Vietnamese National Army) started in late 1946. From the beginning, the struggle for the independence of Vietnam was inter-related with the evolution of the Cold War. Communist China and the Soviet Union supported the Vietminh, while the United States (from 1949 onwards) backed the French forces. The prolonged fighting and the increasing unpopularity of the war eventually led the French to disengage from the conflict. Negotiations between France and the Vietminh started in Geneva in April 1954 (see Chapter 2). Vietnam was divided along the 17th parallel, with internationally supervised elections scheduled to take place in 1956. After the Geneva Accords, the

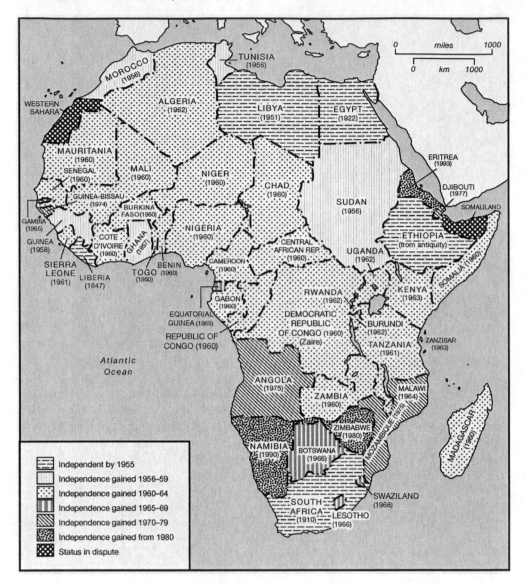

Source: adapted from Brown and Louis (1999)

Figure 3.2 Map of decolonization in Africa since 1945

newly created Republic of Vietnam in the south increasingly relied on the Americans, rather than French, for assistance. The date for the scheduled elections passed without the sides complying with the Accords. The United States gradually started assisting South Vietnam in the creation of its army. In 1959, the communist factions decided to relaunch the fighting for the unification of Vietnam. But at this point the war in Indochina was no longer a war of decolonization. It had become part of America's efforts to contain the expansion of communism (see Chapter 4).

Decolonization and transatlantic relations

The impact of the decolonization process on the transatlantic relationship was twofold. First, the United States stepped in to compensate the withdrawal of the European influence in the areas it considered strategically important, confirming its emergence on the world scene as a leading global power. The European countries, on the contrary, retreated to a predominantly regional role. Second, as many countries became independent – with newly established governments that appeared fragile and potentially exposed to outside interference – the Cold War rivalry increasingly moved into the Third World. Starting in the mid-1950s, following the stabilization of the Cold War order in Europe, the battle for supremacy between the superpowers moved into areas previously considered peripheral. Consequently, the bipolar antagonism started to acquire an additional meaning. The competition between the United States and the Soviet Union became also a competition on the most suitable model of development – capitalist versus socialist – for the Third World countries. This aspect became all the more important after 1960, the so-called 'year of Africa' during which 17 former colonial territories were granted independence. The crisis that ensued in the Congo (after declaring its independence from Belgium) and, later during the 1970s, the wars in Angola and Mozambique (former Portuguese colonies) confirmed a greater American–Soviet competition in the Third World (as both sides entered these conflicts, which effectively became proxy wars between the two superpowers). In contrast, the European powers, for the most part, disengaged. As a result, the issue of how to collectively deal with the multiplication of 'out of area' crises remained unaddressed by the transatlantic alliance.

The nuclear arms race escalates

The decolonization process amplified the potential fields of confrontation between the superpowers, changing the dynamics of the Cold War. As a result, Washington and Moscow had to face the increased political and economic costs of sustaining an increasingly global presence. Each side's military strategies had to be adapted to the change in the political context. In the second half of the 1950s, the superpowers adjusted to these developments in an analogous way: by decreasing their conventional forces (thus cutting the costs related to maintaining troops abroad) and, in parallel, by investing in the development of their nuclear arsenals. The diminished capacity to intervene in crises with conventional forces was thus compensated by a greater reliance on nuclear weapons (considered more cost-effective, and therefore maximizing the cost–benefit ratio in the rationalization of military resources). Consequently, the nuclear competition between the superpowers became an always more central aspect of the bipolar relationship and, in general, of the entire international system.

The nuclear competition, which had started in 1945 with the explosion of the atomic bombs on Hiroshima and Nagasaki, had rapidly evolved in the course of a decade, first with the end of the US monopoly in 1949 (when the Soviets exploded their first device) and then, in the early 1950s, with the development of hydrogen bombs (more powerful nuclear devices). By the 1960s, the number of nuclear weapons possessed by the superpowers (and France and Britain, which had entered the nuclear 'club') had significantly increased.

The nuclear arms race encompassed two distinct but inherently related issues: one was the possession of an arsenal with greater destructive power than that of the adversary; the second was the development of delivery vehicles in order to effectively target the enemy's territory. Initially, the superpowers had relied only on airplanes to deliver the bombs (as had happened in Japan), but from the mid-1950s they started to develop missiles capable of

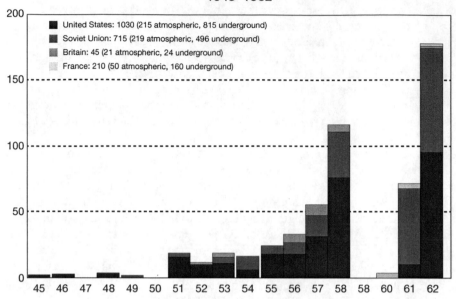

Global Nuclear Weapons Tests
1945–1962

Legend:
- United States: 1030 (215 atmospheric, 815 underground)
- Soviet Union: 715 (219 atmospheric, 496 underground)
- Britain: 45 (21 atmospheric, 24 underground)
- France: 210 (50 atmospheric, 160 underground)

Notes:
US total does not include the two atomic bombs dropped on Hiroshima and Nagasaki in August 1945. The US and the Soviet Union conducted 27 and 124 'Peaceful Nuclear Explosions', respectively, which are included in the above totals. India conducted an underground test in 1974.

Source: US Department of Energy; Natural Resources Defense Council, Nuclear Weapons Databook Project

Figure 3.3 Countries testing nuclear weapons

carrying a nuclear device. When both the US and the USSR developed intermediate-range missiles (i.e. missiles that could reach Soviet territory from the US bases in Europe, and vice versa), the issue became of crucial importance for European security. In fact, the realization that a nuclear war in Europe was possible had obvious repercussions on the evolution of the transatlantic relationship. Having become the potential target of Soviet missiles, some Western European countries started to question the effectiveness of relying solely on America's nuclear guarantee.

An autonomous nuclear capability for Europe?

The American stance during the Suez crisis had left a bitter taste not only in France, but also in other Western European countries. German Chancellor Adenauer, for example, assessed the US position as totally heedless of European interests and started to share the general feeling of distrust circulating in Europe towards the US strategic doctrine. If the Suez crisis had been perceived in Washington as a threat to US interests in the Middle East and, concurrently, the American leadership had stood idle in face of the Soviet action in

Hungary, it seemed difficult to foresee what kind of crisis could be grave enough to trigger Washington's 'massive retaliation' in defence of Europe. The doubts concerning US willingness to employ its nuclear forces only deepened when the rapid technological progress made by the Soviet Union became evident.

Although the production and deployment of intermediate-range missiles on the part of the superpowers had been important, the development of longer-range missiles (or intercontinental ballistic missiles, ICBM) was an even more critical turning point. Considering the inviolability of American territory – because of the absence of Soviet bases close to the United States – the development of missiles theoretically capable of directly striking American soil would totally revolutionize the basic assumptions upon which the US had founded its Cold War posture. In the second half of the 1950s, both superpowers were testing the production of ICBMs, but Washington was confident in its technological lead. In October 1957, the successful launch of the first Soviet satellite into space – the Sputnik – therefore came as a shock. The launch of the satellite highlighted Moscow's progress in missile technology, a sector in which the Americans considered themselves more advanced. Most importantly, the launch exposed the US territory to a potential missile strike for the first time in its history. This aroused deep concerns in America. A pervasive sense of pessimism came to dominate the last years of the Eisenhower administration, despite the fact that the actual gap between the superpowers' forces was less worrying than the Sputnik launch seemed to indicate. But the Soviets had won an important propaganda victory.

For the Western Europeans, the launch of Sputnik only deepened the concerns about their strategic vulnerability. Now that American cities were directly in danger, would the US leadership risk exposing them in order to defend Europe? If an American massive retaliation to a Soviet aggressive act in Europe would trigger an equally devastating Soviet reaction targeting America, then the credibility of the US nuclear guarantee was greatly diminished. Such considerations accelerated the major Western European countries' assessment of the possibility of developing their own autonomous nuclear capability.

The British nuclear programme

For the British, the problem had already been addressed in the early 1950s, when they tested their first nuclear weapon. In contrast to other European powers, the British nuclear programme developed in close cooperation with the United States. In 1958, the US and the UK signed a Mutual Defence Agreement on nuclear weapons cooperation, which enabled the parties to exchange classified information in order to improve the design, development and production of atomic weapons. It was by far the most comprehensive agreement on nuclear collaboration between the United States and any other country. This area of cooperation between London and Washington was a tangible demonstration of the special relationship between the two countries.

The French nuclear programme

For the French, however, the search for an autonomous nuclear capability was the consequence of the diminished confidence in the American deterrent. The first steps towards the development of the French nuclear programme were taken in 1957. In parallel, Paris proposed a Franco-German-Italian nuclear cooperation agreement, in large part viewed as a means to compensate for the deepening of the Anglo-American cooperation. The trilateral agreement was signed in November 1957 and could have potentially been the basis for the

Box 3.1 The impact of Sputnik on civil society

In the mid-1950s, the popularity of the proposals on disarmament and neutrality had signalled the emerging discontent within certain sectors of European public opinion. These started to question the legitimacy of the Cold War division of Europe and the reliance on the American 'nuclear umbrella'. The launch of Sputnik in 1957 and the subsequent escalation of the nuclear arms race deepened the dissatisfaction in parts of European civil society, contributing to the emergence of protest movements against the proliferation of nuclear weapons. Movements that advocated arms control agreements and a greater emphasis on disarmament (rather than rearmament) emerged, for example, in Great Britain, Italy and Germany. In Britain, the pacifist movement – supported by the Labour Party – grew in size and, for the first time, advanced the idea of unilateral disarmament. In the early 1960s, the so-called Aldermaston marches attracted tens of thousands of people. These were protest demonstrations – the first was organized in April 1958 – in which the crowd would march from Trafalgar Square in London to Aldermaston in Berkshire (a distance of over 80 kilometres) to the headquarters of the Atomic Weapons Research Establishment.

   In Germany, protest movements supported by the Protestant Church and by the Social Democratic Party opposed the proposal – advanced by Defence Minister Franz Josef Strauss – to deploy tactical nuclear weapons in the FRG. In Italy, the protest movement emerged in clear opposition to the decision to deploy intermediate-range nuclear missiles. It was supported by the left-leaning Christian Democrats and the Communist Party – which launched an intense anti-nuclear campaign during the 1958 elections.

   While these movements only partially influenced the action of governments, their importance was, at least, twofold. First, they demonstrated a significant shift in Europe towards positions critical of the perceived excessive American emphasis on the militarization of the Cold War. Second, they contributed (either directly or indirectly) to triggering the arms control process. In fact, after 1958 even in the United States more emphasis was given to developing arms control as a means of enhancing national security. Professional organizations – such as the Federation of Atomic Scientists and the Pugwash Conferences on Science and World Affairs – emerged as strong advocates of arms control and disarmament.

   This was the beginning of a process that developed further, after the Cuban Missile Crisis, with the signing in 1963 of the first arms control treaty (the Limited Test Ban Treaty).

creation of a distinctly European nuclear community. However, after Charles de Gaulle returned to power in France in 1958 he terminated the ongoing Franco-German-Italian negotiations and pursued the sovereign French way. According to de Gaulle, an independent nuclear deterrent was indispensable for France. It alone could allow an effective national defence free from outside pressures or interference. This rationale was the basis for the development of the so-called 'force de frappe'. The first French nuclear weapon was tested in early 1960.

Germany and NATO

While France moved to develop its own nuclear programme, the Germans and the Italians hesitated because of the obvious consequences of the issue on the relationship between the superpowers and on the fragile post-war order that had emerged in Europe. The precarious state of Germany was, once again, at the crux of the problem. The potential acquisition of a nuclear capability by West Germany obviously called into question its relationship with the United States. In other words, if the Federal Republic of Germany had to give up the possibility of having its own nuclear weapon because of US pressure or opposition, then the burden of defending Germany had to be totally taken up by the United States. This meant that the American leadership had to undertake complete responsibility for the defence of West Germany (and, by extension, of Europe as a whole). Any residual hopes to reunify Germany had to be indefinitely postponed, while strengthening NATO and totally abandoning the notions of the neutrality of Central Europe advocated by the Soviet Union.

In October 1957, the Polish Foreign Minister Adam Rapacki had proposed to the United Nations the creation of a denuclearized zone composed of East and West Germany, Czechoslovakia, and Poland (initially the proposal entailed a nuclear-free zone, then to be extended to conventional armaments). By creating an essentially neutralized Central Europe, the proposal opened the way for German unification and for a complete modification of the post war order that had emerged between East and West. The Soviet Union backed this so-called 'Rapacki Plan', which, predictably, was not accepted by the NATO countries. In fact, given the Warsaw Pact's superiority in conventional weapons, any reduction of the West's nuclear deterrent was seen as meant to weaken NATO. Moreover, the West did not want to withdraw its defensive line (moving back from the West German border), and more directly expose the other Western European countries to the Soviet threat.

Nuclear missiles deployed in Europe

Although the unity of the Alliance and the strong ties between the United States and the European members of NATO was not seriously questioned, the effects of Sputnik on the cohesion of the Alliance were long-lasting. The American leadership understood that confidence in the United States had to be restored and rapidly moved to reassure the European allies. These confidence-building measures went beyond verbal rhetoric. In late October 1957, the US defence department searched for means to promote the coordinated production of short-range weapons in Europe. Most significantly, the United States negotiated agreements with Britain, Italy and Turkey for the deployment of nuclear missiles. The first American intermediate-range ballistic missiles (the Thor IRBM) were deployed in bases in the United Kingdom (active from 1959 to 1963), followed by the deployment of a second type of missile (the Jupiter) in bases in southern Italy and Turkey (from 1961 to 1963). Concurrently, US Secretary of State Dulles advanced the idea that these intermediate-range nuclear weapons – now present in Europe, but solely controlled by US forces – could be made available for use also by the Alliance (the thorny issue of the control of nuclear weapons in Europe remained topical and was to re-emerge during the Kennedy administration).

The Soviet launch of Sputnik had deepened the tensions already present within the Alliance, opening the way for future crises. On the one hand the United States hurried to reassure its allies of its continued commitments. In this context, the deployment of IRBMs was a tangible means of reassuring the European allies. But on the other the greater US investments in the defence of Europe were accompanied by unmistakable signs of discontent, as the Americans repeatedly called for better sharing of the burden of expenses for the common defence. From the Europeans, instead, came the complaint that the control of nuclear forces remained uniquely in American hands. These issues created tension within the transatlantic community, which would resurface more dramatically in the following years.

The impact of Sputnik on Europe

The deployment of tactical nuclear weapons in Europe had a strong impact on European civil society. Pacifist movements emerged in Western Europe which advocated disarmament and the consideration of other options for the defence of the continent, such as its (at least partial) neutralization. Such propositions had until then been advanced only by the Soviet Union and its Eastern European allies. The emergence of these movements revealed a shift in European public opinion towards positions more critical of the American ally.

This change inevitably also partially influenced the action of governments. In Britain the ideas on European disarmament and neutrality – of the type advanced by the Rapacki Plan – were openly considered and in part endorsed. At the end of the visit by British Prime Minister Harold Macmillan to the Soviet Union in February 1959 (the first visit of a British prime minister since the end of the war), the Anglo-Soviet joint communiqué in fact referred to the need to further explore the possibility of enhancing European security by limiting both conventional and nuclear forces in an area in Europe to be defined in future negotiations. These ideas – which circulated as tentative possibilities and not in opposition to the special relationship with the United States – became central in the foreign policy debates during the 1959 British elections. Also the Conservatives supported some of these views in order to secure more electoral votes (because of the popularity of the ideas on disarmament and neutrality circulating in the country and supported by the rival Labour Party).

Similar tendencies had emerged also in Italy, until then considered a cornerstone of traditional Atlanticist views. While never repudiating the country's participation in the Atlantic Alliance, a policy of so-called neo-atlanticism emerged within the ruling Christian Democratic Party, advocated mainly by Italian President Giovanni Gronchi. The excessive emphasis on security and the exclusive military character of NATO was criticized in favour of the emergence of a transatlantic community based on more broad political and economic cooperation. While these positions remained generic and unspecified, they concealed sympathy for the notions of neutrality and for a more open policy towards the Third World (in those years Italy's oil company ENI was expanding in Africa and in the Arab countries). In the aftermath of Suez, and considering the effects of decolonization, the Atlantic Alliance's reliance on military force alone seemed to be no longer a sufficient means to guarantee peace and security. The same themes had also been emphasized by French Prime Minister Guy Mollet (in power until June 1957), who criticized the US leadership for its excessive preoccupation with the military aspects of security, while disregarding the possibility and the opportunity of negotiations on disarmament.

However, it is important to underline that the emergence of these positions within the major Western European countries took place within a context of undisputed adherence to the Atlantic community. These tendencies simply reflected the change in public opinion taking place in Western Europe, where the Cold War tensions and the East–West division had most directly affected the life of ordinary people. It was a tentative and initial shift, which would more openly surface only during the 1970s. It had been triggered by the different climate that emerged with the Geneva conferences (see Chapter 2), which had opened the way for at least considering means to govern Europe other than its indefinite division. But in the late 1950s such views did not seriously call into question membership in the transatlantic community and the overall leadership exercised by the United States.

The one country in which the notions of neutrality and disarmament were constantly criticized and openly rebuked was the Federal Republic of Germany. Chancellor Adenauer had based his policies on West Germany's NATO membership, on the rearmament of

Germany within the Atlantic framework and on a close relationship with the United States. Accordingly, he was uncompromising towards any option that would jeopardize these choices and would diminish Germany's security guarantee. A neutralized Germany would mean the withdrawal of US troops and a unified country exposed to the Soviet threat – a prospect which, for Adenauer (and for the vast majority of West Germans), was totally unacceptable. Considering that the strengthening of West Germany, its rearmament and participation in the Western security structure had been crucial elements of America's policy towards Europe for years, it was not difficult for Adenauer and for the Germans to receive Washington's reassurances.

In general, the ideas on promoting disarmament and the potential neutralization of Europe remained tentative pronunciations, which never developed into concrete alternatives. Any realistic consideration of these views was then indefinitely postponed when, in November 1958, Soviet leader Nikita Khrushchev demanded the withdrawal of the Western powers from Berlin. This provoked another severe Cold War crisis, which would definitely reconfirm the division of Europe and, for the time being, strengthen the cohesion of the transatlantic community.

The evolution of the EEC

The European aspirations for greater autonomy were therefore frustrated by the bipolarity governing the international system. However, such aspirations had been the underlying motivation for the revival of the European integration project, which had led to the creation of the EEC. The rapid growth of the European economy, and the concurrent emergence of disagreements and dissatisfaction in the relationship with the United States, had, in fact, contributed to triggering the pan-European views discussed at the Messina conference in 1955 (see Chapter 2). The Suez and Hungarian episodes had then motivated the participants' search for agreement, while the launch of Sputnik contributed to the rapid ratification of the treaties by the national parliaments. The creation of the European Economic Community came to represent the means for its member states to assert greater autonomy and independence from their American ally.

In the United States, the detached but definite support for the EEC had given way to some reservations during the negotiations for the treaties. Washington was concerned about the external tariff that the EEC would adopt towards third countries that, in the long run, would make the US and EEC competitors on the global market. The US was also critical of the clauses of the treaty that associated the territories of former colonies (or current colonies in the case of France) to the EEC, thus discriminating against other producing countries of the Third World. These clauses contradicted the US support for free trade and indirectly affected American interests in Latin America. However, while raising some objections on these restrictive clauses, the United States still expressed a general and enthusiastic support for the European community. The political considerations on the potential long-term advantages deriving from the unity of Europe and of the West clearly overshadowed the more limited economic interests.

The American support for the EEC also emerged in Washington's concomitant distancing from the newly created EFTA. In fact, as soon as it became evident that the British intention was to undermine the evolution of the EEC by proposing an enlargement of the Free Trade Area, the US leadership became openly critical. This factor, together with the first evident positive evolution of the EEC, induced the British government to shift its position towards the European institutions. London had been sceptical towards the EEC, convinced that the ambitious project would have little practical success. The doubts and hesitations had only grown with de Gaulle's return to power in France since the British thought that the French general would paralyse the evolution of the European community.

Conversely, the rapid implementation of the EEC and de Gaulle's political support for the project induced the British to reassess their position. By mid-1960, the government, led by Harold Macmillan, started to express support for the EEC. The internal debate in Britain on the advantages and opportunities of joining the community had started, despite the simultaneous establishment of EFTA. A year later, in July 1961, at a speech at the House of Commons, Macmillan announced the British intention to join the EEC provided mutually beneficial conditions were negotiated by the parts (the British application to enter the EEC would later be vetoed by French President de Gaulle in 1963; see Chapter 4). This represented a significant shift for British policy, which coincided with the election in the United States of John F. Kennedy. The new president entered the White House promising a new and reinvigorated American policy towards Europe.

De Gaulle's return to power in France

The difficult decolonization process in Indochina and Algeria had contributed to the political instability of the French Fourth Republic (1946–1958). Within the context of a general political fragmentation, an increased sense of frustration and hostility towards the United States started to characterize the French political scene. The Americans were criticized for having denied France support during the more critical phases of decolonization – in Indochina, Suez and Algeria – where the US policies were assessed as exclusively focused on countering the Soviet and communist threat, while sacrificing the interests of the European allies. The more radical critics advanced the idea that France's forced retreat from Africa had been caused by the economic and political interests of the United States. The more moderate criticism instead targeted the foreign policy of the Fourth Republic for its lack of autonomy and subordination to the United States, even if within the context of NATO.

General Charles de Gaulle's return to power in 1958 therefore occurred within a context in which French public opinion was already somewhat critical of American foreign policy (especially when compared with the sentiments of the other Western allies). In the following decade, de Gaulle's policies would only deepen the tension and, at times, cause severe ruptures between France and the United States. As the crisis in Algeria worsened, de Gaulle had been called to return to power to deal with the crisis and implement the much needed internal reforms in France. The general was convinced that the country needed a new constitution in order to end the fragmentation and political instability of the Fourth Republic. He was given emergency powers by the French parliament in June 1958 and, in September, the French people voted in a landslide referendum for the creation of the Fifth Republic.

The new form of government created a presidential republic, with more power and authority to the president (and therefore to de Gaulle himself). Internally, the new government implemented measures to stabilize the political system and revitalize the economy. In foreign policy, de Gaulle refused a close integration into the Atlantic system and asserted the absolute independence and sovereignty of France, especially on matters of security and defence. In November 1959, in a speech in Strasbourg, the French leader set forth his vision – which was to become famous – of a Europe from 'the Atlantic to the Urals', a Europe that would decide 'the destiny of the world'. The notion of a strong Europe that would stand as a third force between the United States and the Soviet Union was in sharp contrast with the

Atlanticism of the United States and Britain. De Gaulle's expression implicitly opened the way for negotiations with the Soviet Union and was interpreted as excluding Britain from the future Europe (for more on de Gaulle's policies see Chapter 4).

An important element in the Gaullist vision of France was the development of the French nuclear programme. While the new and more assertive leader gave a clear-cut political significance to France's independent nuclear force, the project had already been approved earlier and supported by various governments of the Fourth Republic. De Gaulle, however, better defined the initial vision and spelled out the concept of a 'force de frappe' capable of independently protecting France from a Soviet (or any other) attack. The motivations behind the development of the programme were directly related to the lack of confidence in the United States. According to the French general, Washington would never risk the destruction of American cities in order to defend Europe; therefore it was important to reinforce French autonomy and independence from its most powerful ally. The acquisition of nuclear weapons was an important element in the process of strengthening the international standing and prestige of France. In this context, de Gaulle aimed also to assert French political and military supremacy in continental Europe, thus attaining a nuclear weapon before any other power. Also the policy of rapprochement with Germany – which would lead to his historic visit to Bonn in 1962 – was part of the overall vision pursued by the general geared towards creating a 'European Europe', separate and independent from the United States.

Crisis looms over Berlin

After the crisis caused by the blockade and airlift of 1948–1949, the city of Berlin had recovered and developed, despite its division and the difficulties this obviously entailed. The potential test case of peaceful coexistence, side by side, of East and West was, however, to prove too difficult to sustain. The Western parts of the city, still administered by the Anglo-French-American forces, had been completely integrated into the Federal Republic of Germany. They had developed rapidly and successfully, due to the massive investments of the Western powers. It therefore stood as a model of the Western way of life, with democratic standards and economic entrepreneurship showcased in the face of the less developed eastern part of the city. The contrast between the two parts of Berlin was, in fact, more than evident, as East Berlin struggled to emerge from the devastations of the war, with standards of living dramatically lower than in the western part of the city.

In this situation, the German Democratic Republic came to increasingly perceive the precarious state of Berlin as a threat to the economic and political stability of its regime. Every year thousands of East Berliners would abandon their homes and jobs to cross into the West, then to rapidly resettle in parts of West Germany. The losses – often of middle-class professionals – were a severe blow to the already fragile East German economy. And the damage done to the image of the communist regime was equally devastating. Ending this exodus therefore became a priority for both East German leader Walter Ulbricht and for Soviet leader Nikita Khrushchev.

The Soviet 'ultimatum'

In November 1958, during a speech in Moscow, Khrushchev surprised the West by announcing that the Soviet Union would transfer the administration of its section of Berlin to the German Democratic Republic. A few weeks later, the Soviet leader sent a note to the American government calling for negotiations on the status of Berlin. He denounced the

Western powers' policies – the creation of the FRG and its participation in NATO – which were responsible for the continued division of Germany. According to Khrushchev, the West had violated the Potsdam agreements, which advocated the unification of Germany.

Consequently, the Soviet Union no longer considered itself obliged to respect clauses related to access to Berlin. The division of the city and the Western presence – which undermined the security of the GDR and of other Soviet allies – could no longer be tolerated. The Soviet leader thus asked for the withdrawal of American, British and French occupation forces, and proposed to turn West Berlin into a free city, demilitarized and neutralized (a status that would have to be monitored by the United Nations). In order to negotiate such a proposal, Khrushchev gave the Western powers six months, after which the Soviet Union would transfer full sovereignty to the German Democratic Republic (this meant that the communication and access routes to Berlin from West Germany would be controlled by the GDR).

The timing of the Soviet note – interpreted in the West as an ultimatum – had been well chosen. Following the launch of Sputnik, the Soviet Union was in a perceived position of strength compared with the United States and its allies. Moreover, tensions between Europeans and Americans had surfaced, worsened by the return to power of Charles de Gaulle. The Soviet leader seemed to take advantage of this moment of uncertainty within the Western bloc by proposing to change the status of Berlin, and with it the entire structure that emerged after the end of World War II. The proposal on Berlin was in fact part of the broader plans on the disarmament and neutralization of Europe – of the type of the Rapacki Plan – which had been circulating for a few years. Considering the adherence and sympathy that these ideas had found in the governments and public opinion of the Western European countries, it is likely that Khrushchev hoped to use these as a lever to break the unity of the transatlantic bloc.

The Western response

The Western powers, however, refused to yield to Soviet pressure. In December 1958, the United States replied to the Soviet note by refuting all accusations. The failed implementation of the Potsdam agreements, according to Washington, was the responsibility of Soviet, not Western, policies, and could therefore not be used as a justification by Moscow to repudiate other agreements made relating to Germany and to Berlin. In particular, the US referred to the four-power agreement made in June 1949 – at the end of the Berlin blockade (see Chapter 1) – according to which the Soviet Union undertook an obligation to allow the normal functioning of transport and communication between Berlin and the western parts of Germany. The United States was not prepared to relieve the Soviet Union of such obligations and refused to negotiate under the threat of unilateral action. The western rights and responsibilities over its sections of Berlin were undisputable. The American view was that the status of Berlin could only be modified in the wider framework of negotiations on Germany and European security. The declaration of the North Atlantic Council in December 1958 underscored the position expressed by the United States. The American, French and British governments reaffirmed their rights over West Berlin, and the other NATO member countries supported such rights. The text of the declaration stated:

> The Council declares that no state has the right to withdraw unilaterally from its international engagements. It considers that the denunciation by the Soviet Union of the inter-allied agreements on Berlin can in no way deprive the other parties of their rights

or relieve the Soviet Union of its obligations. Such methods destroy the mutual confidence between nations which is one of the foundations of peace … The Council recalls
the responsibilities which each member state has assumed in regard to the security and
welfare of Berlin and the maintenance of the position of the three powers in that city.
The member states of NATO could not approve a solution of the Berlin question which
jeopardized the right of the three Western powers to remain in Berlin as long as their
responsibilities require it, and did not assure freedom of communication between that
city and the free world. The Soviet Union could be responsible for any action which
had the effect of hampering this free communication or endangering this freedom. The
two million inhabitants of West Berlin have just reaffirmed in a free vote their overwhelming approval and support for that position.[1]

However, despite the expressions of consensus, the position of the Western powers was not
unanimous. While the French, British and Americans agreed on remaining in Berlin and
not withdrawing from their rights, they differed on the issue of recognition of the German
Democratic Republic and how to respond to the Soviet challenge. The British government
was seemingly the most willing to open a dialogue with both the East Germans and the
Soviets. During Macmillan's visit to Moscow in February 1959 the British prime minister
sought to widen the framework of the negotiations from the status of Berlin to the overall
situation of Germany (a position which the other Western powers shared). Although this
visit remained explorative and no concrete agreement emerged, the British confirmed that
potential demilitarization options could be considered in future negotiations. The French,
however, were more intransigent. De Gaulle was convinced that Moscow would not follow
through and provoke a crisis. He thus advocated indifference to Soviet pressure. But at the
same time the West had to be prepared to respond rapidly, with military force if necessary,
should a crisis ensue.

The American position was to mediate between the French and British while unambigu-
ously reassuring the West Germans. In March 1959, President Eisenhower stated publicly
that the United States 'would not retreat one inch from our duty. We shall continue to exercise our right of peaceful passage to and from West Berlin.' At the same time, the president
stated that he remained committed to negotiations that would 'respect the existing rights
of all and their opportunity to live in peace.' More specifically, the president advocated the
convening of a conference of foreign ministers, which could open the way for a summit
meeting (at the same time he stated that the US and its allies would 'never negotiate under a
dictated time limit or agenda or on other unreasonable terms').[2]

The Geneva conference and Khrushchev's visit to the United States

As the principle of negotiating within the broader framework of European security was
accepted by the Western powers (including the reluctant West German chancellor), the
conference of the four foreign ministers (of the nations still present in Berlin) convened in
Geneva in May 1959. But the positions of the West and of the Soviets were irreconcilable.
The Western powers insisted that a peace treaty with Germany could only be possible after
the reunification of the country with free elections. In the meantime, the four-power occupation of Berlin would remain in force. The Soviet Union instead proposed that West Berlin be
transformed into a demilitarized free city and that separate peace treaties had to be signed
with the two German states. After failing to reach agreement, the conference recessed for
an indefinite period of time.

As the impasse over Berlin lingered, the initiative was taken by the US leadership. Eisenhower invited Khrushchev to visit the United States (the topic of a summit meeting between the two leaders had already been circulating for some months). The Soviet leader promptly accepted and visited the United States in September 1959. The objective of the American president was to negotiate on the overall topic of European security and on the question of Berlin. Nevertheless, Adenauer and de Gaulle reacted with consternation to the prospected high-level bilateral dialogue, which excluded the Europeans.

The summit between Eisenhower and Khrushchev at Camp David was held in a generally cooperative atmosphere. The joint communiqué stated that the leaders 'agreed that these discussions have been useful in clarifying each other's position on a number of subjects'. On Berlin, the two leaders agreed that there would be no firm deadline (the Soviets therefore shifted away from the tone of the 'ultimatum') and that a summit would be convened to deal with the issue. Accordingly, in December 1959, Macmillan, de Gaulle, Adenauer and Eisenhower – who were meeting in Paris – invited Khrushchev for a summit to be held in the spring of 1960.

The summit in Paris was scheduled and took place, but it never went beyond the preliminary procedural meetings because it coincided with the controversy over the U-2 incident. On 1 May 1960, a Soviet surface-to-air missile had shot down an American U-2 spy plane over Sverdlovsk, deep in Soviet territory. Controversy followed over the violation of Soviet airspace, made worse by the White House's initial denial of knowledge of the flight, which was soon to prove false. The US had authorized a number of similar spying missions over Soviet missile installations. The Cold War tension and mutual suspicion once again came to dominate the US–Soviet bilateral relationship. Khrushchev went to the summit, but left in protest, withdrawing the invitation to Eisenhower to pay a return visit to the Soviet Union later that the year.

The question of Berlin remained unresolved. The weighty legacy was left to the incoming Kennedy administration.

The election of John F. Kennedy

The American elections of 1960 marked the end of eight years of Republican presidency. In the United States, the Eisenhower years had been characterized by economic expansion, optimism and confidence in the American way of life. US public opinion supported the administration's foreign policy, viewed as successful in containing the expansion of communism while ensuring America's growth and leadership. However, after 1957 – with the launch of Sputnik and with the beginning of an economic recession in the US – the optimism and confidence in the superiority of the American model started to vacillate. This was a consequence not only of the emotional shock caused by Sputnik but also, and most importantly, of a series of other factors which – when assessed together – triggered a process of self-criticism within the American society.

With his notion of 'peaceful coexistence', Soviet leader Nikita Khrushchev had, in fact, launched a different kind of challenge to the United States. His policies were outlined more concretely at the 21st Congress of the Communist Party held in 1959. According to Khrushchev, the economic development and the military power of the Soviet Union, combined with the popularity of the Soviet model in the newly independent countries, created the basis for a shift in the international balance of power. Contrary to the legacy left by Lenin – according to which the socialist model could be established only through conflict – the prospect of a peaceful triumph over capitalism was emerging. The Soviet

leader asserted that after a period of peaceful competition the socialist model would ultimately emerge as superior to the capitalist one. Its ideas, ideals and economic structure
would conquer the majority of the world.

In this way, Khrushchev's challenge hit the very basis of the American way of life, from
the economic structure to the educational and social system. While the gap between the
superpowers (particularly in economic terms) was still huge, in many sectors the Soviets
seemed to be developing rapidly. And the Soviet leader was able to convey to the outside
world the image of a country governed by optimism and renewed enthusiasm. At the
Congress, Khrushchev famously declared that by the year 1970 the Soviet Union's per capita
production would overtake that of the United States.

While the Soviet challenge – military, economic and social – would prove to be ephem-
eral, in 1960 America did seem to have lost some of its global appeal. Eisenhower had
successfully governed through eight years with skill and moderation (despite the initial
calls for greater aggressiveness), but these qualities seemed no longer sufficient to contain
a Soviet offensive that appeared more insidious and multilayered than the one launched
by Stalin. This was the situation inherited by John F. Kennedy, the incoming American
president, who seemed to possess the credentials to match the enthusiastic Soviet leader.
America, and with it the Western world, called for a renewed and reinvigorated leadership.

The grand design

At 43, John F. Kennedy, the Democratic victor in the election of 1960, was the youngest
man ever to win the American presidency. On television, in a series of debates with rival
Republican opponent Richard Nixon, he appeared able, articulate and energetic. In the
campaign, he spoke of moving assertively into the new decade: 'We stand today on the
edge of a new frontier,' stated the future president, 'the frontier of the 1960s, the frontier
of unknown opportunities and perils, the frontier of unfilled hopes and unfilled threats.'[3]
Once elected, the slogan of the new frontier came to characterize the incoming presidency's
ambitious programmes – both domestic and foreign – intended to improve the US economy,
provide international aid packages, fill the alleged 'missile gap' with the Soviet Union and
boost the American space programme. During his brief presidency (Kennedy would be
assassinated in November 1963), he set the basis for America's increased global responsibilities and for an unprecedented extension of US power.

While Kennedy's programmes invested in many sectors, one of the most ambitious was
the so-called grand design for the Western Alliance. The scope of Kennedy's policy towards
Europe was to create the conditions for the establishment of a truly transatlantic partnership.
Ultimately, this would lead to the creation of a solid political, economic and military bloc
composed of a unified Western Europe and the United States (together with their respective
links and special relations with the Commonwealth, Africa, Canada and Latin America).
Once this bloc had attained the necessary cohesion, its power would definitely neutralize
the communist threat. Although Kennedy's design appeared fascinating and captivating, it
came to focus almost exclusively on the military and strategic aspects of transatlantic cooperation, thus eventually undermining its long-term political significance.

The dilemmas of flexible response

In order to translate the design into policy, the US leadership in fact assigned a priority to
the redefinition of NATO's military strategy. Kennedy modified the doctrine of massive

retaliation – which had been already deprived of significance in the aftermath of Sputnik – in favour of 'flexible response'. This policy offered alternatives to total nuclear war by diversifying America's strategic options. It introduced the concept of limited nuclear war and an increase in conventional weapons systems. While Kennedy was convinced that nuclear deterrence remained paramount, he also believed that limited wars and low-intensity conflicts should be fought with conventional weapons (thus overturning the previous rationale of relying predominantly on nuclear weapons).

In order to increase America's flexibility in dealing with limited crises, the Kennedy administration decided to invest in the strengthening of conventional forces. This led to an increase in the US defence budget. The consequences of the new American posture on the transatlantic relationship were twofold. First, facing an increase in its financial spending in order to make the US deterrent more effective, Washington started to demand, with increasing insistence, that the Western European allies 'do their part'. In fact, the pressures on NATO allies for greater burden-sharing multiplied during the Kennedy administration and continued into the Johnson presidency. These created serious tensions within the Alliance.

Second, while the European allies had sought reassurances after 1957 and had questioned the effectiveness of the US doctrine of massive retaliation, the shift to flexible response did little to satisfy their fears. The new American posture was interpreted in Europe as a means for Washington to assert a greater margin of independence from the obligations towards the Atlantic Alliance. The Europeans viewed greater investment in conventional forces as inducing the enemy into launching a limited offensive, which for obvious geographic reasons would be directed against Europe. Thus, having reluctantly accepted the precepts of massive retaliation, and despite the dilemmas it had triggered, the Europeans now demanded a continued reliance on a strong nuclear deterrent. France and Britain in particular (which from the mid-1950s had chosen the nuclear option) and Germany (which totally relied on the US nuclear protection) were reluctant to move away from a heavy reliance on nuclear weapons.

Moreover, the dilemma of the exclusive American control of nuclear weapons remained alive. In order to counter the criticisms of the Europeans, the Americans proposed the creation of a so-called multilateral force (MLF) that would consist of a fleet of nuclear-armed ships under NATO, not US, command. But the proposal never translated into an actual policy due to the divergences between the US and the European allies over the strategy and financing of the force. These issues undermined Kennedy's desire for greater transatlantic unity. De Gaulle, in particular, refused the notion of integration of Europe's military defence into a force mostly controlled by the United States, and assertively defended France's independence. Ultimately, the grand design lost its appeal. Transatlantic divisions were only to deepen in the years to come.

The Berlin Wall

Although the Kennedy administration tried to reinvigorate the transatlantic relationship – and in this task the new US president only partially succeeded – his presidency left a long-lasting impact on America's European policy because of the decisions related to Berlin. The ongoing crisis in the divided German city had been left unresolved by Kennedy's predecessor. It was the central topic of the first and only meeting between the American president and Soviet leader Nikita Khrushchev held in Vienna in June 1961. Kennedy entered the meeting determined to convey intransigence, a stance motivated by the US president's renewed anti-communist assertiveness following the Bay of Pigs fiasco (in April 1961 the

Kennedy administration had sponsored an intervention of Cuban exiles with the intention of triggering a revolt to depose Cuban communist leader Fidel Castro). For his part, Khrushchev restated his position on Berlin. No progress was made.

Throughout July 1961 the Western powers remained passive. The American position seemed to advocate the continuation of the stalemate, motivating the prolonged inaction with the need to demonstrate intransigence to Soviet pressure. Should the Soviets follow through with their threat to cut the access routes to West Berlin, then the Western powers would be ready to react. In a speech to the American people delivered on 25 July 1961, Kennedy called for further increases in US defence spending needed to face the challenges threatening the free world. According to the American president, the Soviet pressure on Berlin was part of a global challenge that the West had to counter. The German city had become the test case of the West's courage and determination.

The unexpected way out of the impasse was offered by the Soviets and East Germans on 13 August 1961. The border between East and West Berlin was closed and, in the next few days, the construction of a wall began, which would isolate the eastern part of the city from the western sectors. In this way, the exodus from East Germany was stopped, without causing a major international crisis. Surprised, and with limited options available, the West did not react. West Berlin's mayor Willy Brandt wrote to Kennedy protesting and demanding energetic countermeasures, but the US president responded that only a war would deter the Soviet action.

The tension that had risen over Berlin thus abated with a decision that was to confirm the division of the city (and of Germany) for almost three more decades. The status quo in

---

Box 3.2 Document extract: John F. Kennedy's radio and television report to the American people on the Berlin crisis (25 July 1961)

On 25 July 1961, in a speech delivered from the president's office, John F. Kennedy warned the USSR against aggressive moves in Berlin and called for increased US military spending in order to counter the Soviet threat:

West Berlin – lying exposed 110 miles inside East Germany, surrounded by Soviet troops and close to Soviet supply lines – has many roles. It is more than a showcase of liberty, a symbol, an island of freedom in a Communist sea. It is even more than a link with the Free World, a beacon of hope behind the Iron Curtain, an escape hatch for refugees.

West Berlin is all of that. But above all it has now become – as never before – the great testing place of Western courage and will, a focal point where our solemn commitments stretching back over the years since 1945, and Soviet ambitions now meet in basic confrontation.

… And the challenge is not to us alone. It is a challenge to every nation which asserts its sovereignty under a system of liberty. It is a challenge to all those who want a world of free choice. It is a special challenge to the Atlantic Community – the heartland of human freedom.

We in the West must move together in building military strength. We must consult one another more closely than ever before. We must together design our proposals for peace, and labor together as they are pressed at the conference table.

And together we must share the burdens and the risks of this effort.

… Today, the endangered frontier of freedom runs through divided Berlin.

Europe was maintained and confirmed. The wall became the symbol of the Cold War order in Europe – an order which, once again, was not challenged, but rather endorsed, by the United States and its Western European allies.

Conclusion

The late 1950s witnessed the emergence of the first serious tensions within the transatlantic relationship. This was a consequence of the sense of vulnerability caused by the Soviet launch of Sputnik and the subsequent adjustments to the American strategic posture, which only partially satisfied the Europeans. While these tensions did not yet lead to major ruptures within the transatlantic community, they did anticipate more serious problems that would emerge in the following years. Concurrently, the impact of the decolonization process changed the map of the world. Many new countries became independent and were subject to the pressure or influence (direct or indirect) of the two superpowers. Conversely, the former colonial European powers progressively lost their influence. In the early 1960s, the Cold War competition started to move into the Third World while, in Europe, the building of the Berlin Wall definitely confirmed that the superpowers had accepted the status quo.

Box 3.3 The significance of the West's acceptance of the Berlin Wall

The construction of the wall came as a complete surprise to the Western Allies. After 13 August 1961, it separated East Berlin from the West and was protected by armed guards ordered to shoot East Germans attempting to cross over to the Western sector. The West's implicit – and pragmatic – acceptance of the wall's creation was motivated by the belief that a challenge would risk open conflict. Although pressed by some hawkish voices in America and severely criticized by West Berlin's mayor Willy Brandt, President Kennedy decided against armed intervention to halt the construction of the wall. Whether he was right or wrong was a subject of fierce debate for many years.

For Kennedy's critics, the Berlin Wall was the latest in a series of Soviet-inspired provocations allowed to pass without a firm response from the West. Moreover, the West's acceptance of a divided Berlin legitimized the Communist East German regime and indefinitely postponed the prospect of a unified Germany.

Despite the criticism and the moral condemnation of accepting such a crude symbol of Cold War division, historians have highlighted that Kennedy's decision was in line with the overall policy of normalization of superpower relations that had been ongoing since the mid-1950s. Rhetoric aside, throughout the Berlin crisis the US leadership had been committed only to defending its rights in West Berlin and not to rolling the Soviets back from the Eastern part of the city. The US policy was guided by the principle of containing the further expansion of the Soviet influence, not by the desire to free East Berlin. As had been the case in 1953 (during a revolt in East Berlin) and in 1956 (during the Hungarian crisis), the United States, and with it the Atlantic Alliance, recognized – and did not challenge – the Soviet sphere of influence. As Kennedy told his advisers, 'It's not a very nice solution, but a wall is a hell of a lot better than a war.'

The West's acceptance of the status quo motivated future West German Chancellor Willy Brandt's search for improved East–West relations (the policy that later become known as *Ostpolitik*) and opened the way for the era of détente in the 1970s (which ultimately led to the recognition of the post-World War II European borders in the 1975 Helsinki Final Act).

As the United States was becoming an increasingly global power, the European countries retreated, concerned predominantly with regional affairs and with the development of the EEC. While the Kennedy administration had hoped to launch a new vision of cooperation and unity between Europe and the United States, the two sides of the Atlantic were, instead, developing divergent interests. Economically and politically more assertive, Europe was in search of its role. Although militarily still dependent on the United States, the main Western European powers more energetically wanted their voices to be heard within the Atlantic Alliance.

Suggested further readings

Beschloss, Michael (1991) *The Crisis Years: Kennedy and Khrushchev 1960–1963*. New York: HarperCollins.

Costigliola, Frank (1992) *France and the United States: The Cold Alliance Since World War II.* New York: Twayne.

Gearson, John and Kori Schake (eds) (2002) *The Berlin Wall Crisis: Perspectives on Cold War Alliances*. Basingstoke, UK: Palgrave.

Harrison, Hope M. (2003) *Driving the Soviets Up the Wall: Soviet–East German Relations, 1953–1961*. Princeton, NJ: Princeton University Press.

Suri, Jeremi (2003) *Power and Protest. Global Revolution and the Rise of Détente*. Cambridge, MA: Harvard University Press.

Winand, Pascaline (1993) *Eisenhower, Kennedy, and the United States of Europe*. Basingstoke, UK: Macmillan.

4 Challenged America, 1961–1972

Setting the stage: The Wall and Cuba

Two East–West crises marked the early 1960s: the building of the Berlin Wall in August 1961, and the Cuban missile crisis in October 1962. While both events were handled mainly by Washington and Moscow, they also had profound impacts on the transatlantic community. Not all of these impacts became apparent immediately. In the short run, and especially in the public perception, the Western Alliance closed ranks behind the American leadership when clashing with the common enemy. In the longer run, however, Kennedy's acquiescence regarding the Wall led to a more independent attitude among the West Germans, and his handling of the missile crisis raised the question whether the Europeans and the Americans really shared the same strategic goals. Moreover, superpower agreements on both issues set the stage for a more challenging attitude by the Europeans towards their American protector.

The moral dilemma of US passivity in Berlin

When the East Germans put up a barricade of barbed wire and steel across Berlin in the night of 13 August 1961, the three Western powers reacted rather mildly. The US government, anxious not to provoke the Soviets or the East Germans, dispatched a cautious protest note only four days later. British Prime Minister Macmillan decided to downplay the crisis and not to cut short his golfing holiday in Scotland. Quite similarly, French President de Gaulle remained unperturbed and stayed in his holiday cottage when the East Germans started the operation code-named 'Great Wall of China'.

These slow reactions were not only due to previous occasions when the sector borders between East and West Berlin had been closed and always reopened. By August 19, as the East Germans proceeded to construct a concrete wall, everybody understood that this barrier was meant to last. From now on, and for 28 years to come, people trying to flee over the wall were shot by the East German border troops. But the three Western powers were appeased by the fact that the Eastern actions did not violate any agreement on West Berlin. Compared to his 1958 ultimatum, Khrushchev had backed down. And among the Western allies, nobody was ready to risk a nuclear war to fight for the rights of the East Berliners. 'For us, the Wall resolves the Berlin problem', commented the French foreign minister.[1]

The story was very different for the West Germans. Instinctively they turned to the United States and expected a strong reaction against the oppression of the Berliners. Chancellor Adenauer was disappointed when President Kennedy opened up negotiations with the Soviets instead, to discuss the city's status.

In Berlin, bitterness reigned. The mayor of West Berlin, Willy Brandt, was almost as angry with the Western allies for doing nothing as he was with the East Germans and the Soviets for constructing the Wall. Upon receiving an impassioned letter from Brandt, President Kennedy strengthened the US forces and sent Vice President Johnson to show solidarity with the West Berliners, but he also made clear that he considered a wall a better solution than a war. When students blew up parts of the Wall at night, with homemade bombs, the Western allies even advised the Berlin police to protect the Wall, in order to avoid any escalation of the conflict.

The moral dilemma of American passivity in Berlin became blatantly obvious in August 1962, when 18-year-old Peter Fechter tried to escape over the Wall. He was shot, fell back on Eastern territory and cried for help, unable to move. The American soldiers standing nearby were ordered to stand down. Under the eyes of a horrified population, the young man slowly bled to death. This tragic event brought the frustration of the Berliners to a head. Their anger was directed not only against the 'murderers' in the East, but also provoked an outcry of anti-American sentiment in the West Berlin press and even a small demonstration in front of the US mission. Such anti-American feeling, however, was short-lived.

With his visit to West Berlin in June 1963, Kennedy decisively transformed the accumulated bitterness of the population into courage and ecstasy. His masterful speech and famous claim '*Ich bin ein Berliner*' touched the hearts of the people and inspired them with hope. For the longer-term survival of the isolated city, this was a critical achievement. Leaders in East and West understood Kennedy's speech as an unconditional American security guarantee for West Berlin. Kennedy's speech in Berlin undeniably stands out as one of the most memorable moments in the history of transatlantic relations.

Nevertheless, the events related to the construction of the Berlin Wall triggered a chain of events hardly anticipated by the American government. Willy Brandt admired Kennedy and continued to promote the benefits of German–American friendship. But Brandt also realized that Kennedy – despite his power, his nuclear weapons and his wonderful speech – was unable to remove the Wall. No military build-up of the West would change this simple fact. If Brandt wanted to improve daily life in a divided country, make the Wall 'permeable' and shape the future, he had to talk to the East German authorities, and ultimately to the Soviet authorities. He had already started to do so even before his election as chancellor, a few years later. Brandt recognized that the West Germans had to develop their own political concepts and contacts with the East, if necessary without US support.

Nuclear missiles in Europe, but not in Cuba

The Cuban missile crisis won Kennedy the image of a determined, wise and successful leader of the West. After all, he exposed to the world the nuclear build-up by the Soviets in Cuba, made clear that the US would not accept it, and compelled Khrushchev to withdraw the nuclear missiles. Throughout the crisis, the Europeans acted as model allies. The British, Germans and Italians, and even the French government, demonstrated firm support for Kennedy's actions. Not a single NATO member contradicted the resolute American policy on Cuba in October 1962.

Yet Kennedy's showdown with Khrushchev and their bilateral handling of the affair did produce some collateral damage in transatlantic relations. Most of all, the Europeans were informed but not consulted by the US administration. Even Kennedy's close contacts with British ambassador David Ormsby-Gore did not provide London with any leverage in American decision-making. When it came to the decisions on war and peace, the European allies realized they had no influence on Washington. Would it be any different in a future crisis in Europe?

The Kennedy administration argued that the missile crisis was handled by the Americans alone because of Cuba's geographical closeness to the US. But this explanation was not entirely convincing. Although Kennedy managed to avoid actual combat, repercussions had already emerged in Europe. Turkey was most directly concerned. The Americans maintained military bases with nuclear missiles on Turkish territory, close to the border with the USSR. When Kennedy made clear that he would not tolerate nuclear warheads on Cuba, the Kremlin pointed out the analogy of American deployments and threatened to launch a nuclear strike against Turkey. As a result, the Turkish government took measures to evacuate the cities of Istanbul, Ankara and Izmir. Furthermore, American bombers stationed in Britain, France, Italy and Germany were alerted during the crisis and equipped with nuclear arms. The host countries of these US air bases thus became prime targets in case of military action. Even a more limited confrontation in Cuba could easily result in a Soviet close-down of access routes to West Berlin. As the Europeans realized how directly they would suffer the consequences of American actions, they started doubting whether the key decisions of the Atlantic Alliance should be left to Washington alone.

Another fact dawned on the European leaders in October 1962. The United States considered nuclear missiles on Cuba a *casus belli*, while it routinely consented to huge numbers of Soviet missiles on the borders of Western Europe. American vulnerability was unacceptable, but threats against Europe were habitual. Obviously, the protection of the American mainland and of Western Europe did not have the same priority level for Washington. This naked truth momentarily shook the foundations of the Atlantic Alliance. However, lacking any real alternative to oppose the aggressive Soviet Union, most Europeans preferred to go back to NATO business as usual. Except for de Gaulle, who kept asking: would the United States really fight for Western Europe if this could lead to the destruction of American cities in return?

The tacit agreement between Khrushchev and Kennedy on the Berlin Wall and their successful negotiations over Cuba made a nuclear war less likely. On the downside, the Europeans feared being left out in these superpower dealings. It later turned out that Kennedy had indeed bartered the removal of American Jupiter and Thor missiles from Turkey and Italy against the withdrawal of Soviet missiles from Cuba, behind the backs of the Europeans.

The Gaullist challenge

The most obvious sign of European uneasiness with the state of transatlantic affairs in the 1960s was French President de Gaulle. He openly challenged the American way of dealing with the Europeans on many levels. While de Gaulle provocatively spoke up against American dominance within the Western camp, essentially he did not question the need for close transatlantic cooperation and partnership as long as the Soviet threat existed. The Gaullist challenges were thus limited in scope. Also, they were quite successfully countered by the United States.

Provocative moves

As seen in the previous chapter, de Gaulle came back to power in 1958. But it was not until 1963 that his confrontation with Washington became virulent. Meanwhile, de Gaulle had consolidated his domestic position and managed to bring the Algerian revolt to a peaceful conclusion. With Algeria's independence treaty signed in March 1962 and the French economy prospering, de Gaulle could turn his attention to European and world affairs from a position of relative strength. European economic integration was now under way, with France the leading country of the six who had formed the EEC.

The global context had also changed and opened up new possibilities for smaller powers. In times of Soviet aggression, Western Europe needed to stand at America's side. But the handling of the Berlin affair and especially the outcome of the Cuban missile crisis had shown that neither of the superpowers wanted to go to war. De Gaulle now saw the moment fit to articulate French interests and ambitions more freely. In his opinion, wars were to be fought against enemies, but peace was the time to challenge one's friends.

In a press conference on 14 January 1963, de Gaulle launched his first direct attack against the American design of the transatlantic framework. He rejected the idea of a US-controlled nuclear cooperation within NATO and bluntly dismissed British plans to join the EEC. De Gaulle asserted that Britain's entry would fundamentally alter the EEC's structures and transform it into 'a colossal Atlantic Community under American dependence and direction'. Instead, he wanted the EEC to be strictly European.

President Kennedy had come to support British EEC membership partly because of de Gaulle. Even though he had restored stability to his country, the French president was no longer considered a positive force for the West. Washington perceived de Gaulle more and more as a rival and a threat to transatlantic unity. Kennedy also set aside his predecessor's fear that Britain would dilute the supranational elements inherent in the European integration process and instead emphasized the traditionally close Anglo-American cooperation, the 'special relationship'. From an American perspective, British EEC membership had become a means to oppose Gaullist tendencies of weakening Europe's ties to the United States.

De Gaulle's veto against British entry not only disconcerted the Americans, but defied the core of Kennedy's European policy. According to his grand design, proclaimed on Independence Day 1962, Kennedy regarded a strong and united Europe as a partner with whom he wanted to deal 'on a basis of full equality'. For this to happen, he made the conditions very clear: 'The first order of business is for our European friends to go forward in forming a more perfect union which will some day make this partnership possible.' This more perfect union obviously included British membership and the EEC's Atlantic orientation. Should the EEC not develop in this way and dismiss the United Kingdom, the condition for American–European partnership on the basis of equality would not be fulfilled. Admittedly, Kennedy's sense of equality was flawed as he intended to monopolize control over Western nuclear armaments. Even so, it was de Gaulle's press conference that was about to undermine the pillars of JFK's grand design.

More was to come. Just a week later, on 22 January 1963, de Gaulle and Adenauer signed a Franco-German friendship agreement, the Elysée Treaty. The text of the treaty itself was fairly modest in scope, merely creating a framework for regular consultations on foreign policy, defence and culture. It also sealed the reconciliation of France and Germany after a century of wars, an objective basically supported by the United States. What transformed the Elysée Treaty into a threat to the transatlantic community and threw the American government into a state of 'shock' mostly derived from the political context.

The consultation mechanism created by the Elysée Treaty had originally been drafted for all six members of the EEC, in order to develop their political cooperation. But during the negotiation process, the Dutch, the Belgians and the Italians had become

Box 4.1 The Special Relationship

The term 'special relationship' was coined by Winston Churchill in his famous Iron Curtain speech of March 1946, to describe the close links between the United States and the United Kingdom. This term has been used ever since, although more often by the British than the Americans. According to Churchill, the nature of Anglo-American bonds was as follows:

> The British and the American peoples come together naturally, and without the need of policy and design. That is because they speak the same language, were brought up on the same common law, and have similar institutions and an equal love of liberty. There is often no need for policy or statecraft to make British and Americans agree together at an international council table. They can hardly help agreeing on three out of four things. They look at things the same way. (Winston Churchill, 7 November 1945)

The exact nature of the special relationship has been questioned by many scholars, and some of them doubted its very existence. It has been argued that the close relations between the UK and the US were of a temporary rather than enduring nature, or that they had not existed before World War II. Others pointed out that Britain's special relationship with the United States was in fact no more special than Canada's, Israel's or Germany's. Furthermore, the question has been raised whether the Anglo-American special relationship since 1945 was based on mutual influence or rather on an asymmetric dependence by the United Kingdom. In response to these arguments, the exceptional longevity of the contact has been emphasized (going back to the colonization of North America), along with the unprecedented and crucial cooperation during World War II, and the comprehensive consultations ever since.

During the 1960s, the invocation of the special relationship between Britain and the United States contrasted starkly with the virulent discourse between the French and the Americans. President Kennedy indeed referred to British Prime Minister Macmillan as his favourite interlocutor, and their signing of the Nassau Agreement in December 1962 exemplified the close military and nuclear cooperation between the two countries. Yet the British and the Americans hardly looked at things the same way, as Churchill had suggested. In the second half of the 1960s, President Johnson had particularly strained relations with Prime Minister Wilson, as a result of the latter's refusal to send British troops to Vietnam. But even then, the existence of a special relationship was not denied, and the United States continued to rely on the British to strengthen the Atlanticist orientation of Western Europe. President de Gaulle picked up on the issue and raised the question whether the Anglo-American special relationship was even compatible with the United Kingdom being a full European member of the EC – a question that resurfaced in later decades.

Despite open questions about the exact nature and the concrete implications of the special relationship, British and American leaders have continued to this day to refer to their nations' parallel or identical self-interests with remarkable regularity and perseverance.

reluctant to back the French proposal. They feared that de Gaulle intended the new body to supersede the institutions of the EEC, and maybe even emancipate it from NATO. It appeared to be a counter-project to the American design for Western Europe. When Adenauer signed the Elysée Treaty one week after de Gaulle's press conference, West Germany seemed to adopt an anti-American policy and opted for French leadership instead.

American counters

The White House was seriously alarmed. For a moment, President Kennedy even considered modifying the foundations of American foreign policy, remarking at a National Security Council meeting in late January 1963: 'If the Europeans do not wish to continue with us, then, indeed, a turning point is here.'[2] However, no turnaround was to happen. Instead, Kennedy made it clear to the German leaders that they faced a choice between either working with the United States or cooperating closely with France. His emissaries threatened American withdrawal from Europe and 'the end of Berlin', if the Germans should make the wrong choice. US pressure was especially high on the potential successors of Chancellor Adenauer, aged 87 at that time and scheduled to step down soon.

The American strategy proved successful. Adenauer's pro-French course did not get a majority and the German Bundestag (parliament) added a preamble to the Elysée Treaty, stressing the overriding importance of transatlantic cooperation. From an American point of view, this was a major victory against the Gaullist challenge. It meant that ultimately, West Germany would favour the US over France.

In retrospect, the 1963 showdown between France and the United States over their influence on Germany was decisive. If de Gaulle wanted to put into practice his long-term ideas of a more European and less Atlantic Europe, he definitely needed German support. France alone was too small to achieve de Gaulle's lofty plans. As the Kennedy administration had foreseen, de Gaulle's influence over his European partners diminished substantially once Adenauer left the German chancellery in October 1963. The subsequent German governments showed no intention of jeopardizing their good relations with Washington for the sake of unduly close relations with Paris.

Indeed, France was increasingly at odds with the rest of Western Europe. Paul-Henri Spaak and Joseph Luns – the foreign ministers of Belgium and the Netherlands – passionately rejected de Gaulle as a 'grave-digger' of Atlantic cohesion and European integration. France's isolation within the EEC peaked in the summer of 1965, when de Gaulle ordered the French representatives to boycott common meetings until the others came round to French views on the EEC's future. Paradoxically, the six EEC member nations shared relatively similar approaches to the processing of the community's daily issues, yet de Gaulle's aggressive attempt to impose French policy further antagonized his partners.

French relations with the British were even worse. De Gaulle's 1963 veto against the United Kingdom's EEC membership left a scar that never healed. The British public tended to see de Gaulle as a leader obsessed with French grandeur and tainted by an irrational grudge against the United Kingdom. While the British establishment remained divided on the prospect of joining the EEC, de Gaulle's renewed veto of November 1967 was perceived as even more condescending than the first one, and provoked general consternation in the United Kingdom.

Against this background de Gaulle continued to be a thorn in the Americans' flesh, but with his power confined to France he was considered too weak to inflict any serious damage. From mid-1963 to 1968, the American attitude towards the Gaullist challenge thus remained mostly passive. President Lyndon B. Johnson, who took office after Kennedy's assassination in November 1963, basically wanted to wait de Gaulle out. To be sure, Johnson monitored that Gaullist ideas did not spread beyond France, but he refused to speak out publicly against the French president.

Some of Johnson's hard-line advisers struggled to carry out this low-key policy, as de Gaulle continued to criticize the United States and jar American nerves. In 1964, de

Gaulle ignored NATO policy and recognized Communist China. It would not make sense, he explained, to have no relations with the biggest population on earth 'just because the Americans did not like their regime'.[3] De Gaulle also publicly condemned US policy in Vietnam. He had called for the neutralization of the region from early on, and had warned the American leaders against military intervention. When the Vietnam conflict and US engagement escalated by 1965, de Gaulle set out on a veritable anti-war crusade, perceived by many as anti-American.

A multi-polar rather than a two-bloc world

Despite the little international support for de Gaulle's policy, he remained the dominant figure in transatlantic debates throughout the 1960s. Not only was he the president of the (so far) most powerful country of the EEC, but he was also the first Western European leader since the beginning of the Cold War to offer a distinctly European grand design. De Gaulle's breaking of taboos and his efforts to gain more European elbow room in the East–West conflict intrigued the Western leaders more than they cared to admit.

Notably, de Gaulle developed his own approach towards the Soviet Union, instead of letting Washington fulfil the role of the West's only spokesman. After a number of Franco-Soviet contacts at ministerial level, de Gaulle went on a high-profile state visit to Moscow in summer 1966. At that time, French promotion of détente with the USSR made many Western politicians fear that de Gaulle might seek a military understanding with the Kremlin, or even switch sides. But this was not his objective. Well informed of de Gaulle's talks with the Soviets, the American leadership observed with relief that France did not betray any fundamental position of the West.

From de Gaulle's point of view, expressing himself freely on Vietnam and taking the liberty of talking to the Chinese and the Soviets were vital elements of the national independence he claimed for France. This notion of non-dependence lay at the core of de Gaulle's policy. While he acknowledged the usefulness of alliances, he nevertheless aspired to a maximum of national sovereignty. De Gaulle's approach contrasted with the notion of blocs, as promoted by Washington, since a bloc system required the smaller countries to align with the most powerful. He was convinced that the emergence of national entities would make the world more peaceful and contribute to a new balance of power. By Gaullist definition, a multi-polar world was more peaceful than a bipolar world. De Gaulle also saw a historical necessity for the Europeans to develop a genuinely European position, because a world in equilibrium needed a strong European pillar.

Within the Atlantic community, de Gaulle's withdrawal from the NATO command structure triggered the major irritation. In a handwritten letter dated 7 March 1966, de Gaulle asked President Johnson to remove the NATO headquarters and all American troops from French territory, while insisting that France remain a member of the Atlantic Alliance. In the future, France would only fight in case of 'unprovoked aggression' against a NATO member. Behind this somewhat imprecise condition lay the Gaullist view that the French president – and not the American president – should decide whether or not France would go to war. De Gaulle wanted to make sure that France would not be dragged into other countries' conflicts, in Vietnam or elsewhere. And again, his actions aimed at increasing French sovereignty, by ensuring his own control over the French nuclear force, and by reassuming command over the French troops previously assigned to NATO orders.

De Gaulle's announcement of March 1966 hardly came as a surprise. He had already withdrawn the French Mediterranean fleet from NATO command in 1959, and the Atlantic fleet in 1963. After the unsuccessful proposal of a triumvirate leadership in 1958, de Gaulle had continually criticized American domination within NATO. In 1964 and 1965, he had revealed the forthcoming French withdrawal to German and American representatives.

Nevertheless, reactions in spring 1966 included a wide range of surprise and disbelief, mingled with outright anger and fear of the consequences for other NATO members. The British and the Dutch openly voiced their resentment against the French move, whereas American policymakers even dreaded the collapse of NATO. They anticipated that de Gaulle's decision might resuscitate nationalist movements in Germany and push countries like Italy or Denmark into neutralism. Not for the last time in history, many Americans felt betrayed by the French. When discussing the removal of US soldiers from France, State Secretary Dean Rusk scornfully asked de Gaulle whether this also included the dead Americans from the military cemeteries. In New York, some restaurant owners poured out their bottles of French wine in the street as a sign of protest.

The American president weighed up his options and again chose to respond calmly to de Gaulle. Rather than explaining any details, Johnson formulated his conclusions in a characteristic one-sentence parable that he would recall in his memoirs: 'When a man asks you to leave his house, you don't argue; you get your hat and go.'[4] Wisely, he refrained from a reaction that would further divide the Europeans and explicitly kept the door open for a French return to NATO's command structure in the future.

Barking more than biting

De Gaulle's partial withdrawal did not lead to the fragmentation of the Atlantic community or the end of NATO, as some of Johnson's close advisers had feared. With French opposition gone, the other NATO members could finally agree on the new strategy of flexible response. In December 1967, the Atlantic Council also redefined the organization's purpose in the context of East–West détente by adopting a plan elaborated under the leadership of Belgian foreign minister Pierre Harmel.

Some remaining clouds of uncertainty hanging over NATO's future were dispelled in August 1968. The Warsaw Pact's invasion and brutal repression of reform movements in Czechoslovakia shifted NATO's focus back on its primary purpose as a defence organization. Disconcerted by the Soviet Union's aggressiveness, the Western allies closed ranks again and European governments willingly increased their financial contributions to American NATO troops stationed on their territory. In autumn 1968, US officials observed a surprising solidarity within the Atlantic Alliance. This also included France, whose representatives continued to participate in most committees and sub-committees of the organization. When, after 20 years, the treaty of the Atlantic Alliance expired in April 1969, France and all other members tacitly renewed the agreement. It was one of de Gaulle's last actions as French president before he stepped down on 28 April 1969 for internal reasons.

The Gaullist challenge to American foreign policy had already lost some of its intensity. In 1967, de Gaulle still fired off verbal broadsides against Washington and took counter-positions on monetary policy, on Vietnam, the Middle East and Israel, even on Canada. But the tide turned in 1968. De Gaulle was much impressed when Johnson announced a de-escalation policy on Vietnam in April 1968. Student and worker unrest in France undermined French economic power and de Gaulle's authority, while West Germany was on the rise. The Czech events and the election of Richard Nixon to the White House in November 1968 further mended the strained relations between Washington and Paris.

Box 4.2 Document extract: The Harmel Report on 'The Future Tasks of the Alliance' (14 December 1967)[5]

3   The [Harmel] exercise has shown that the Alliance is a dynamic and vigorous organization which is constantly adapting itself to changing conditions. ...
4   Since the North Atlantic Treaty was signed in 1949 the international situation has changed significantly and the political tasks of the Alliance have assumed a new dimension. Amongst other developments, the Alliance has played a major part in stopping Communist expansion in Europe ... Although the disparity between the power of the United States and that of the European states remains, Europe has recovered and is on its way towards unity. ...
5   The Atlantic Alliance has two main functions. Its first function is to maintain adequate military strength and political solidarity to deter aggression and other forms of pressure and to defend the territory of member countries if aggression should occur. Since its inception, the Alliance has successfully fulfilled this task. But the possibility of a crisis cannot be excluded as long as the central political issues in Europe, first and foremost the German question, remain unsolved. ...

In this climate the Alliance can carry out its second function, to pursue the search for progress towards a more stable relationship in which the underlying political issues can be solved. Military security and a policy of détente are not contradictory but complementary. ...

9   Accordingly the Allies are resolved to direct their energies to this purpose by realistic measures designed to further a détente in East–West relations. The relaxation of tensions is not the final goal but is part of a long-term process to promote better relations and to foster a European settlement. The ultimate political purpose of the Alliance is to achieve a just and lasting peaceful order in Europe accompanied by appropriate security guarantees.

Overall, the Gaullist challenge of the 1960s remained a confrontation within limits, despite some heated reactions at the time. While de Gaulle condemned Europe's subordination to America and called on the Europeans to shoulder their own responsibilities, he never questioned the basic usefulness of the Atlantic Alliance as long as the 'totalitarian system' in the Soviet Union persisted. Even at the apogee of his tirades, de Gaulle instructed his officials never to cross a certain line when dealing with the United States, who remained France's ally after all.

Washington effectively countered the Gaullist challenge, with a sharp reaction in early 1963 and a forbearing attitude thereafter. De Gaulle's France faced growing isolation from its European allies, to a large extent because they shared American objections against de Gaulle's 'nationalist' policy. Clearly, the other West Europeans did not wish to endorse French leadership at the expense of American authority. They reckoned that France would not be powerful enough 'to keep the Germans down' if needed, let alone 'to keep the Soviets out'. From political and strategic points of view, France was thus no real alternative to the United States. Moreover, de Gaulle's model of a European Europe stretching 'from the Atlantic to the Urals' aroused suspicions among the others, as he never explained what exactly this notion stood for and when in the future he planned to achieve it. Last but not least, de Gaulle's aggressive style and his overemphasis on France alienated even benevolent Western partners.

In hindsight, several political actors of the 1960s have expressed significantly milder judgements on de Gaulle and given him some credit for contributing to a greater European self-confidence, notably vis-à-vis the Americans.

The economic challenge

The Kennedy and Johnson administrations stuck to the American premise that the political and strategic spheres took priority over economic relations with Western Europe. Thus, the Gaullist challenge to the Atlantic framework was clearly considered the most serious one of the 1960s. But during the same time period, a second European challenge also emerged on the economic and monetary level. It was structurally linked to the economic integration of Western Europe and to the gradual decline of the preponderance of the US dollar in the international monetary system.

EEC and US become competitors

The United States had been a major driving force behind the process of European integration since the end of World War II. Besides the more idealistic motives of reconciling wartime enemies in Europe, and of exporting the American model of democracy and free markets, some more practical interests remained integral parts of Washington's reasoning in the 1960s. To be sure, the new European structures provided a suitable international control over German evolution, but a unified Western Europe was also expected to be a better partner for the US, and to strengthen the American camp in the East–West conflict.

Even from an economic point of view, European integration was thought to be beneficial, in the sense that it would stimulate American exports and the world economy in general. Moreover, with the European status quo now approved by East and West, economic performances became likely to play decisive roles in the Cold War. The prosperity of Western Europe should eventually manifest the inferiority of the communist system to the Eastern Europeans. When it came to the principle of European integration, the interests of the trans-atlantic partners thus seemed to converge.

But frictions appeared as soon as the EEC started to implement its programme. Even faster than originally planned, the six EEC members advanced towards a customs union. Starting in 1959, they abandoned the EEC's internal border taxes on industrial goods at an average of 10 per cent per year until, by 1968, these taxes completely disappeared. With the merger of the executives of the EEC, the ECSC and Euratom in July 1967 the six countries adopted a new name: 'European Communities' (EC). And, more seriously for American export business, the Europeans managed to pass over their own dissensions on agricultural products. By the mid-1960s, they gradually elaborated compromises leading to a common policy even in this sector. Parallel to the elimination of all internal tariffs, the six countries harmonized their import policies and established a Common External Tariff. This in turn had a negative effect on US exports, as American products became less competitive on the booming EEC market. In the 1960s the average GDP growth rates of the six EEC countries did indeed surpass those of the United States and of Britain (albeit not reaching the skyrocketing Japanese figures). All these developments were inherent consequences of the emerging customs union in Western Europe. Nevertheless, they weighed heavily on transatlantic relations during the 1960s.

American annoyance over the EEC's protectionist tendencies became evident for the first time in 1962. 'We are not going to stand by and allow our historical markets to be taken

Table 4.1 GDP per capita annual growth rates (%)

	1961	1962	1963	1964	1965	1966	1967	1968	1969	1970	1971	1972
United States	1.0	3.6	2.6	4.1	4.3	4.7	1.6	3.2	1.7	−0.9	2.2	4.5
Belgium	4.4	4.6	3.6	6.0	2.7	2.5	3.3	3.8	6.4	6.1	3.4	4.9
France	4.4	4.8	3.5	5.4	3.8	4.3	3.9	3.5	6.1	4.8	4.2	3.7
Italy	7.5	5.5	4.8	2.0	2.4	5.2	6.4	5.9	5.5	4.8	1.3	3.1
Luxembourg	2.6	0.1	2.5	6.4	−1.6	0.6	0.1	3.8	9.3	1.3	1.1	5.6
Netherlands	−1.0	5.3	2.2	6.8	7.2	1.4	4.1	5.3	5.2	4.4	3.2	1.6
West Germany	4.6	4.7	2.8	6.7	5.4	2.8	−0.3	5.4	7.5	5.0	3.3	4.1
United Kingdom	1.7	0.4	3.3	4.3	2.1	1.5	1.7	3.5	1.6	2.0	1.5	3.3
Japan	11.0	7.9	7.4	10.5	4.7	9.6	10.1	12.5	10.2	9.5	3.4	6.9

Sources: data from World Bank; Statistisches Bundesamt Deutschland

away', declared US Secretary of Agriculture Orville Freeman, referring to American poultry and grain exports to Western Europe.[6] By 1963, economic retaliatory measures between the US and the EEC had developed into a fully fledged 'chicken war'. After the Europeans had raised tariffs on imported American chicken, the US responded by imposing taxes on French cognac and German Volkswagen vans. In the course of the dispute, the United States imposed extra tariffs on European products such as carpets, bulbs and blue cheese, whereas the EEC six countered with tariffs on American synthetics and paint. This first trade war between the EEC and the US was temporarily resolved by an arbitration committee. Even so, it was only the first one in a series of similar disputes to follow.

In order to make sure that the EEC complied with the rules of world trade laid down by the General Agreement on Tariffs and Trade (GATT), and to avoid trade discrimination against the US, Washington initiated a new round of GATT negotiations. This 'Kennedy Round' took place in Geneva from 1964 to 1967 and involved some 40 countries, but mainly opposed the EEC and the US. Both sides fought hard and bitterly for more than three years.

These negotiations entailed much more than just harmonizing different tariff systems. For the Europeans, the success of the EEC project was on the line. The EEC six were still unsure whether they would be able to create a lasting and competitive economic unit. Core interests were also at stake on national levels, especially when it came to agriculture. France threatened to leave the EEC if there were no truly European agricultural policy. The Italians became staunch defenders of national agricultural interests, after their initial concessions had backfired. The Dutch, like the French, vigorously defended the creation of a protected European market in order to sell their agricultural goods. The German government had to balance the needs of their industries for worldwide exports on the one hand, and the pressure from their farmers to maintain the highly protected and inefficient German agriculture on the other. The curtailing of farmers' privileges had already led to an increase in protest votes for a German right-wing party, a matter that was taken very seriously at the time.

In the United States, resentment against the EEC's protectionist trade policy was fuelled by an increasing deficit in the flow of money and gold. Put simply, more dollars and gold left the US than came in. President Kennedy was reportedly 'obsessed' with the balance of payments, and similar concerns continued during the Johnson administration. In order to cover the growing expenses from investments and defence costs overseas, Washington opted for an ambitious export strategy. Hence, the US launched the Kennedy Round with the aim of reducing the money outflow and of boosting American exports to Europe. From Washington's point of view, buying products from the US should have been the European contribution to financing NATO defence. Now that the Common Market was flourishing, the Europeans were expected to bear a heavier financial burden, and to focus on the wider context of the East–West conflict.

But the EEC was reluctant to liberalize world trade in the way Washington had hoped for. While the Kennedy Round did result in 35 per cent tariff reductions, the drain of US gold and dollars continued. In hindsight, the American goal of reducing the payments deficit through international trade might not have been the most pertinent strategy, since the roots of the deficit were in politics rather than trade. More fundamentally, trade measures did not stop the international monetary system from gradually collapsing.

Crises of confidence in the US dollar

Since the 1944 conference in Bretton Woods, where the post-war monetary order was established, the world had changed significantly. Japan and Western Europe had recovered from the war and turned into booming economies. Throughout the 1960s, their growth rates surpassed those of the US economy. Partly as a result of this evolution, the leading international role of the American currency also came under attack. The Bretton Woods system fixed the value of the US dollar at $35 per ounce of gold, and pegged the other currencies to the dollar. The American currency thus served as the numerical standard of the international monetary system. While this special role of the dollar had remained uncontested after World War II, when the US had amassed more than 65 per cent of the world's gold stock, some critics now called for a revision. De Gaulle especially claimed that the initial rationale of the Bretton Woods system no longer applied, as the gold reserves held by the EEC six equalled or even exceeded the American stocks by 1965.

The international monetary order was becoming obsolete for further reasons. With the rise of economic mobility and the proliferation of short-term movements in international capital, a static system based on fixed exchange rates became increasingly difficult to handle. Central banks and national treasuries struggled to keep up with the fast-changing realities. Not only the role of the US dollar, but even the basic idea of gold as the ultimate value seemed outdated. The expanding international economy was in desperate need of monetary liquidity and thus of more US dollars. According to the Bretton Woods logic, the printing of more paper dollars should have been accompanied by a parallel increase in newly mined gold, which turned out to be impossible. Regardless, the US printed more dollars.

From an American point of view, Western Europe had largely benefited from the Bretton Woods system, which had provided the framework for prosperity and economic recovery after the War. The American elites therefore expected the Europeans to sustain the monetary order instead of criticizing it. But the US officials were also slow to change, because the Bretton Woods system was generally considered beneficial to American interests.

From a European perspective, the inflationary costs of US monetary policy became alarming burdens for the economies. Large-scale speculations against the main European currencies only added fuel to the flames. With the devaluation of October 1967, the British pound sterling practically lost its previous monetary role and any real impact on the system. France had initially been the loudest critic. De Gaulle's efforts to exchange the French US dollar reserves for gold had earned him the nickname 'Gaulle-finger', after Goldfinger, a James Bond villain obsessed with gold. But in 1968, a social and economic crisis significantly weakened the French franc and deprived de Gaulle of any basis to fight against 'dollar imperialism'.

By the end of 1968, the Deutschmark (DM) emerged as the incontestably strongest European currency, thereby putting the West Germans in an exposed position. They generally felt little inclined to challenge Washington. And yet they did do so when American monetary policy became a cause of inflation. In November 1968, the West Germans rejected an urgent request by the US government, and refused to revalue the Deutschmark. The deeply rooted German aversion to inflation proved stronger than the will to cooperate with the Americans. The nightmare memory of the hyperinflation of the early 1920s, which had paved the way for the rise of Adolf Hitler, was still fresh in German minds.

Although the DM was finally revalued in 1969, German–American antagonism over monetary issues continued. In 1970 and 1971, a crisis of confidence in the dollar led to a massive outflow of capital from the United States, mostly to Germany. The six EC ministers of finance were united in their anger against the US, but unanimous about concrete responses. Hence the Germans felt compelled to act on their own. When traders dumped billions of dollars for Deutschmarks in early May 1971, the German currency markets were closed and the purchase of dollars officially stopped.

In the United States, the German move brought anti-European feelings to boiling point. Senator Mike Mansfield had already gathered considerable support in Congress to reduce the costs of the American military presence in Europe. President Richard Nixon was under the impression that Western Europe was pursuing unfair economic policies and he intended to end America's 'benevolent' approach to the world. In July 1971, a public data release confirmed that for the first time since the end of World War II, the US balance of trade had become negative. Another wave of heavy dollar selling was the result. In order to prevent a full-blown panic on the financial markets, Nixon suspended the dollar–gold convertibility on 15 August 1971.

President Nixon thus ended the premises of the Bretton Woods system. He did so without consulting any of his allies, even though consultation lay at the core of the Bretton Woods system. The Europeans were shocked by Nixon's unilateral action. Some perceived it as a declaration of economic war. Although American officials and European leaders tried to mend the fences in the following months and to partly restore the monetary system, their attempts were ultimately unsuccessful. By March 1973, the major currencies were floated and the idea of fixed exchange rates definitely abandoned. With the Bretton Woods system, a powerful tool of American leadership was lost.

Washington questions European integration

The various economic and monetary rivalries between the EC and the US also caused President Nixon to take a more hesitant approach towards European integration than his predecessors. While Lyndon B. Johnson had still prioritized security cooperation, and thus put the greater good of Atlantic cohesion before economic disputes with the Europeans, Nixon concluded that the Europeans could not have it both ways. 'They cannot have the United States' participation and cooperation on the security front and then proceed to have confrontation and even hostility on the economic and political front', Nixon would complain.[7] The objective of European unity now looked much less profitable to the United States. Nixon and his security adviser, Henry Kissinger, doubted whether the goals of a supranational Europe and a US-dominated Atlantic community were even compatible. The often-quoted question 'Who do I call if I want to call Europe?' conveys an erroneous impression of Kissinger's attitude. Instead of having one interlocutor, he actually preferred to talk to each European government separately and to exert American influence as directly as possible.

Not only were economic and monetary priorities evolving differently, but the European developments seemed to escape American control even politically. After the US had struggled with de Gaulle's stubborn independence throughout the 1960s, yet another form of European autonomy had emerged in West Germany by the end of the decade. Chancellor Brandt's new *Ostpolitik* (Eastern policy) and his bold initiatives to promote détente in Europe now risked undermining Washington's pre-eminent role in the East–West dialogue.

The challenge of détente

By the end of the 1960s, the members of the Atlantic Alliance generally agreed on the need for détente, or for a reduction of East–West tensions. Despite this basic consensus, détente did not make the relations between the Western allies any easier; quite the contrary.

Dangers of alliance: entrapment and abandonment

Political scientists have applied the useful theory of 'security dilemma' to explain the complex repercussions of détente. This model asserts that a security alliance holds benefits as well as dangers for its members. In the case of the Atlantic Alliance during the Cold War, the main benefit expected by the United States was European support for American leadership in the world – on diplomatic, economic and logistic levels. From a European perspective, protection against the Soviet threat stood out as the chief advantage, complemented by access to world markets and advanced technology. On the negative side, membership of the alliance also involved the two dangers of 'entrapment' and 'abandonment'. Entrapment refers to the risk of being dragged into a conflict against one's own interests. Abandonment basically means to be deserted by the other members of the alliance. According to this model, the security dilemma of the Europeans consisted of a permanent effort to balance the hazard of abandonment and the risk of entrapment.

This reasoning leads to the first conclusion that détente reduced the benefits and pre-eminence of the alliance. Indeed, the Europeans did not value American protection as highly as in earlier times of East–West crises, and the United States struggled harder to implement its leadership. In the early 1970s Kissinger often warned that détente must not endanger Atlantic unity and Western cohesion. For some European governments, on the other hand, the rise of détente offered a welcome opportunity to sidestep American tutelage and to initiate direct talks with the Soviet Union and Eastern Europe.

In addition, détente shifted the dominant risk of the alliance from entrapment to abandonment. In times of peaceful negotiations between the superpowers, the European NATO partners surely worried less about having to suffer the consequences of a conflict triggered by excessive American bellicosity. Consistent with the model of security dilemma, the danger of abandonment now loomed more prominently over the members of the alliance. American withdrawal from Europe became a viable option, notably in the deliberations of the US Congress in 1969–1971. And as soon as Washington and Moscow engaged in serious talks on peace and arms reductions, the Europeans feared being left out by the United States. Paradoxically, many Europeans had pushed for better relations between the two superpowers during the 1960s, but warned against a 'superpower condominium' in the early 1970s. With the notion of balancing the dangers of entrapment and abandonment, the seemingly contradictory shifts in European attitudes towards the United States may become more understandable.

Détente creates room for German Ostpolitik

West German *Ostpolitik* under Chancellor Willy Brandt offers the best example that not only the Europeans, but also the Americans dreaded abandonment during détente. Especially in the first two years after the advent of *Ostpolitik* in October 1969, the Nixon administration entertained lively suspicions that Brandt might go too far in his negotiations with the Soviets. Would the Bonn government be tempted to leave the Western framework if Moscow held out hopes of German reunification?

Concretely, *Ostpolitik* meant normalization of the FRG's hitherto hostile relations with Eastern Europe and the USSR. Brandt started by complying with the Soviet demands all previous West German governments had rejected. He acknowledged the de facto loss of German territories ceded to Poland in 1945, he accepted that the Federal Republic would never possess any nuclear weapons, and he recognized the German Democratic Republic as a state (although not as a nation). Unfolding an unprecedented dynamism of West German foreign policy, Brandt went on to sign the first of his Eastern treaties with the USSR in August 1970. Both parties pledged to respect the frontiers of all states in Europe as 'inviolable', to refrain from using force against each other, and to work towards international détente. Over the next months and years, Brandt signed similar treaties with Poland, the GDR and Czechoslovakia.

None of these concrete aspects of *Ostpolitik* jeopardized the political agendas of Germany's Western partners. Their uneasiness stemmed more from Brandt's new political style and a general uncertainty about the long-term effects of *Ostpolitik*. Brandt defended German interests with more self-confidence than his predecessors, and called for America's cooperation rather than advice. His opening up to the East had also emerged in a wider context of politically left-wing and societal changes in Germany, with America's image tarnished by the Vietnam War. Indeed Brandt repeatedly emphasized the friendship with America and the vital importance of NATO. But the underlying assumptions of *Ostpolitik*, notably the principle of 'change through rapprochement' and the long-term goals of a European peace order and German reunification, sparked off some animated speculations in Washington, Paris and London.

The reactions to Brandt's *Ostpolitik* were not all negative, however. The governments of many smaller European countries and large sections of public opinion admired the German initiatives aiming at reconciliation with the East. The photo of Chancellor Brandt kneeling in front of the Warsaw Ghetto memorial in December 1970 quickly spread to the front pages of newspapers. The whole world could see how much Germany had changed since the Nazi era.

While Brandt's policy also enjoyed some sympathy in America, the US government struggled hard to reaffirm its leading role in East–West negotiations. Kissinger bluntly instructed the Germans that 'if a course of détente is to be pursued, we do it'.[8] His own efforts to link détente-oriented concessions in Europe with Soviet backing down on Vietnam proved futile, however. Nixon and Kissinger realized that they had no alternative to offer to Brandt's dealings with the East. But they could at least try to control the pace of *Ostpolitik* and give the inevitable a 'constructive direction'. In this endeavour, the US government was fairly successful.

Kissinger identified Berlin as an effective tool for supervising *Ostpolitik*. Control of the divided city still lay with the four powers, and Brandt depended on an agreement to fill the legal void of Berlin's status. Therefore, Kissinger skilfully linked any progress on the Berlin question to the substance of Brandt's bargaining with the East, and to Strategic Arms Limitation Talks (SALT) between the United States and the Soviet Union. As Moscow had a major interest in the ratification of Brandt's Eastern treaties by the Bundestag, Washington thereby created indirect leverage against the FRG and the USSR. After Kissinger's first visit to China in July 1971 he judged the time fit and unlocked the negotiations on Berlin. The subsequent Quadripartite Agreement, which entered into force in June 1972, confirmed the four-power control over the city and finally guaranteed free civilian access from West Germany to West Berlin.

From the American perspective, the challenge represented by *Ostpolitik* was partly tamed by 1972. Washington managed to reaffirm its leadership role in the East–West talks, Brandt acted more in line, and inner-German frictions slowed down the chancellor's initial dynamism. Thus *Ostpolitik* did not lead to a redefinition of transatlantic relations, and not even to a major crisis. Yet it did elevate West Germany within the Atlantic Alliance. The FRG had initiated fruitful ties with the Soviet Union and had acted to push Washington into serious negotiations with Moscow.

The example of German *Ostpolitik* also illustrates some differences in the European and American understanding of détente. For the Germans, and in a broader sense for the Western Europeans, détente policies were geographically limited, and focused on the regional context of Europe only. But in terms of substance, European détente covered a wider range of issues and had a higher significance than on the other side of the Atlantic. Brandt's *Ostpolitik* not only resulted in diplomatic meetings with the East but also, at long last, formalized Europe's post-war borders. It resolved the knotty German question for the time being, reduced the danger of war on European soil, and set in motion a variety of economic and cultural exchanges through the Iron Curtain. With the Conference on Security and Cooperation in Europe and the Helsinki Declaration of 1975, all European countries would become involved in the process. Not surprisingly the Europeans clung to détente much longer, from the mid-1960s until well into the 1980s, while American praise for détente did not stretch far beyond the Nixon administration (1969–1974).

For Washington, détente basically consisted of bilateral summits with Moscow, and represented a change of means rather than ends. Containment of the Soviet Union prevailed as the foremost objective of US foreign policy. In times of social upheaval, American self-doubts over Vietnam and feelings of decline, détente appeared to be an adequate means to that end. Although American détente did produce some spectacular global results, like Washington's opening to China and the SALT agreement with the USSR, Americans and Soviets merely shared the will to avoid a nuclear war that would kill them all. The vast differences in their thinking remained irreconcilable. Hence the persistent American resistance towards Brandt's close ties with the East. The Germans failed to recognize that Moscow's forthcoming attitude only aimed at loosening the FRG's anchoring in the Western framework, Nixon complained repeatedly. He considered Brandt's good relations with the USSR to be latently incompatible with West Germany's Atlantic ties. In general, Europeans and Americans would continue to approach the East–West conflict from different angles.

Out-of-area challenges

In Western terminology, 'out-of-area' stands for all territories not covered by Article 5 of the 1949 NATO treaty. It reads: 'The Parties agree that an armed attack against one or more of them in Europe or North America shall be considered an attack against them all'. Hence the NATO treaty applies to Europe and North America only. Attempts by any member to gain support through the Alliance for conflicts in other parts of the world led to very limited results throughout the Cold War. This was also the case with the Vietnam War, despite President Lyndon Johnson's strenuous efforts to pressure the Europeans to 'share the burden of Free World responsibility in Vietnam'.[9] As the US leadership, and especially President Johnson, tended to view transatlantic ties through the lens of Vietnam, the lack of European response led to major resentment in Washington. In return, American engagement in the war impacted heavily on America's public image and in varying degrees on Western European governments.

Alone in Vietnam

Since the defeat of the French colonial power at Dien Bien Phu in May 1954 and the subsequent split of Vietnam into two halves, American patronage of South Vietnam had aimed at containing the spread of communism in Indochina. If the 'domino fell' in Vietnam, President Eisenhower maintained, neighbouring Laos and Cambodia would follow, and eventually all of Southeast Asia. The United States relied on South Vietnamese leader Ngo Dinh Diem, an anti-communist, former colonial administrator. Ho Chi Minh, on the other hand, the communist leader of the north, appealed to the historic hopes of Vietnamese self-determination and by far exceeded Diem's popularity. While the United States and the Soviet Union supplied the opposing sides of a civil war ravaging Laos in the early 1960s, the corrupt Diem regime lost more ground in South Vietnam. To stabilize the situation, President Kennedy decided to raise the number of American 'military advisers' from 700 in 1961 to 16,700 in the autumn of 1963. Matters deteriorated nevertheless. As a consequence, Diem was killed on 1 November 1963 in a coup endorsed by the CIA. A series of incompetent military juntas succeeded Diem in the governance of South Vietnam.

Although the Europeans preferred not to subscribe to the American credo of the falling domino in Vietnam, Washington's perception of events was not groundless. In the summer of 1964, all of Southeast Asia seemed to be threatened by communism. President Sukarno of Indonesia announced a 'year of living dangerously' in August 1964, moved closer to Beijing and initiated an 'anti-imperialist' process, while his troops were engaged in a conflict with the Federation of Malaysia. Chinese influence increased in Vietnam, Cambodia and Burma. Even the future developments in Western-friendly Thailand and Singapore appeared to be uncertain. The Asian scenario thus contrasted with conditions in Europe, where the end of communist expansion had opened the door to détente.

On 1 May 1964, US President Johnson launched the 'More Flags' programme and called upon other nations to show support for the South Vietnamese government. Johnson intended to demonstrate to the American and South Vietnamese peoples, as well as to the enemy, the determination of the free world to fight against communism. Washington was also reluctant to be left alone in South Vietnam, in a colonialist position. But the result of the More Flags call was meagre. Only Australia and New Zealand eventually participated with their own combat troops, while the contingents sent by South Korea, Thailand and the Philippines were paid for by the United States. Even when the US president personally urged his allies – notably the British and the West Germans – to understand the overbearing significance of the task, not much came of it. All European governments declined to provide a manpower contribution, even a symbolic one. British intelligence support and some German non-combat-related assistance to the South Vietnamese regime remained the most noteworthy European involvement during the following years. By 1965, Johnson understood that he had to cope with the escalating Vietnam War without the Europeans, a matter that irrevocably poisoned his relations with the allies. For instance, President Johnson never agreed to pay official visits to his European partners.

The sympathies of the European leaders for the US commitment to Vietnam varied. In NATO meetings, Greece applauded America's defence of South Vietnam against the communist infiltration from neighbouring countries, and pointed out the similarity of Greek experiences after World War II. Portugal, facing insurgencies in its African possessions of Angola and Mozambique, offered eloquent support for a global strategy against the communist offensive. On the other side of the spectrum, Denmark and Belgium expressed serious concern over the war escalation. In neutral Sweden, the Social Democrats harshly criticized US involvement in Vietnam on moral grounds, and Minister Olof Palme eventually marched in the streets of Stockholm together with the ambassador of North Vietnam in protest.

The West German government drew an analogy between the American commitment to the protection of South Vietnamese and German territories, especially West Berlin. The FRG therefore provided assistance to the American war effort in Vietnam, albeit limited to economic aid. The idea of sending out troops only 20 years after World War II was anathema to the entire German leadership. Britain opted for a wait-and-see approach, wavering between friendliness towards the United States and deeply rooted scepticism about the adequacy of the American war strategy. The delicate relations with different members of the Commonwealth also kept London from taking a clear stance. With the escalation of the Vietnam War from 1965 onward, the uneasiness of the Italian government found expression in various attempts to mediate between the war parties. Still, if many European leaders privately experienced embarrassment about the Vietnam War, they nevertheless seconded the American policy line in their official statements. For the US government, such rhetorical support also mattered.

The one major exception was French President de Gaulle. Since 1959, he had urged Eisenhower and then Kennedy to recognize the impossibility of a military solution for Vietnam. In August 1963 he started to publicly criticize the Americans. De Gaulle proposed to keep the superpower rivalries out of Indochina and advocated neutrality for the whole peninsula. In light of French experiences a decade earlier, he was convinced that the Vietnamese population would turn against any foreign power trying to succeed by force. The French activism reached its peak in September 1966, when de Gaulle blamed the United States for the Vietnam War in front of a cheering crowd of 100,000 Cambodians in Phnom Penh. Johnson held de Gaulle partly responsible for the low morale of the US troops in Vietnam, but was powerless to stop him. A turning point in Franco-American relations occurred in the spring of 1968, when Johnson announced a de-escalation policy in Vietnam and agreed to initiate peace negotiations. De Gaulle acclaimed Johnson's 'courageous' act and ceased the harsh French criticism at that stage. In return, Johnson accepted Paris as the site for the forthcoming peace negotiations, a choice which implicitly honoured the European efforts to bring about a diplomatic solution to the conflict. Georges Pompidou, who succeeded de Gaulle in 1969, continued to promote the neutralization of Indochina, but took care not to jeopardize his valued role as mediator between the Americans and the North Vietnamese.

Richard Nixon had taken office with the pledge of ending the Vietnam War honourably. Yet the peace negotiations lasted almost five years, not least because of communist offensives in Laos and Cambodia, and the north's maximalist demand to unite Vietnam under communist rule. The Paris Peace Accords of January 1973 finally ended the American war in Vietnam and signified the complete withdrawal of US troops, but brought no lasting peace to the Vietnamese people. After a two-year interim to let Washington save face, North Vietnam overran the South in 1975. Wars continued to ravage Indochina for another 15 years.

The experience of failure in the Vietnam War added to a general American perception of decline, and contributed to a more modest and inward-looking definition of US interests in the 1970s. Eventually, this resulted in a period of less intense relations across the Atlantic.

The Western European governments never considered the defence of South Vietnam essential for their own security. Quite the opposite: they feared being dragged into a war that might escalate to China or go nuclear (entrapment). Despite the differences among them, the European leaders fundamentally agreed to focus their own ambitions on Europe, now that the former colonies had gained independence. The Vietnam War also raised doubts about the American ability to lead the Alliance wisely, which in turn was conducive to European self-reliance in the years to come.

Conclusion

After the United States had largely dominated the build-up of the Western framework during the 1950s, the 1960s witnessed an increase in European self-confidence and challenges to American hegemony. Several factors contributed to increasing the European leeway within the transatlantic partnership. The cementing of the European status quo by the Berlin Wall and the initiation of American–Soviet contacts after the Cuban missile crisis made a war on European soil less likely. In times of superpower détente, lining up behind Washington's leadership became less of an imperative. America's military engagement in Vietnam also provoked a wave of anti-Americanism among the Western European public. On an economic level, the European integration process and the successful creation of the Common Market further reduced dependencies on the United States.

While this constellation produced challenges in all aspects of transatlantic relations, the 1960s and early 1970s also showed that the ties were strong enough to avert a major crisis, and flexible enough to adapt to new developments. For example, despite the economic wrangling between the US and the emerging EEC, transatlantic trade continued to prosper thanks to new GATT agreements and reciprocal investments increased virtually every year.

The European challenges were also limited in scope. As long as the Soviet threat persisted, America's main Western opponent of the 1960s, French President Charles de Gaulle, never questioned the need for close cooperation with the United States. German Chancellor Willy Brandt temporarily took the lead in East–West contacts by launching *Ostpolitik* in 1969, but in the longer run he depended on the Americans to make German–Soviet détente a lasting reality.

Overall, the years from 1961 to 1972 were a period of intense and demanding debate among the Western partners, with the European voices gaining more weight in the transatlantic balance. The following period, starting in 1973, was to be characterized by more distant relations, with both the European and American sides concentrating primarily on their internal developments.

Suggested further reading

Bozo, Frederic (2010) 'France, "Gaullism", and the Cold War', in Melvyn P. Leffler and Odd Arne Westad (eds), *The Cambridge History of the Cold War*, vol. 2, pp. 158–78. Cambridge, UK: Cambridge University Press.

Buffet, Cyril (2002) 'De Gaulle, the bomb and Berlin: How to use a political weapon', in John Gearson and Kori Schake (eds) *The Berlin Wall Crisis: Perspectives on Cold War Alliances*, pp. 73–95. Basingstoke, UK: Palgrave.

Dumbrell, John and Axel Schäfer (eds) (2009) *America's 'Special Relationships'*. London: Routledge.

Logevall, Fredrik (2003) 'The American effort to draw European states into the war', in Christopher Goscha and Maurice Vaïsse (eds), *La Guerre du Vietnam et l'Europe, 1963–1973*, pp. 3–16. Brussels: Bruylant.

Lundestad, Geir (2003) *The United States and Western Europe: From 'Empire' by Invitation to Transatlantic Drift*. Oxford: Oxford University Press.

Schwartz, Thomas A. (2003) *Lyndon Johnson and Europe: In the Shadow of Vietnam*. Cambridge, MA: Harvard University Press.

Vaïsse, Maurice (1993) *L'Europe et la Crise de Cuba*. Paris: Armand Colin.

Winand, Pascaline (1993) *Eisenhower, Kennedy, and the United States of Europe*. Basingstoke, UK: Macmillan.

5   Atlantic distance, 1973–1983

The widening ocean, 1973

The year 1973 prefaced a period when the Atlantic Ocean seemed to grow wider. While the fundamental framework of transatlantic cooperation persisted, in the following years the Western Europeans and the Americans clearly prioritized their own concerns over Atlantic unity. The different meanings attributed to détente thereby became increasingly apparent. After 1979, the United States engaged in the 'Second Cold War' in order to repel the Soviet Union, even if the Europeans doubted the appropriateness of American belligerence. This chapter ends at the high point of East–West tensions, and the low point of transatlantic relations, in late 1983.

In 1973, three specific events signalled the growing distance between Western Europe and America: the first enlargement of the European Communities (EC), Kissinger's heavy-handed 'Year of Europe', and especially the Arab–Israeli War of October 1973.

Britain turns to Europe

The number of EC members rose to nine on 1 January 1973. Britain, Ireland and Denmark joined the original six after many years of exploratory talks and intricate bargaining. Norway had also applied for membership but withdrew due to an unfavourable plebiscite. Both Ireland and Denmark had close economic ties with Britain and to a large extent followed London's lead. In terms of political influence and economic weight, Britain was by far the most significant new EC member. It was also influential in transatlantic relations.

Edward Heath, British prime minister 1970–1974, recognized that his country needed to take some distance from the United States in order to get into the EC. During the 1960s, France had consistently blocked British entry on two grounds. First, because it would change the nature of a community still in the making; and second, because Britain was not yet 'European' enough and too much attached to America. De Gaulle had even called Britain a 'Trojan horse' engineered by the United States. With the common market completed, de Gaulle gone and West Germany launching *Ostpolitik*, the international constellation had finally come to favour Britain's entry. Pompidou wanted London to counterbalance Germany's growing influence, while Brandt counted on the British to endorse his Eastern policy. Public opinion in the six member states had long been urging the community's enlargement. When Britain finally entered the EC in January 1973, Heath was keen to demonstrate that his country was no American Trojan horse. He acquiesced to many EC regulation demands, notably by adhering to the Common Agricultural Policy, and promoted the creation of a European Regional Development Fund. Heath was fully determined to be a good European and aware that London's 'special relationship' with Washington would suffer for it.

The Americans had discreetly encouraged the British application, and were careful not to mar the outcome. They expected the enlarged EC to evolve in a more liberal and westward-looking way instead of turning into 'Fortress Europe'. The Nixon administration, hesitant about the core idea of integration, saw the British as insurance against a closed and potentially supranational Europe. National security adviser Henry Kissinger had hoped to maintain close ties with London while building up similar 'special relationships' with other European capitals, although his concept defied the very idea of any relationship being special. And yet, the state of Anglo-American relations palpably deteriorated after Britain's entry into the EC.

An unappreciated Year of Europe

Kissinger himself unwittingly contributed to the degeneration of affairs not only with Britain but with the Western European countries in general, when he announced 'The Year of Europe' on 23 April 1973. Kissinger's speech at a journalists' meeting in New York was actually meant to encourage transatlantic dialogue and to strengthen the Western framework. In Nixon's name, Kissinger called upon the other Western leaders to jointly work out a new Atlantic Charter and to develop 'a shared view of the world we seek to build'. He aimed at widening the Atlantic community in a geographical sense, by including Japan, and also in substance, by extending cooperation beyond security.

Kissinger's analysis of world affairs was fairly accurate. However, his mode of expression alienated the other leaders and prompted harsh responses, similar to the negative results provoked by de Gaulle's hectoring style a few years earlier. The part of Kissinger's speech stating that the European allies had 'regional' and the United States 'global interests and

---

Box 5.1 Document extract: 'The Year of Europe'

The following remarks are extracted from the address by Henry Kissinger to the annual meeting of Associated Press editors in New York on 23 April 1973.[1]

Nineteen seventy-three is the year of Europe because the era that was shaped by decisions of a generation ago is ending. The success of those policies has produced new realities that require new approaches ...

Today the need is to make the Atlantic relationship as dynamic a force in building a new structure of peace, less geared to crisis and more conscious of opportunities, drawing its inspirations from its goals rather than its fears. The Atlantic nations must join in a fresh act of creation equal to that undertaken by the postwar generation of leaders of Europe and America. ...

The problems in Atlantic relationships are real. ... The United States has global interests and responsibilities. Our European allies have regional interests. These are not necessarily in conflict, but in the new era neither are they automatically identical. ...

We must strike a new balance between self-interest and the common interest. We must identify interests and positive values beyond security in order to engage once again the commitment of peoples and parliaments. We need a shared view of the world we seek to build.

responsibilities' caused the greatest consternation. The American initiative was widely perceived as condescending, as if the United States suddenly remembered the Europeans while its real interests lay elsewhere. According to the historian Daniel Möckli, French President Pompidou criticized Kissinger's proposal as an 'imperious' attempt to subordinate Europe to America's authority, by convening a 'ballet of the Nine before Nixon' like a meeting of 'Roman vassals' with Caesar.[2] All European leaders now started to voice their accumulated disapproval of Kissinger's methods. Even the British, formerly the most vehement supporters of America, sided with the Europeans and criticized Washington's effort to subdue the EC.

From Washington's point of view, the Year of Europe had been intended to increase the Europeans' financial share of the 'burden of common defence', but not to degrade them. Still, after the United States had prioritized the USSR and Asia for several years, the European allies justifiably doubted the seriousness of the American resolve to refocus on Europe.

Kissinger's ambitious project ended up in a modest Declaration of Atlantic Relations one year later, but, more significantly, it provoked a new sense of unity among the Europeans. Coinciding with the nine EC members' struggle to find a European identity, the Year of Europe speech contributed to the forming of a European identity distinct from the United States. For once, Britain, France and Germany saw eye to eye; the nine countries' consensus naturally ensued. Washington followed the discussions on European identity with growing concern, suspicious of their potentially anti-American edge. The new sense of Europeanness indeed became a main ingredient of the transatlantic confrontation over interests in the Middle East, triggered by the Arab–Israeli War of October 1973.

Middle Eastern clashes

The 1973 war in the Middle East arguably resulted in the most serious crisis between Europeans and Americans since the founding of NATO. As Kissinger later commented in his memoirs, 'each side's unilateralism fed the other's and turned into a self-fulfilling prophecy'.[3] And yet the transatlantic clash was only a sideshow of the real conflict. Essentially the war was an effort by a coalition of Arab states, led by Egypt and Syria, to reclaim the territories Israel had occupied six years earlier (the Sinai Peninsula, the Gaza Strip, the West Bank and the Golan Heights), or at least to consolidate the Arab position after the humiliating defeat of 1967.

The hostilities lasted three weeks in total. On 6 October 1973, Egyptian and Syrian forces launched a surprise attack against Israel, crossing the Suez Canal and invading the Golan Heights. Israel was close to defeat during the first week of the war, then managed to counterattack thanks to American supplies. The hostilities ended on 26 October, when the warring parties accepted a ceasefire called by the United Nations. A series of negotiations followed.

The core aspects of the war were complicated by their connections to the wider issues of the East–West conflict and American–Soviet rivalry over influence in the Middle East. Moscow had gained ground with the 1956 Suez crisis and maintained close relations with Nasser's Egypt as well as Syria. After succeeding Nasser in 1970, Sadat initiated secret contacts with the US and considered realigning with the West. During the war of October 1973, the United States followed a double strategy of militarily siding with Israel while also attempting to draw Egypt closer to the West, a fact the Israeli leadership remained completely unaware of.

From a transatlantic perspective, another highly complex matter entered the equation: the historical relations between the United States and the European powers with the different warring parties. Britain had exerted a dominant influence over the Middle East since the 19th century, and France had been Israel's chief mentor and arms supplier between 1956 and 1967. Both Britain and France sceptically witnessed America's gradual take-over of their former roles. At the same time, the French were eager to re-establish their traditional ties with the Arab world, which had suffered badly from much bloodshed on the road to Algerian independence. Israel's victory and dramatic expansion during the Six-Day War of 1967 prompted a shift in Western policies. While Washington had tended to perceive Israel as an obstacle to American interests in the Middle East until 1967, the growing Soviet penetration of the region and Israel's new strategic importance reversed the premises. Washington came to rely on Israel as its main partner in the Middle East, now considered strong enough to extend American influence and bring stability to the sub-continent. By contrast, the French government condemned Israel's aggression in 1967 as 'imperialistic' and shunned its former partner. When Syrian and Egyptian forces entered the Golan Heights and the Sinai in October 1973, they were only advancing into their own territories in French and British eyes. In the context of emerging European identity, the nine EC countries consequently formed a like-minded bloc opposing America's military support for Israel.

During the war of October 1973, the Arabs also discovered the political weight of their oil assets and thus added another explosive element to the transatlantic dispute. The Arab coalition doubled (and later quadrupled) oil prices, announced reductions of 25 per cent in production and issued an embargo against countries supporting Israel. Since the Europeans were far more dependent on Arab oil than the Americans, this move significantly widened the gap within the Atlantic community.

The aforementioned rifts between the EC and the US deepened as soon as the fighting in the Middle East started. Washington focused on countering the Soviets, who airlifted military supplies to Syria, and requested the use of NATO bases and airspace to assist the Israelis. But the Europeans, sensing entrapment, refused to be involved in the hostilities. With the peculiar but ultimately pointless exception of Holland, the EC nine rejected the American demand. Even the British denied access to their ideally located bases on Cyprus. The Nixon administration was furious with the European allies, and especially Britain. Pressured by Kissinger to follow Washington's lead, the British Ambassador to the United States, Lord Cromer, coolly responded in mid-October that 'Europe would not be content to be without Middle East oil because of American actions.' [4] Heath feared a parallel build-up of Arab and Soviet strength in the Middle East and Western Europe's economic decline due to the oil shortage.

America's relations with the other European allies were not much better at that point. The Germans protested against the US covertly shipping arms from their territory to Israel, and France took the lead in elaborating a distinctly European policy for the Middle East. The transatlantic dispute grew even worse by the end of the month. On 25 October, Washington put the American nuclear forces in Western Europe on alert, for the second (and last) time, after the Cuban missile crisis. The Soviets had alerted 50,000 parachutists the day before, and Nixon considered his move the best response in the interests of the Alliance. However, his failure to consult the allies on this major issue indicated to many Europeans that transatlantic dialogue was a one-way street. Washington claimed influence on European affairs while granting no access to American decision-making.

With the end of the hostilities on 26 October, Kissinger saw himself as the logical spokesman of the West in the forthcoming, highly complex negotiations, only to discover that the Europeans preferred to launch their own agenda. In early November, the EC nine called for direct European–Arab discussions and for peace negotiations within the framework of the United Nations. Washington criticized the EC's solo performance as a sell-out of Western unity due to the Arab 'oil weapon'. Particularly displeased, Kissinger accused the Europeans of sabotaging the peace process in the Middle East and predicted that Nixon would be the last American president emotionally attached to Europe.

The future of the Atlantic community was not really so grim, however, and the acrimony died down after a few months. The Europeans were unable to develop a common or pertinent strategy for the Middle East and soon discovered that they could not solve their energy problems without America. By 1974, the governmental changes in the four major Western powers would help turn the page on the violent transatlantic clash of October 1973.

In the Middle East, the outcome of the Arab–Israeli War corresponded to American wishes. Israel had achieved a limited victory, Egypt's pride was restored and it now agreed to sit down at the negotiation table supervised by Washington. In the long process of peace talks, which ultimately resulted in the Camp David accords of 1978, Egypt moved from the Soviet to the American camp. The moderate Arabs began to see in Washington's services a possible way out of the regional stalemate. The USSR was excluded from the Israeli–Egyptian discussions and lost much of its influence on the region.

Nevertheless, the evolution in the Middle East had also its negative aspects, from a Western viewpoint. Egypt paid a price for its new orientation and was suspended from the Arab League, Sadat was eventually assassinated by militant Islamists, and the oil crisis served to boost Soviet energy production. The soaring values of hydrocarbon fuel and natural gas helped finance foreign expenses and to some extent explains the USSR's return to a more aggressive stance after 1975. Moscow's successful support for Marxist-inspired forces in Angola and Ethiopia indeed created the impression that the 'class struggle' was now on the rise in Africa. The impacts of this communist offensive would hit transatlantic relations a few years later, in late 1979.

Alliance in times of introspection, 1974–1979

Between March and August 1974, an almost simultaneous shift occurred in the Western capitals. Heath's Conservative Party lost the general election in Britain, and the new Labour government of Prime Minister Harold Wilson (and later James Callaghan) re-emphasized cooperation with Washington. French President Georges Pompidou died suddenly. His successor, former minister of economy Valéry Giscard d'Estaing, adopted a more pragmatic attitude towards the English-speaking world, and developed close ties with the new German Chancellor Helmut Schmidt. Willy Brandt had stepped down upon the exposure of an East German spy in his inner circle. Richard Nixon was facing an impeachment procedure due to his being implicated in the Watergate scandal, a break-in at the Democratic Party's headquarters in 1972, and resigned on 8 August 1974. Gerald Ford assumed the US presidency. He had been appointed vice president just a few months earlier, by Nixon, after the previous vice president, Spiro Agnew, had stepped down due to allegations of fraud. All these governmental changes converged towards less passionate, more practical and overall friendlier relations within the alliance.

Moreover, as suggested by the events of 1973, during the next few years the partners on both sides of the Atlantic followed fairly self-reliant policies. The Europeans were mostly busy operating their enlarged community, and the Americans suffered a period of economic setbacks and rising inflation while striving to recover from the Vietnam debacle. Remarkably, during this time of more self-centred policies, the structures of transatlantic cooperation not only survived but silently developed. When struggling with internal issues,

none of the allies wished to alienate friends on the other side of the Atlantic. And the fundamental reasons for alliance were still valid.

Modest America

Gerald Ford was well aware that his presidency lacked the democratic legitimation of an
election. He hadn't even been elected vice president. Mindful of his standing as interim
president as well as his personality, Ford accepted diversity within the Alliance more readily
than his predecessors. The Europeans found in Ford an inconspicuous leader with an ear
attentive to their concerns. Transatlantic relations therefore improved during Ford's presidency (August 1974–January 1977). At the same time, Europe was not among his priorities.
Studies of Ford's tenure have not brought to light any momentous statement or initiative
he may have taken towards Europe. Ford lacked experience in foreign policy and initially
opted for continuity. Henry Kissinger, who had assumed the office of secretary of state a
year earlier, thus retained his position with even greater responsibilities and also continued
to preside over European affairs.

During the Ford presidency, Kissinger's biggest worry about Western Europe was the
apparent rise of leftist tendencies. Three previously authoritarian regimes in southern
Europe – in Portugal, Spain and Greece – collapsed in 1974–1975 and were replaced by
democratic governments. In the turmoil of transition, Greece withdrew from NATO's military command, and in Portugal, a founding member of the Atlantic Alliance, communists
temporarily entered the government and took over key positions in the army. Meanwhile
the communist parties of Italy and France seemed to be on their way into national governments. Clearly overestimating the appeal of communism to Western Europe's youth and
electorates, Kissinger warned President Ford that 'we could face in ten years a socialist
Europe whose cement is anti-American'.[5] This prediction proved wrong, however, and Euro-
communism never became a serious challenge to NATO.

The most memorable act of President Ford's European policy was his signing of the
Helsinki Accords on 1 August 1975, along with the representatives of all European states
except Albania, as well as the USSR and Canada. These documents represented the fruits
of two years of diligent negotiations within the Conference on Security and Cooperation
in Europe (CSCE), and dealt with issues as diverse as the 'inviolability' of borders,
economic and cultural relations, and human rights. Initially, the Soviets had promoted
the idea of an all-European security conference with the aim of excluding the United
States and driving a wedge between the Western Europeans and the Americans. But by
the early 1970s, Moscow had abandoned that objective and no longer tried to force the
Americans out of Europe. German *Ostpolitik* had provided further groundwork in favour
of an East–West conference.

For the Western Europeans, the Helsinki Accords of 1975 marked the high point of détente
and consequently proliferated into a multitude of Helsinki Groups all over the continent –
although hardly anybody foresaw the abrasive effects the human rights agreements would
eventually have on the Soviet bloc. The US government saw no crucial importance in the
CSCE discussions, at least not in the mid-1970s, and primarily used them as a means to
keep Soviet–American bilateralism running smoothly. 'They can write it in Swahili for all I
care', Kissinger commented to his staff members on the Helsinki agreements.[6] Nevertheless,
the Americans did care about improving transatlantic relations and came to back up the
Western Europeans' efforts at the Helsinki conference, which, in retrospect, symbolized a
breakthrough in the East–West conflict.

After August 1975, while still shining bright in Europe, the star of détente fell rather quickly in the United States. Ford's fellow Republican Ronald Reagan reached a wide audience by denouncing the Helsinki Accords as a sell-out of American power and acquiescence to Soviet domination over Eastern Europe. The prestige of the architect of US détente, Henry Kissinger, also faded away. Democrat Jimmy Carter repeatedly attacked him for the moral compromises of détente. Under the impression of communist advances in the so-called Third World, notably in Angola and Vietnam, and of a stalemate in arms reduction talks with the USSR, the American public turned away from détente. In March 1976, President Ford banned the use of the word and instead announced a policy of 'peace through strength'. During the presidential elections of 1976, Ford narrowly defeated Reagan in the Republican primaries, then lost the general election to Carter in a close race.

In theory, one would have expected the Europeans to like Carter and his high moral ideals. In his inaugural address of 20 January 1977, he pledged himself to fight for human rights and against poverty, to 'walk humbly' and to aspire to 'a lasting peace, built not on weapons of war but on international policies'. Carter promoted closer cooperation by paying early visits to the European Commission and NATO headquarters in Brussels, and indeed got off to a good start with the Europeans. Nevertheless, transatlantic relations soon became problematic. Despite his initial promises, Carter paid little attention to consulting the allies and displayed ambiguous tendencies in foreign policy. He had wanted to abandon the East–West thinking, but eventually he would end up in an arms race with the Soviet Union. Rather than reducing the North–South imbalance he tried to handle, somewhat unfortunately, a domestic economy shaken by 'stagflation' (high unemployment and high inflation). Instead of liberating the world from the atomic threat, as he had set out to do, Carter found himself advocating a new generation of nuclear weapons just a few months after his inauguration.

The affair of the 'neutron bomb' (as it was popularly called) vividly exemplifies the general problematic of transatlantic relations during Carter's presidency, namely the detrimental effects of American vacillation on the Alliance. Relations with German Chancellor Helmut Schmidt were most directly affected in this case. The affair began in June 1977, when the *Washington Post* printed a story of an enhanced radiation warhead (ERW) designed to destroy tanks and leave buildings intact. Carter was apparently not familiar with that specific weapons programme the Pentagon had been developing for more than 15 years. However, as the matter escalated in the press, Carter gave the ERW option a half-hearted endorsement. The Senate took this as a statement of support and approved further financing. Still hesitant about the whole project himself, but hoping for a trump card vis-à-vis the Soviets, Carter pushed Schmidt to give the green light for the ERW's future deployment in West Germany. In return, Carter accepted Schmidt's proposal of linking deployment of the new weapon with arms control negotiations between the superpowers.

Carter was scheduled to officially announce ERW production in March 1978, but he changed his mind, ignored his advisers and put the whole project on hold, to the German chancellor's great embarrassment. Carter thought it would be futile to spend money on a weapon that, if arms limitation talks proved successful, would go directly from the production facilities to the scrapyard. For Schmidt, on the other hand, the outcome of this affair represented a major personal and political defeat. Facing an aggressive opposition to the ERW from within his own Social Democrat Party, a burgeoning and latently anti-American peace movement, and a press in favour of disarmament, Schmidt had invested all his personal prestige in gaining support for Carter's new weapons programme. All for nothing. The trust between the two men was irretrievably lost, and Schmidt would henceforth view Carter as an unpredictable maverick.

The controversy over the neutron bomb also illustrates another dilemma that was simmering between the Europeans and the Americans. Schmidt's version of détente policy, similar to Brandt's but less daring and more pragmatic, found wide support in Western Europe. On the whole, the governments as well as public opinion perceived the effects of German *Ostpolitik* as beneficial and détente worth retaining. Daily life on the divided continent and especially in divided Germany had improved, and war seemed less likely due to closer East–West contacts. In the years 1977–1979, the European partners thus came to endorse Schmidt's ambition to approach the East on the basis of a dual strategy. This included the will to manifest Western strength, notably by countering the deployment of Soviet SS20 medium-range nuclear missiles along the Iron Curtain, and at the same time to exploit the fruits of détente and to pursue disarmament negotiations with Moscow. All NATO members would adopt this rationale in the 'double-track decision' of 12 December 1979.

Carter had come a long way to support the double-track decision. He had wanted to improve US–Soviet relations on the precondition that Moscow show greater respect for human rights and international agreements. Understanding that these conditions would not be met, Carter vacillated between self-imposed restraint and half-hearted attempts to build up a front of Western pressure on the Soviet Union. For example, in the CSCE follow-up conference of 1977–1978, the American representatives harshly criticized the Eastern bloc's violation of human rights. Carter also tried to enlist the European allies in an effort to coerce the Soviets by means of economic embargoes. The Europeans, sceptical about the goals of American policy, rejected such initiatives as counterproductive. By the end of 1979, a number of events would finally tip the balance in favour of a confrontational American attitude to the Soviet Union, and Washington's understanding for the Europeans' wish to save détente would fade.

EC embroiled in Euro-pessimism

After the enlargement of 1973 and until the early 1980s, the nine EC member states lived through a period widely perceived as the EC's decline. This slow-down of the integration process not only meant that the member states spent a lot of time dealing with the European malaise, but also that the United States was facing an overall quiet time in its relationship with the EC. Devoid of obvious progress, European unification posed neither an economic nor a political challenge to the US.

One reason for the spread of Euro-pessimism was the enlargement itself. British membership had turned out to be more problematic than expected. As soon as the Labour Party returned to power in March 1974, Harold Wilson endeavoured to reset his predecessor's European course and re-emphasized British ties to the United States and the Commonwealth. He asked his EC partners for a renegotiation of the (already implemented) entry agreements and demanded better conditions for British agriculture and Commonwealth products. After a year of acrimonious bargaining, Britain held a referendum in June 1975 with a 67 per cent vote to stay 'in Europe'. Despite this favourable outcome, the political elite in the United Kingdom remained deeply divided over EC membership. Ambivalent positions would continue, with Prime Minister Margaret Thatcher famously protesting 'I want my money back' (from Brussels) in the 1980s, and later with Prime Minister John Major's partial adherence to the Maastricht treaty. Many of the European partners were deeply disappointed by such British indecisiveness. The Americans, on the other hand, conveniently resumed their role as Britain's special ally, once the intermezzo of the Heath government was over.

The degeneration of the European Commission was a further stumbling block for the EC. Originally conceived as an agenda-setter and a potential seed for a European government, the supranational-oriented commission had suffered a defeat against de Gaulle in 1965–1966 and appeared to sink into oblivion in the following years. After the EC's enlargement, the French and the British heavyweights braced themselves against any further loss of national sovereignty, and the very idea of a supranational Europe now appeared outmoded. Furthermore, the EC's major goal for the 1970s was silently shelved. In the face of economic disparities triggered by the oil crisis, high unemployment and inflation in the member states, the creation of a single currency within an economic and monetary union (EMU) by 1980 had become an illusion. The slowing down of the integration process thus had its roots in the Europeans' inability to develop a homogeneous community, not in an American attempt to prevent European unification from happening.

Still, in view of the EC's subsequent take-off, the struggles of the 1970s appear in a more positive light than they did at the time. While the nine member countries fell short of reaching monetary union, they did lay important groundwork. In response to the weakness of the dollar and soaring oil prices, the Western Europeans anchored their currencies to the Deutschmark with floating rates. By 1979 the EC leaders instituted the European Monetary System (EMS), which successfully served as an agency for adjusting exchange rates among the community's currencies. The EMS eventually paved the way for the euro.

The nine EC members also assisted Greece, Spain and Portugal in setting up democracies, and thereby prepared the EC's southern enlargements of 1981 and 1986. And finally, the roles of the European institutions were readjusted. The nine members held popular elections to the European Parliament in 1979 as a first step towards the democratic legitimization of the EC. Under the presidency of Roy Jenkins, the Commission re-emerged by the end of the decade as skilful administrator, and the Franco-German motor with Schmidt and Giscard d'Estaing acting as agenda-setter. Most importantly, the nine found a pragmatic way out of the EC's paralysing leadership vacuum, and decided to institutionalize regular meetings of the heads of state and government in 1974. This European Council, a purely intergovernmental body, failed to meet the hopes of the European federalists. Yet it provided the EC with the highest authority and de facto leadership, able to assume international tasks. The capital holding the presidency of the European Council, rotating every six months, would henceforth represent the EC in negotiations with the United States.

Washington welcomed this (partial) clearing up of responsibilities. But overall, the Ford and Carter governments, as well as Reagan's first administration, reflected a high degree of American indifference with regard to European unification. Questions related to NATO and the common framework were clearly of greater interest to the Americans.

The Atlantic framework confirmed

In that respect, transatlantic ties were in place, and even developed. Above all, a substantial number of US troops continued to be based in Western Europe, most of them in West Germany. After lengthy debates in Congress during the Johnson and Nixon administrations, and despite Senator Mansfield's lobbying to bring the troops home, their number was only moderately reduced during the Vietnam War and partly rebuilt afterwards. This fact was highly significant for the stability of the Atlantic Alliance. Against all plans from the founding years of NATO, American troop presence in Europe remained surprisingly steady throughout the Cold War. US forces in West Germany totalled about 300,000 soldiers in 1953, dropped to 245,000 by 1970, and fluctuated between 261,000 and 292,000 in the 1980s.

Table 5.1 US army and air force levels in Germany

1945	2,680,860
1950	98,931
1955	288,650
1960	259,632
1965	299,654
1970	245,436
1975	263,195
1980	261,643
1985	291,212
1990	244,200
1995	86,600
2000	67,140
2004	69,200

Source: Zimmermann (2009)

Neither side had any interest in reducing or getting rid of these troops during the 1970s. Nixon maintained them not least to preserve his autonomy against Congress; Ford and Carter were reluctant to disturb the alliance or lose strategic assets at a time of relative American weakness. West Germany's growing financial power helped secure the costly deployment. More fundamentally, the three elements of NATO's raison d'être hadn't lost their validity. The Europeans now contributed more than 80 per cent of NATO's conventional forces, but they still wanted to 'keep the Americans in' to preserve the nuclear umbrella. In addition, the presence of American GIs on the continent remained important as a symbol of alliance and a guarantee that the mighty ally would indeed fight in case of an attack against Western Europe.

The creation of an autonomous European defence seemed too expensive and hardly feasible in a period of economic turmoil and frail European unity. Hence, NATO was still the best means to 'keep the Russians out'. And Brandt's *Ostpolitik*, especially its unforeseeable long-term effects, had imbued the motive of 'keeping the Germans down' with new significance. Even though the West Germans behaved like good allies, they were nevertheless the only ones with an interest in changing the European status quo. Nobody really knew if the division of Germany would last for ever or in what kind of framework the country could be unified in the future. All Western Europeans, including the French, preferred to think that the Americans should be present at that moment.

In the economic field the transatlantic partners generated new approaches. In order to respond to the coordinated actions of the Organization of Petroleum Exporting Countries (OPEC), Kissinger launched the idea of a Western counterpart in December 1973. His initiative led to an energy conference in Washington and the formation of the International Energy Agency (IAE) in 1974. However, France stayed out, and the IAE never became the tool of American leadership Kissinger had hoped for. Another proposal proved to be more fitting to discuss the effects of the oil crisis and the collapse of the Bretton Woods system. Giscard d'Estaing's idea of a forum for the leaders of the big industrial states was taken up by Ford and institutionalized as the G5 in 1975. Initially composed of the United States, Britain, France, West Germany and Japan, the

G5 turned into the G7 by 1977, when Italy and Canada (as well as the president of the European Commission) also joined the group. The annual economic meetings of the G7, less US-dominated than Kissinger's IAE, eventually became an inherent part of the Western framework.

Apart from a few unavoidable agricultural tensions between the United States and the EC, transatlantic trade and mutual investments were evolving well in the 1970s. Between 1960 and 1980, US annual exports (goods and services) to the EC had gone up from $7.2 billion to $70.3 billion, imports in the other direction from $4.2 billion to $48 billion. While trade over the Pacific developed even faster than trade over the Atlantic, the foreign direct investments (FDI) between Western Europe and America increased significantly, also as a percentage of overall investments. American annual FDI in the EC amounted to $6 billion in 1960 and $79.9 billion in 1980, rising from 18.3 per cent to 37.4 per cent of total FDI. The EC countries' direct investments in the US grew in the same time period from $4.1 billion (47.1% of total) to $40 billion (58.5%). Furthermore, by the 1970s the Europeans' latent resentment of American wealth and economic domination subsided. They were now just as able to buy cars and washing machines as their transatlantic allies.

Hence the transatlantic framework, security cooperation and economic exchanges were less in the limelight than in the 1950s and 1960s, but overall still in good shape.

Good cop versus bad cop, 1979–1983

The turning of Iran against America and the Soviet invasion of Afghanistan in December 1979 put an end to internal debates within the Carter administration and caused the President's resolve to confront the USSR in 'competitive engagement'. Washington concluded that the period of détente was now definitely over and that a 'Second Cold War' had started. In the following years, and more prominently after Ronald Reagan's accession to power in January 1981, the United States placed emphasis on hard power and military measures, whereas the Europeans were more inclined to rely on soft power and diplomatic negotiations in their contacts with the East. Until the end of 1983, when Reagan unexpectedly abandoned his confrontational stance, the question of how to deal with the Soviet Union was to be the major bone of contention within the Atlantic community.

Historical evidence suggests that the transatlantic differences stemmed from diverging foreign policy choices rather than the supposedly opposing natures of peace-loving Europeans and bellicose Americans. For example, the French had killed hundreds of thousands of Algerians just two decades earlier. Even the West Germans, the most reluctant to use force, did not refrain from shooting the hijackers of a Lufthansa plane to liberate the hostages in 1977.

While in the years 1979–1983 the Western Europeans and the Americans still agreed that the Soviet Union was the common enemy, their strategies differed. The tactic applied by the United States, clearly in the lead, may be compared to confrontation and a 'bad cop' attitude. The Europeans tended to personify the 'good cop', and cared more about maintaining positive relations with the adversary. With the hindsight of the USSR's turnaround in the mid-1980s and eventual collapse, the combined Western strategy could even be judged complementary. At the time, however, the good cop and the bad cop did not play their roles as faithfully as in detective stories, and eventually got into rather heated arguments about the suitability of their respective tactics.

Iran and Afghanistan tip the global balance

Taken completely by surprise, Carter witnessed in 1979 how Iran was transforming from his closest regional ally into a bitter enemy. Curiously, Moscow was not even implicated in the fall of the Shah and the subsequent 'loss' of Iran by the West. This experience nevertheless impacted heavily on Carter's perception of a renewed Cold War.

Iran had been a stronghold of Western positions since the early days of the East–West conflict. Muhammad Reza Shah Pahlavi had outlawed the opposing Communist Party in 1949 and gradually improved his relations with Britain and the United States, who aimed at containing Soviet expansion in a strategically important region. In 1953, the CIA was involved in restoring the Shah's regime against nationalist Muhammad Mossadiq, a fact that undermined the Shah's legitimacy in the eyes of the population.

The Iranian–American cooperation extended over the years to a 'special relationship' with close military and economic ties. Washington perceived the Shah as a 'man of mission' to keep radical Arab and Soviet influence in Southwest Asia under control. The US maintained up to 40,000 technical advisers in Iran and granted access to high-tech arms systems. In the years 1972–1976, Iran bought almost one-third of the total US arms sales. In return the United States benefited from military transit rights and intelligence facilities close to the Soviet border, as well as access to Iranian oil. The last element became even more important for the West after the oil crisis of 1973, as the Shah did not participate in the Arab embargo.

The United States remained unaware of the Shah's increasingly precarious domestic position. Relying on American contacts with only the Iranian government, Carter visited Tehran in December 1977 and praised Iran as 'an island of stability in one of the more troubled areas of the world'.[7] Just a few weeks later massive riots against the Shah started. The Iranian people demonstrated against his oppressive regime and his course of modernization and Westernization, which increased the gap between rich and poor, and provided the country with sophisticated weapons rather than everyday goods. With all aspects of political life heavily controlled, the mosques became the meeting points of the revolutionaries.

In 1979 events unfolded rapidly. Carter had considered the use of force to save the Iranian regime, but finally refrained. In January, the Shah fled the country. Many Iranians (and Arab leaders) assumed that the United States had let down a close ally, despite previous promises of support. In February, the pro-Western government collapsed and Ayatollah Ruhollah Khomeini proclaimed the Islamic Republic of Iran. The anti-American edge of the Iranian revolution reached a peak when in November 1979 hundreds of students stormed the US embassy in Tehran. They took 66 American hostages and released 52 of them only 444 days later.

Almost simultaneously, the Soviet Union endeavoured to take control of neighbouring Afghanistan. On Christmas Day 1979, a total of 75,000 Soviet air and ground forces invaded the country. Babrak Karmal, the leader of an Afghan communist party, was declared president two days later. The Soviet troops maintained a presence in Afghanistan until Soviet leader Mikhail Gorbachev withdrew them in 1989.

The Kremlin's motives for the 1979 invasion were presumably more defensive than Washington understood at the time. Afghanistan had entertained close political and economic relations with the Soviet Union throughout the 1970s. After a military coup in April 1978, the infighting between different Afghan fractions degenerated into a civil war. Moscow was facing a choice between military invasion and recalling all 7200 Soviet advisers. The latter option would have left Afghanistan in a political vacuum likely to be filled by either a fundamentalist Islamic regime or by the Americans, eager to find a new foothold in the region. Apparently, the decisive argument in favour of the Soviet invasion was to forestall the deployment of US missiles on Afghan territory along the border of the USSR.

Diverging strategies to cope with the 'Second Cold War'

The American government interpreted the move into Afghanistan as a prelude to further Soviet expansion. Advances into Pakistan and Iran, providing the USSR with access to the Indian Ocean, appeared to be likely next steps. Carter's security adviser Zbigniew Brzezinski argued that the 'loss' of Iran represented a farther-reaching setback for the United States than the Vietnam debacle and recommended resolute action to defend Western interests. In December 1979 Carter did indeed start to perceive the Soviet Union in a different light. He resolved to end a period of American restraint and to challenge the USSR more aggressively. This new course would eventually be consolidated and heavily promoted by Carter's political opponent and successor, Ronald Reagan, and antagonize the transatlantic partners. The Europeans proved unwilling to implement Washington's global strategy of subduing the USSR, and instead tried to keep détente alive in Europe.

The Carter administration elaborated four levels of action against the Soviet Union. The first, most obvious level involved active containment of the supposed Soviet expansion. In his State of the Union speech of 23 January 1980, Carter declared that America had 'vital interests' in the Persian Gulf region and would repel 'by any means necessary, including military force' any outside power attempting to gain control over that area. The new emphasis on Southwest Asia and hard power measures entailed secret American aid to the anti-communist Afghan resistance, the *mujahidin*, as well as an increased US military presence in the Indian Ocean. At the same time, Carter started to support Somalia in its war against Soviet-sponsored Ethiopia, and activated America's strategic relationship with China to contain the USSR. Washington lifted the relevant trade bans in early 1980, and henceforth provided China with sophisticated military technology and equipment.

The second level of action entailed building up the Western defence. President Carter introduced an ambitious modernization programme and initiated new American weapons systems, such as the Trident submarines, the B-2 Stealth Bombers, and the Pershing II missiles. In 1978 Carter had already called on the European allies to increase their defence budgets by 3 per cent every year. At the end of 1979 he raised that figure to 5 per cent.

Third, the US strategy encompassed an economic level. Carter intended to use the superiority of the Western market system to his advantage and to exploit the Soviet dependence on Western goods. In January 1980, he announced economic embargoes against the Eastern bloc and urged the other Western countries to do the same. From an American perspective, these economic sanctions not only aimed at forcing the USSR out of Afghanistan, but were increasingly meant to undermine the Eastern economies. Some American experts even hoped to trigger a major economic crisis in the Soviet Union by the mid-1980s.

Finally, a fourth level of action was designed to rhetorically challenge the Kremlin's rationale. This included attempts to promote human rights and diversity within the Soviet sphere of influence, notably by encouraging autonomous tendencies in Hungary, Poland and Romania. Carter also expected his allies to endorse the American boycott of the summer 1980 Olympic Games to be held in Moscow.

The Western European governments assessed the situation differently. Although they tried at first to appear supportive of Washington and condemned the invasion of Afghanistan, they perceived Carter's reaction as excessive and the new American course, which had been decided without allied consultation, as unsuitable.

Britain, true to tradition, showed most support for the United States. The new prime minister, Margaret Thatcher, certainly sympathized with Carter's resolve to oppose the Soviets. Yet even the British government had reservations about a purely confrontational stance in the East–West conflict and feared that US policy might provoke anti-Western sentiment, especially in India.

Among the European allies, West Germany depended most on American protection and could least afford to dismiss Washington's demands. Hence the Federal Republic was the only European country to take part in the Olympic boycott. But Germany also had much to lose from ending détente. Carter's new course risked the annihilation of some previous achievements, namely freer access to West Berlin and East Germany, and conflicted with the fundamentals of the generally appreciated *Ostpolitik*. The assumption that a peaceful unification of Germany would only become possible with and not against Moscow had been a starting point of *Ostpolitik*. It thus seemed pointless to abandon the dialogue with the Kremlin or to push for Eastern European autonomy. Close diplomatic contacts and lively trade across the Iron Curtain had played important roles in West Germany's reconciliation with the East and had also proved beneficial in economic terms. Therefore, the Carter administration tried in vain to 'whip' the Germans 'into line' and to end their trading with the Soviets. Chancellor Schmidt also suspected that Carter had hardened American foreign policy in order to improve his chances in the presidential elections of November 1980. However, Carter ultimately lost to Ronald Reagan.

The French openly distanced themselves from American policy. They argued that reviving the Cold War would be the wrong choice for Europe and would only serve to tighten the Soviet grip on Eastern Europe. Like Schmidt, in 1980 Giscard d'Estaing personally met with the Soviet leader Brezhnev to keep détente and East–West communication active.

The other EC countries acted more discreetly on the international scene and were also less subjected to American or Soviet pressure. The smaller European powers generally tended to support the Franco-German approach of maintaining good contacts with the East. For example, Norway in 1980 feared that an extensive deployment of US weapons would provoke the Kremlin and re-emphasized the Scandinavian effort to serve as 'bridge-builder' between East and West.

Overall, the European allies found it difficult to understand why the Red Army's move into Afghanistan, located within Moscow's sphere of influence, should be so different from the previous Soviet invasions of Hungary (1956) and Czechoslovakia (1968). NATO had hardly shown any reaction then. Also, most importantly, the Western Europeans did not wish to provoke new confrontations in Europe because of out-of-area issues, or by blindly embracing America's 'Second Cold War'.

Sabre-rattling Ronald Reagan frightens the Europeans

The first years of Reagan's presidency, from January 1981 until late 1983, continued to be characterized by transatlantic friction over the strategy to follow in the East–West conflict. Reagan stepped up America's hard-line foreign policy and added a tough rhetoric against the USSR. The governments of the European allies tried to keep up the two tracks of negotiating with the enemy while showing Western strength, and deplored Reagan's almost exclusive emphasis on the second aspect. Domestically, they were facing massive peace movements claiming that the arms race itself had become more dangerous than the enemy. The antagonism between Western Europe and Reagan's America was widely perceived as serious. At the same time, the basic framework of transatlantic cooperation remained solid, and none of the allies developed sympathies for Soviet policy. The Western Europeans continued to rely on American protection and preferred to use most of their resources to relaunch their struggling economies instead of building up a costly defence.

Reagan's confrontational policy against the Soviet Union resembled Carter's blueprint more than the new administration cared to admit. Most of all, Reagan energetically promoted the rebuilding of America's military strength. Showing little interest in arms control, the Reagan government enhanced American strategic capabilities and modernized the conventional arms sector. US defence expenditures in 1981–1985 were boosted to the tune of 30 per cent of the federal budget.

Washington also amplified its attempts to undermine Soviet influence in Asia, Africa and Latin America, and supported 'freedom fighters' who resisted or challenged communism within the Soviet sphere of influence. Reagan notably authorized paramilitary operations against the (elected) left-wing Sandinista government in Nicaragua, a policy widely deplored by the Europeans as illegal. When in December 1981 the Polish regime imposed martial law to suppress the Solidarity protest movement, the United States endorsed the protesters by imposing economic sanctions against Poland. Quite oppositely, the Western Europeans did not want to give false hopes to the Polish people and stuck to the long-established NATO policy of respecting the Soviet sphere of influence.

The Reagan administration eventually conducted a veritable campaign of economic warfare to harm the Eastern camp. Washington banned the transfer of Western technology (including devices as simple as toasters), infiltrated Eastern business with faulty equipment and endeavoured to reduce the Soviets' benefit from their energy sources. American attempts to impede East–West trade were not always successful. In the case of a gas pipeline deal between the USSR and Western Europe, the Reagan government ultimately had to yield. Even Margaret Thatcher, Reagan's only committed supporter in Europe, in 1982 rejected such American interference in European matters. In contrast to Washington, the European governments considered East–West trade an effective contribution to political stability in Europe.

The one element that most obviously poisoned the transatlantic atmosphere in the early 1980s was Reagan's war-like rhetoric. Without even giving the impression of seeking consultation with the allies or caring about European concerns, Reagan took the public denunciations of the Soviet Union to a new level. In May 1981, he self-confidently declared that the West was about to dismiss communism 'as some bizarre chapter in human history whose last pages are even now being written'. The US president called the deployment of SS-20 missiles in Eastern Europe 'Soviet aggression' and accused the USSR of being 'plainly offensive in nature'. In March 1983, Reagan famously proclaimed that the Soviet Union was an 'evil empire' and 'the focus of evil in the modern world'.[8]

From European perspectives, such simplistic language was dangerously heating up the atmosphere and likely to provoke further Soviet aggression instead of improving the Western position. The Reagan government's casual talk of nuclear warfare and of winning the Cold War clearly frightened the European public. During a visit to Washington, West German Chancellor Schmidt tried in vain to appeal for moderation, saying 'Our country lies within the range of Soviet intermediate-range missiles. It is no bigger than the state of Oregon, but six thousand nuclear weapons are deployed there which are not under our control.'[9] Reagan did not seem affected by such fears of nuclear annihilation. Not yet.

President Reagan's personal contacts with the German government became more cordial after Schmidt lost his chancellorship to Helmut Kohl (Christian Democratic Union) in the autumn of 1982. Kohl was less concerned about demonstrating good relations with Moscow. At the same time, he was under significant pressure from critical and rapidly growing German peace movements. American–French relations improved momentarily after François Mitterrand (Socialist Party) won the presidential elections of 1981. Mitterrand wanted to demonstrate Western firmness vis-à-vis the Soviet Union, not least to prevent Germany from slipping into neutrality. Yet the underlying discord with Reagan's foreign policy remained. The French establishment resented the decline of East–West contacts and the renewal of Cold War thinking, which left little room for an independent French policy.

In 1983, East–West tensions reached a critical level when accidental nuclear warfare entered the realms of possibility. The transatlantic debate over the handling of the 'Second Cold War' and the massive European peace movements peaked in the same year. In this heated context, the most controversial issues were Reagan's announcement of a 'Star Wars' laser shield, and the deployment of US Euromissiles (Pershing II and Tomahawk cruise missiles), scheduled for November 1983.

Star Wars and Euromissiles

The planned deployment of Euromissiles originated in NATO's dual-track decision of December 1979. The members of the Atlantic Alliance had then committed themselves to the European deployment of new American medium-range missiles, if arms negotiations with the USSR were not successful within four years, and the Soviet SS-20 missiles withdrawn from Eastern Europe. The talks with Moscow remaining fruitless by 1982, the Western governments emphasized their intention to stick to the scheduled deployment despite widely hostile public opinion.

At the same time, the European allies suspected the Reagan government of single-mindedly aiming at deploying new weapons and reinforcing US nuclear capabilities, and of following the negotiation track for the sake of appearances only. European doubts about American sincerity were not unfounded. Reagan had indeed presented the Soviets with a 'zero option' proposal that US Secretary of State Alexander Haig later described as 'absurd' and a 'frivolous propaganda exercise', since the USSR would have to dismantle their SS-20s while getting virtually nothing in return. Therefore Moscow's dismissal of the proposal hardly came as a surprise.

The prevalent impression of Reagan's bellicose nature was reinforced in March 1983 when he announced the Strategic Defense Initiative (SDI), immediately dubbed 'Star Wars' by the media. The goal of SDI was to develop a defensive laser shield in space that would protect the United States against ballistic missiles and nuclear attacks. Reagan himself viewed SDI as an initiative to abandon the doctrine of Mutually Assured Destruction (MAD) and to break with the customary belief that no country could protect itself from nuclear destruction. He wrote in his memoirs: 'It was like having two westerners standing in a saloon aiming their guns at each other's head – permanently. There had to be a better way.'[10]

The Western Europeans very much doubted that SDI would be a better way. Their reactions to Reagan's announcement ranged from surprised scepticism to overt opposition. Like many American officials, the Europeans (correctly) doubted the technical feasibility and the strategic adequacy of the project. Thatcher officially supported SDI but also feared that it would lead to a decoupling of American and European security, and that it would destroy the fragile balance of terror, which she perceived as effective. The other European allies criticized SDI more openly. They argued that it would extend the arms race into space and cause a new round of East–West competition in offensive arms.

The SDI project also gave new ammunition to protest movements on both sides of the Atlantic. In the United States, the 'Freeze' movement had assembled 750,000 demonstrators in New York's Central Park in late 1982, calling for a freeze of nuclear weapons at present levels. The Reagan administration narrowly defeated the freeze resolutions in Congress by arguing that they would mean a fatal American disadvantage in intercontinental arms. Nevertheless, the Freeze movement continued to be supported by established figures like George F. Kennan and McGeorge Bundy, Senator Edward Kennedy and future secretary of state Madeleine Albright, and celebrities such as Bruce Springsteen and Meryl Streep.

In Western Europe, anti-nuclear protests reached formidable dimensions and peaked in the weeks before the arrival of the first Euromissiles in November 1983. Nevertheless, the European governments abided by the NATO decisions. On 22 November 1983, the German

---

Box 5.2 Anti-nuclear protests in Western Europe

In Western Europe, the anti-nuclear protests emerged from several existing environmentalist movements. Especially after the accession of Ronald Reagan to the American presidency, these movements turned their attention to the nuclear arms race and reached a rapidly growing part of the population. Many Europeans shared the fear that Europe would become the theatre of a nuclear war. On 10 October 1981, a first wave of protests culminated in an international demonstration of some 250,000 people in Bonn, calling for drastic arms reductions and a nuclear-free Europe.

Influenced by the stalemate in the superpowers' arms talks, Reagan's announcement of SDI, and the forthcoming implementation of the double-track decision, the European protests regained momentum in 1983. Demonstrators with a variety of backgrounds now gathered in the peace movements: priests and feminists, pacifists and housewives, students and artists, 'greens' and 'reds', young and old. Interestingly, the manifestations were mostly directed against the Americans and the complicit Western European governments rather than against the Soviets, who covertly encouraged the peace movements.

The protests were strongest in West Germany, where a total of 108 American Pershing II missiles were to be based. Massive demonstrations also took place in the countries designated to host additional Tomahawk missiles – Britain, Italy, Holland and Belgium. The protestors feared that the purpose of these new missiles would be offensive and that they might be used to unleash a nuclear war confined to Europe. The United States, on the other hand, would be protected by the futuristic SDI shield. The protests were organized or spontaneously articulated in many forms: faking mass-scale death in public places ('die-ins'), selling of lottery tickets for access to nuclear shelters, ringing of bells, starving or marching for peace, assembling in candlelit vigils, human chains and sit-ins. Singers like Joan Baez and Udo Lindenberg, and many other celebrities, supported the events.

In November 1983, hundreds of thousands of Europeans protested in the streets against the deployment of Euromissiles. Up to half a million people gathered in Bonn and Rome, and about 300,000 in Brussels. With slogans like 'This time we shall not be silent!', or 'Do you want total peace?', German demonstrators warned against addressing conflicts by military means and what they perceived as a repetition of past mistakes. Protesters blockaded a US military base in Germany (Mutlangen) and held out for several months, yet they could not prevent the missile deployment. The anti-nuclear movements still had some political impact, in the sense that they put a lot of pressure on West European governments and NATO's overall strategy for years to come.

Bundestag confirmed the deployment of the Pershing II missiles by a vote of 286 to 226. The following day the Soviet delegation marched out of the arms negotiation talks in Geneva. Soviet leader Yuri Andropov, who had succeeded Brezhnev the year before, publicly declared that he could no longer interact with the Reagan administration.

Unknown to the public, in the very same month of November 1983, East–West tensions reached a critical and potentially disastrous point. At a time when the Soviet Politburo considered the international atmosphere 'thoroughly white-hot', NATO conducted a nine-day nuclear-readiness exercise of unprecedented scope. Exercise 'Able Archer 83' stretched from the Mediterranean to Norway and Turkey, and involved a variety of new military patterns. Soviet intelligence misconstrued the exercise as a possible cover for a nuclear strike against the USSR, and fears in Moscow escalated to the point where a nuclear attack against the West became a serious possibility. The world came close indeed to Armageddon in November 1983. Secret reports about the Soviet perception of Western war scenarios left Reagan aghast. He suddenly realized what his firmness had caused. In this sense, Able Archer played a significant role in Reagan's subsequent decision to abandon his provocative and confrontational 'bad cop' behaviour against the Soviet Union. The American turnaround in East–West matters would come as a complete surprise to the incredulous Europeans in January 1984.

Conclusion

After the first enlargement of the European Communities in January 1973, the distance between the transatlantic partners widened. The nine EC members wished to create a European identity, which in American perception was directed against the United States. In this context, the Arab–Israeli war of October 1973 provoked a momentary split within the Atlantic Alliance, and one of the most serious crises in the history of NATO. Unlike in the 1960s, when the Europeans had been divided into different factions, the EC nine now formed a like-minded bloc and openly disagreed with America's involvement in the war on the Israeli side.

The heated debates on Western unity and American leadership dissipated in the course of the 1974 governmental changes, and gave way to a general attitude of self-reliance on both sides of the Atlantic. While the Europeans concentrated on the inner consolidation of their community, and the Americans on recovering from the Vietnam debacle, the structures of transatlantic cooperation persisted silently but beneficially.

This period of introspection came to an end in 1979 when Soviet forces invaded Afghanistan, and Iran changed almost simultaneously from an American ally to a bitter enemy. The East–West conflict once again became the primary focus of attention, and America re-emphasized its leadership in the alliance. While the European leaders disapproved of America's return to a purely confrontational Cold War policy, the international setting once again manifested their dependence on American protection. Earlier attempts at 'Europeanizing' Europe were shelved.

At the same time, the 'Second Cold War' revealed fundamental differences in European and American approaches to the Soviet Union and the Eastern bloc. The Western Europeans generally perceived steady contact, political détente and economic exchange across the Iron Curtain as an essential factor for the preservation of peace. The United States, on the other hand, especially after Ronald Reagan's accession to the presidency in 1981, placed strong emphasis on military measures and engaged in war-like rhetoric in order to force the Soviet 'evil empire' into submission.

The rift thus created between Americans and Europeans was widely perceived as serious, yet there was no option but to stick to the Atlantic Alliance. Hence the NATO partners endeavoured to demonstrate public solidarity, notably by implementing the 'double-track decision' in November 1983. But they did so at the heavy cost of antagonizing large sections of the European public and of accentuating the East–West conflict. Tensions with the Soviet Union did indeed reach a dangerous peak in late 1983. In parallel, transatlantic relations touched a low point. All Western European governments rejected Reagan's bellicosity and interventionism. Even British–American relations cooled after Reagan unilaterally ordered the invasion of Grenada in October 1983, in an attempt to forestall a leftist revolution. However, Grenada was a member of the British Commonwealth, and Reagan had not even bothered to consult his British allies.

In hindsight, 1983 was the final culmination of Cold War hostility. In early 1984, a first and unexpected step towards de-escalation occurred in Washington, and a fundamental change took place in Moscow only one year later.

Suggested further reading

Garthoff, Raymond (1994) *Détente and Confrontation: American–Soviet Relations from Nixon to Reagan*. Washington, DC: Brookings.

Hanhimäki, Jussi M. (2010) 'Détente in Europe, 1962–1975', in Melvyn P. Leffler and Odd Arne Westad (eds), *The Cambridge History of the Cold War*, vol. 2, pp. 198–218. Cambridge, UK: Cambridge University Press.

Loth, Wilfried and Georges-Henri Soutou (eds) (2008) *The Making of Détente: Eastern and Western Europe in the Cold War, 1965–1975*. London: Routledge.

Ludlow, N. Piers (2010) 'European integration and the Cold War', in Melvyn P. Leffler and Odd Arne Westad (eds.), *The Cambridge History of the Cold War*, vol. 2, pp. 179–97. Cambridge, UK: Cambridge University Press.

Möckli, Daniel (2010) 'Asserting Europe's distinct identity: The EC nine and Kissinger's year of Europe', in Matthias Schulz and Thomas A. Schwartz (eds), *Strained Alliance: US–European Relations from Nixon to Carter*, pp. 195–220. Cambridge, UK: Cambridge University Press.

Schulz, Matthias and Thomas A. Schwartz (2010) 'The superpower and the union in the making: US–European relations, 1969–1980', in Matthias Schulz and Thomas A. Schwartz (eds), *Strained Alliance: US–European Relations from Nixon to Carter*. Cambridge, UK: Cambridge University Press.

Spohr-Readman, Kristina (2010) 'Germany and the politics of the neutron bomb, 1975–1979', *Diplomacy and Statecraft*, 21(2): 259–85.

Thomas, Daniel (2001) *The Helsinki Effect: International Norms, Human Rights and the Demise of Communism*. Princeton, NJ: Princeton University Press.

6 Walls come down, 1984–1989

Turn of the tide

In early 1984, nobody imagined that the East–West conflict would change during the following years as dramatically as it did. The apparently irreconcilable differences in American and European dealings with the Soviets disappeared miraculously in the process. Instead of urging US President Reagan to mitigate his aggressive stance to the USSR, as the Western Europeans had done before, by late 1986 they were somewhat concerned about excessively friendly contacts between Washington and Moscow. Even more surprising events occurred thereafter. At the end of the 1980s, an unforeseen chain of events removed the main elements of the Cold War confrontation that had been at the root of close trans-atlantic cooperation since the 1940s. With Mikhail Gorbachev establishing good Soviet relations with the West, and the people of Eastern Europe successfully challenging their communist regimes, the Eastern threat melted away like ice under the sun. Moreover, the fall of the Berlin Wall in November 1989 put the German question in a completely new light. The effects on the Western framework were likely to be unprecedented. After the Europeans and Americans had argued for decades about how to organize the Atlantic community, the year 1989 would leave them wondering whether or not in the new situation the community itself still made sense.

Change in Washington

The first signs of fundamental change appeared as early as in 1984, even though most Europeans were slow to recognize them. In a major speech on 16 January 1984, Reagan proclaimed a new policy of 'cooperation and understanding' with the USSR. He explained:

> Neither we nor the Soviet Union can wish away the differences between our societies and our philosophies. But we should always remember that we do have common interests. And the foremost among them is to avoid war and reduce the level of arms. ... Our countries have never fought each other; there is no reason why we ever should.[1]

The tone of this presidential address contrasted sharply with Reagan's previous threats to bring down the Soviet 'evil empire' and with his calls for a Western arms build-up. Subsequent events showed that the change was indeed significant, and that Washington's new openness to constructive dialogue with the Soviet Union would eventually contribute to dramatic developments. But why this American turnaround in January 1984?

President Reagan, whose personal assessment had been decisive for the policy change, explained that the United States was now in a position to open dialogue with Moscow from a position of strength. He declared that America's decline had been reversed, the national economy and defence rebuilt, the Western values proclaimed to the world. Indeed, some officials in the Reagan administration now hoped to win the Cold War by different means, against a Soviet Union already doomed to lose. A less confrontational foreign policy also seemed fitting in the run-up to the US presidential elections.

At the same time, the American turnaround was also the result of mounting doubts about the suitability of the previous aggressive strategy. A series of incidents proved to Reagan that his hard-line Soviet policy had exacerbated the superpower tensions to a dangerous level. In September 1983, a South Korean airliner coming from Alaska accidentally strayed into Soviet airspace and was shot down, because the Soviets fatally mistook it for a military plane. Two months later, another misperception by the Soviet Union almost led to nuclear Armageddon. Moscow misinterpreted a NATO exercise over Western Europe as an impending attack and came close to launching a pre-emptive nuclear strike. The Soviet leaders had obviously believed in the possibility of a nuclear strike by the Americans. Shaken by this experience, Reagan's perception of the main threat to US security shifted from the Soviet Union to nuclear weapons themselves.

The Western Europeans had long called for attenuation in American foreign policy and for abandonment of the war rhetoric. European resentment against American bellicosity had reached its peak in 1983, and the policy shift announced by Reagan in January 1984 did indeed prevent transatlantic cohesion from deteriorating any further. From 1984 to 1989, the overall quality of European–American relations improved substantially, yet initially very slowly and with several backlashes.

In 1984 the European allies viewed Reagan's reorientation with some scepticism. Like the American public, European leaders also tended to interpret Reagan's new approach as a superficial ploy to win the upcoming elections. Nevertheless, British Prime Minister Margaret Thatcher gave herself credit for deflecting Reagan from his 'evil empire' rhetoric. Washington's new official position also appeared to be more in line with the West German objective, pronounced by Chancellor Helmut Kohl on 13 October 1982, to 'create peace with ever fewer weapons', although in reality the increase in American military spending continued (from 1981 to 1989, the annual defence budget of the US swelled from $158 billion to $304 billion).[2] French President François Mitterrand, who visited Moscow in June 1984, optimistically encouraged Reagan to move further towards détente with the USSR. But even if the most critical point in the 'Second Cold War' had been passed, superpower relations remained chilly until late 1985. So far only a few Western observers detected the first signs of the wind of change that would soon be blowing through the Eastern camp.

Change in Moscow

The transformation of Soviet policy in the mid-1980s was even more fundamental than Reagan's turnaround, and by the end of the decade it developed into the decisive basis for the peaceful ending of the Cold War. However, like the changes taking place in Washington, the metamorphosis in Moscow took some time to impact on international relations and was initially viewed warily by the Western world. The American and Western European leaders – although to varying degrees – entertained similar doubts whether the new thinking in the Soviet Union would prove to be more than just a new appearance.

However, the change in Soviet foreign policy was much more than cosmetics. During the Polish crisis of 1980–1981, when the Solidarity workers' movement challenged Poland's communist regime, Moscow had already been reluctant to fall back on old patterns and to restore order in Eastern Europe. While the Polish regime did indeed declare martial law in December 1981 and suppressed Solidarity, the USSR did not intervene militarily as it had done in East Germany (1953), Hungary (1956) and Czechoslovakia (1968). The West had erroneously expected the Red Army to gun down the Polish protesters and remained unaware that the Kremlin increasingly feared the consequences of military intervention within its own sphere of influence. In the opinion of Yuri Andropov (the new Soviet leader since Leonid Brezhnev's death in November 1982), Soviet interests would suffer more from heightened Cold War tensions than from reforms in Eastern Europe. But Andropov's leadership was short-lived; he died in February 1984, to be succeeded by Konstantin Chernenko, aged 72 and already sick when he took office. Chernenko died only one year later, in March 1985. This time, the Politburo chose a leader who might last longer: 54-year-old Mikhail Gorbachev.

Gorbachev had presented himself as a moderate reformer much in line with Andropov and enjoyed wide support from the other Politburo members. He set out to improve the Soviet economy, to cut back on arms expenditure and thereby to create more advantageous relations with the West. In the first months after his accession to power, Gorbachev indeed appointed a whole new generation of reform-minded advisers and ministers. The Kremlin was relieved to have a dynamic leader again, and the whole world was positively surprised by the well-educated and youthful appearance of the USSR's new general secretary. At the same time, many officials in East and West maintained that Gorbachev not only had a friendly smile but also iron teeth.

The reforms initiated by Gorbachev were ideologically rooted in Leninism and intended to rebuild and strengthen the Soviet Union, not to bring about the demise of the communist camp (although they eventually did). Like Lenin, Gorbachev was driven by a messianic ambition to reshape the world and believed that a reformed socialism would prove superior to the political and economic models promoted by the West. He aimed at providing the Soviet Union with a new role of moral and political leadership in the world. But unlike Lenin, Gorbachev intended to achieve this goal by introducing democratic elements into the domestic structures, and by renouncing the use of force in international affairs.

As early as in March 1985, at Chernenko's funeral, Gorbachev privately told the Eastern European leaders that they should expect no more Soviet military support to keep them in power. Henceforth, Gorbachev called on the Eastern European governments to win the trust of their own people instead of relying on repression. Hardly any leader in East and West, or even the traditional Soviet administration, understood at the time that Gorbachev was totally serious in his renunciation of the use of force. Only in 1989 did the impact of Gorbachev's new foreign policy materialize, when the peoples of Eastern Europe finally realized the freedom of choice before them.

Hesitation in Europe

During his first two years in power, Gorbachev concentrated his efforts on domestic reforms and the introduction of perestroika (reconstruction) in order to reverse the prolonged decline of the Soviet economy. Western Europe initially played a rather insignificant role in his foreign policy. Until the end of 1986, Gorbachev only toyed with the idea of launching a major détente with the Western Europeans, and instead tried to use them to push the United

States towards disarmament. Consequently, the changes initiated by Gorbachev had only a limited impact on European issues, and the Western European leaders remained sceptical whether Gorbachev would indeed be able to substantially modify the USSR's foreign policy. His room to manoeuvre was considered just too small.

Nevertheless, the East–West atmosphere was improving under Gorbachev, and several Western European leaders acknowledged his personal merits. Margaret Thatcher had received Gorbachev for the first time in December 1984 and subsequently praised his genuine desire to reform the Soviet system. This public support from Britain's 'Iron Lady', who was well known for her anti-communist views, amazed and impressed many of her Western colleagues. Paradoxically, West German Chancellor Helmut Kohl figured on the other end of the spectrum, despite his country's political interests in good relations with Moscow. Kohl suspected the new Soviet leadership of changing nothing but their public relations strategy and in October 1986 even compared Mikhail Gorbachev to Joseph Goebbels, the Nazi minister for propaganda. Soviet–German relations obviously suffered from this major diplomatic faux pas.

In comparison, Gorbachev's relations with US President Reagan evolved faster – almost too fast for the taste of the perplexed Europeans. When in November 1985 Gorbachev and Reagan met for the first time in Geneva (Switzerland), Western Europe still unanimously applauded what appeared to be a small step towards superpower détente. Nothing conclusive came of the Geneva summit, yet it helped 'overcome a serious psychological barrier' (as Gorbachev put it in a letter to Reagan soon after the summit) and allowed the two leaders to 'understand each other better' (as Reagan maintained in a speech to the US Congress in November 1985).[3] The two most active European leaders in this context, Mitterrand and Thatcher, promoted further Soviet–American dialogue. In 1986 the French president especially perceived his role as the honest courtier in promoting a new era of détente, and urged Reagan to respond positively to the Soviet calls for (radical) disarmament. However, the talks between Reagan and Gorbachev during their second meeting, in October 1986 in Reykjavik (Iceland), went far beyond anything the Europeans had anticipated.

As it turned out, the American and the Soviet leaders both came to Reykjavik with matching convictions that a world without nuclear weapons would be safer. Both Reagan and Gorbachev had already spoken publicly in favour of total nuclear disarmament, but hardly anybody expected them to take any concrete steps towards this end. Gorbachev and Reagan did indeed share the view that in a nuclear war there were no winners, and they both feared an unintended nuclear Armageddon. Furthermore, in April 1986 a major accident at the nuclear power plant in Chernobyl had cruelly manifested the lethal and long-lasting effects of nuclear radiation. In this context, yet completely out of the blue for the Europeans, on 12 October 1986 Reagan and Gorbachev agreed verbally to eliminate all nuclear weapons within ten years. The Reykjavik talks nevertheless ended without any written agreement because Reagan stubbornly refused to give up the American SDI programme ('Star Wars'), while Gorbachev insisted on its abolition.

The Western European leaders had long hoped for East–West détente, but not for the kind of superpower reshaping of the world that had almost resulted from the Reykjavik summit. For them, contacts with the Soviet Union should always include the two tracks of constructive dialogue *and* maintaining a strong NATO defence, in order to keep Western Europe immune to Soviet intimidation. Most importantly, the Europeans had been completely excluded from crucial security discussions pertaining to their own safety. France felt left out by both Americans and Soviets, and henceforth took a hesitant stance to disarmament negotiations. Margaret Thatcher concluded that Reykjavik had been a Soviet trap to force

Western nuclear disarmament while the USSR maintained superiority in conventional weapons. She even warned her friend Ronald Reagan against a possible catastrophe in transatlantic relations if US military protection for Western Europe became ambiguous.

Overall, the reactions to the Reagan–Gorbachev talks in Reykjavik showed that Western Europe hesitated to believe in the changes that had apparently taken place in Washington and Moscow. Many Europeans doubted whether the USSR was able to change overnight. And Reagan's sudden transformation from cold warrior to ambassador of peace was not entirely convincing, especially since American foreign policy continued to be aggressive and interventionist in other parts of the world.

Scarcely a month after the Reykjavik meeting, on 4 November 1986, the news broke that the Reagan administration had been selling arms to 'moderates' in Iran, despite the loudly proclaimed US arms embargo against Iran. While President Reagan tried to justify the illegal deal by the liberation of American hostages (in Lebanon), his political credibility suffered drastically. Even worse, further reports revealed that some profits of the Iranian arms deal had been used to fund the operations of the rebellious Contra groups in Nicaragua – although the US Congress had officially decreed the termination of such funding.

This Iran–Contra Affair cost Reagan the support of many voters at home, and within the Atlantic Alliance re-emphasized the existing differences on out-of-area issues. The Western European governments and public opinion widely deplored the ongoing American assistance to rebellious 'freedom fighters' in Afghanistan, Cambodia, Angola and Nicaragua. To some extent this reflected the established European attitude of avoiding any strategic responsibility outside of Europe. But it was also the result of different judgements. The Europeans tended to view the military support of ill-assorted groups of rebel factions in other countries as morally and legally wrong, ineffective, and ultimately contrary to Western interests. Whereas the Reagan government aimed at reducing communist influence by covertly intervening in the countries mentioned, the Europeans feared that American intrusion only exacerbated conflict, thereby pushing the challenged regimes closer to the Soviet Union. The Western Europeans also perceived the American bombing of Libya in April 1986 as an excessive response to the killing of American soldiers in a Berlin nightclub by Libyan agents. Only Britain hesitantly supported the US air raid against Libya, while France and Spain denied the use of their airspace.

By the end of 1986, such American out-of-area belligerence was at odds with President Reagan's Icelandic claim of a new era of peace in international relations. From European perspectives, America's tendency to abuse its power also damaged Reagan's credibility as leader of the Western camp.

Progress in European unification

From the American perspective, on the other hand, in 1986 transatlantic relations suffered less from Washington's unpredictable foreign policy than from the Europeans' adoption of the Single European Act, and the ensuing (but temporary) tensions in economic cooperation.

Ever since the first enlargement of the European Communities (EC) in 1973, the integration project had grappled with internal feelings of Euro-scepticism and Euro-sclerosis. The whole European enterprise seemed to stagnate or even to move towards decline, as formerly abolished border taxes between the EC member states reappeared in the form of indirect taxes and non-tariff barriers. Since no obvious progress was achieved within the EC until the mid-1980s, only minor disruption in transatlantic relations resulted. But unsurprisingly, the economic antagonism with the American partners resurfaced as soon as the European unification process was injected with fresh dynamism and the EC set out in pursuit of ambitious new objectives.

A number of reasons contributed to the successful relaunch of the European project. The appointment of Frenchman Jacques Delors to the presidency of the European Commission in January 1985 served as a catalyst. Delors identified the building of a truly barrier-free EC market by 1992 as the community's concrete objective and found immediate backing for this endeavour. European big business leaders came forward with strong support in the hope of catching up with their more productive competitors in the United States and Japan.

Moreover, a consensus had emerged among the EC's national governments in favour of greater economic liberalization, with the idea of emulating the German success model on a European scale. Even France's socialist President François Mitterrand had relinquished his elusive goal of a state-controlled French economy and by 1983 came around to support the European option. Together with German Chancellor Helmut Kohl he became a key promoter of European integration. Reforming the EC also seemed appropriate in the context of the 'southern enlargement' of January 1986, when the relatively new democracies of Spain and Portugal entered the community (Greece had already joined in 1981). Finally, the almost unnoticed structural reforms of the EC during the former decade, namely the creation of the European Council as the supreme authority, now bore fruit. The Council took the necessary steps to implement Delors's plans, and in February 1986 signed a new treaty, entitled the Single European Act.

While rather technical in its content and dealing mostly with the economic reforms to be achieved, the Single European Act nevertheless spurred on a revival of European enthusiasm and EC cooperation. By eliminating all non-tariff barriers and by establishing the free movement of goods, labour, capital and services within their territory until 1992, the twelve signatories gave momentum to a far-reaching enterprise. The new European dynamism would eventually provide the framework for German re-unification in 1990 and lead to the groundbreaking Maastricht Treaty of 1992, which created the modern-day European Union (EU).

Box 6.1 Document extract: The Single European Act

Signed in Luxembourg on 17 February 1986, entered into force on 1 July 1987.[4]

Preamble: Moved by the will to continue the work undertaken on the basis of the Treaties establishing the European Communities and to transform relations as a whole among their States into a European Union, ... determined to improve the economic and social situation by extending common policies and pursuing new objectives, ... have decided to adopt this Act ...

Article 13: ... The Community shall adopt measures with the aim of progressively establishing the internal market over a period expiring on 31 December 1992 ... The internal market shall comprise an area without internal frontiers in which the free movement of goods, persons, services and capital is ensured in accordance with the provisions of this Treaty.

Article 21: ... Member States shall pay particular attention to encouraging improvements, especially in the working environment, as regards the health and safety of workers ...

Article 30.1: The High Contracting Parties, being members of the European Communities, shall endeavour jointly to formulate and implement a European foreign policy.

International impact of the Single European Act

The Single European Act of 1986 for the first time included the scope of a common foreign policy (hence the word 'single', in contrast to separate) and launched cooperation in social welfare. This Western European progress and cooperation, extended to new grounds, also proved significant in light of the Cold War antagonism and later events in Eastern Europe. Whereas the EC members developed a prosperous economic unit combining the goals of free enterprise and social justice, the Eastern European countries suffered from crippling debts, inefficient use of resources, and shaky guarantees of individual rights. The economies of Eastern Europe were heavily dependent on the Soviet Union and were unable to compete on the world market. The Western European model therefore became a considerable attraction for Eastern European people. What they were later looking for, after the collapse of the Cold War structures in 1989–1991, was essentially military protection by the United States (i.e. NATO membership), and economic and social success such as was enjoyed in Western Europe (i.e. EU membership).

It was no coincidence that Mikhail Gorbachev, too, started to take a serious interest in the EC after the passing of the Single European Act. He struggled to revitalize the Soviet economy and discovered Western Europe as a potential partner in reform. In early 1987, Gorbachev complained in his inner circle that 'we have a poor knowledge of Europe' and stressed his interest in thoroughly studying the EC economy.[5] From 1987 onward, the economic dimension contributed to the rising importance of Western Europe in Gorbachev's mind also on a political level.

The United States had become used to routinely paying lip service, but not too much attention, to the cause of European integration, and was slow to realize that a new dynamic had emerged within the EC. The White House generally preferred to deal with the different European capitals bilaterally rather than with the whole community, because the United States carried more weight in direct relations and because the EC just seemed too fragmented and difficult to handle. Richard Burt, an American official, commented: 'we are always a little behind the power curve in understanding what is happening in terms of Europe'.[6] European Community affairs and trade disputes rarely came to the notice of the top officials and President Reagan, who devoted relatively little time to economic questions. Yet when the passing of the Single European Act prompted headlines of a 'Fortress Europe' in American newspapers, and the slogan 'Europe for the Europeans' raised concern in the administration, Reagan became personally involved and cautioned the EC against protectionist tendencies. A number of disputes between the US and the EC followed. As in the past, the main bone of contention was agriculture, since American farmers feared losing their European markets.

The EC project initiated by the Single European Act did indeed have the potential to cause a major upset in transatlantic relations. It was designed to propel the European economy onto equal terms with the US and Japan, and to take more efficient advantage of the community's market power. In other words, the twelve member states attempted to enhance their economic role in the world, following the EC's enlargements and corresponding increase in population. In the second half of the 1980s, the wave of confidence within the EC contrasted strikingly with the unstable picture presented by the US economy, facing at the same time a large 'double deficit' in the balance of payments and the federal budget. 'Black Monday', in October 1987, when American stock markets plummeted, apparently symbolized the uncertain future of the US economy. A shift in the transatlantic balance of power seemed imminent.

Table 6.1 The evolution of US and EU populations (millions of inhabitants)

	United States	EEC/EC/EU
1957	171	167 (EEC-6)
1960	180	172 (EEC-6)
1965	194	182 (EEC-6)
1970	204	189 (EC-6)
1975	216	260 (EC-9)
1980	227	262 (EC-9)
1985	238	274 (EC-10)
1990	250	329 (EC-12)
1995	266	374 (EU-15)
2000	282	379 (EU-15)
2005	296	463 (EU-25)
2010	308	501 (EU-27)

Sources: data from US Census Bureau; Statistisches Bundesamt Deutschland; INED Paris

However, the rise of the EC did not develop into a major transatlantic clash. It did not even result in a substantial policy change by the United States. In hindsight, the contemporary theories of American decline can be dismissed, even though they were fairly popular at the time. Furthermore, the EC's development did not seriously undermine the role of NATO and America's prominence in security questions, which remained the decisive point for Washington. Only France and West Germany in 1988 endeavoured to initiate a European defence identity by uniting a small part of their forces. Last but not least, by 1989 the positive geopolitical aspects of the EC's prospering clearly outweighed the remaining economic concerns in the United States. In a context of disintegrating structures in Eastern Europe, and soon of German reunification, a strong EC framework also appeared beneficial to American policymakers.

The fall of the Berlin Wall

During the final years of the 1980s, transatlantic relations evolved in the shadow of the fast transforming East–West setting. The Western governments often needed to adapt to unexpected developments in the East in order to keep pace with the course of events. While in 1987 and 1988 most changes took place in the realm of high politics, in 1989 the people of Eastern Europe took the lead. Their peaceful revolutions culminated in the breaching of the Berlin Wall in November 1989, the most prominent symbol of the crumbling Cold War structures.

Reagan and Gorbachev: partners instead of enemies

The Reagan–Gorbachev meetings of 1985 and 1986 had produced little apart from a sense of personal trust between the two leaders. Yet, with both Reagan and Gorbachev convinced that neither side was going to attack the other, the foundation for concrete progress in 1987 and 1988 was laid. Especially Reagan's extraordinary anti-nuclear proposals in Reykjavik had signalled to Gorbachev that the US president would be ready to support bold initiatives, and not try to exploit them.

Hence, Soviet–American arms negotiations got quickly under way in 1987. Gorbachev relinquished his opposition to Reagan's (uncertain) pet project, SDI, and on 28 February 1987 surprised the world with an offer to eliminate all medium-range missiles in Europe. Reagan's spontaneous reaction to this 'zero-solution' for European strategic missiles was positive, yet the American defence specialists remained sceptical and considered increasing their short-range weapons instead. In response, Gorbachev proposed the elimination of the short-range missiles as well. Since the Americans and the Western Europeans hesitated, Gorbachev proposed including Asia in the disarmament plans. Thus the Western experts struggled perpetually to keep pace with ever new Soviet proposals. When the American negotiators demanded the guarantee of inspection rights, to make sure that the Soviet missiles would indeed be destroyed, Gorbachev offered to extend inspection rights to all bases at all times. This was too much for the Americans; they feared that Soviet experts would then be allowed to inspect the latest US arms technology.

Agreement between Moscow and Washington was reached nevertheless, mostly due to the persona of Ronald Reagan. He took little interest in the details of arms control, but perceived the scope of Soviet initiatives as reasonable and had the power to override opposition within his own camp. Basically, Reagan had come to see the long-lasting distrust between the superpowers as the essence of the Cold War and was determined to overcome it. As a result, Reagan and Gorbachev met again in December 1987 to sign the Intermediate-range Nuclear Forces (INF) Treaty. It was based on the 'zero-solution' proposal and stipulated the dismantling of all nuclear missiles with a range of 500 to 5500 kilometres, considered as especially destabilizing. For the first time in the history of the Cold War an entire class of existing nuclear missiles was to be scrapped.

The symbolic meaning of the INF treaty even exceeded its concrete significance. Not only arms control, which had been abandoned since 1980, but substantial reductions of nuclear and conventional forces were now on the agenda. Mutual understanding was about to replace the former East–West conflict. When celebrating the signing of the treaty, Gorbachev daringly commented to Reagan on the SDI programme: 'I am of the opinion that you are wasting your money.'[7]

Within only a few years, the relationship between the leaders of the United States and the Soviet Union had changed from aggressive confrontation to partnership in ending the Cold War. Some frictions nevertheless persisted. Much to Gorbachev's irritation, after the signing of the INF treaty Washington showed little enthusiasm for further progress in arms control and instead turned to human rights issues. The Reagan administration also continued to support the fight of the Afghan *mujahidin* against the Soviets, even at a time when the USSR was seeking ways to withdraw its troops.

Notwithstanding the American attitude, in February 1988 Gorbachev announced the complete Soviet withdrawal from Afghanistan within a year. This was another strong signal of international change. From the American perspective, the Soviet invasion of Afghanistan in 1979 had been instrumental in starting the 'Second Cold War'. Now that the Soviet troops were to withdraw, the Second Cold War became history.

Reagan and Gorbachev met two more times in 1988. The Moscow summit in May brought no spectacular novelty, yet it demonstrated how much the two men had become partners in change, even 'friends', in Reagan's words. Margaret Thatcher observed aptly: 'We're not in a Cold War now.'[8]

A few weeks before the end of Reagan's eight-year presidency, the fifth Reagan–Gorbachev meeting took place in New York on 7 December 1988. However, their bilateral talk turned into a sideshow of the landmark speech Gorbachev delivered to the United

Nations the same day. The Soviet leader called on the world community to relinquish the political clashes and national hostilities of the past, and to build a new order for an inter-dependent world, based on peace and the transformation of the arms economy. Gorbachev emphasized freedom of choice and absence of use of force as the new fundamentals of Soviet foreign policy. Furthermore, he concretely sketched out the reduction of Soviet forces by 500,000 persons and a significant withdrawal of Soviet offensive capabilities from Eastern Europe within two years.

The impact of Gorbachev's speech was tremendous. Not only was it proof positive of the USSR's fundamental reorientation to Western leaders, but it also made the Eastern European people understand that their freedom of choice was a reality and not mere rhetoric. To a large extent, Gorbachev's speech at the UN set in motion the Eastern European revolutions of 1989.

Western Europe: from caution to Gorbi-mania

The unusual closeness of Reagan and Gorbachev provoked reactions of different sorts in Western Europe. In early 1987, still in the aftermath of the Soviet–American summit in Reykjavik, the European leaders shared a generally circumspect attitude. Several reasons contributed to their reservations. First, the Europeans dreaded being left out of important decisions. As in former periods of détente, they warned against a 'superpower condominium' or against a revival of 'Yalta' (where the superpowers had allegedly divided Europe in 1945). Thus far, Gorbachev had indeed concentrated his Western contacts on the United States and Reagan was not at pains to consult his allies.

Second, the radical disarmament plans pursued by Reagan and Gorbachev threatened to upset the fragile security balance in Europe and to lead to a decoupling of American defence from the continent. This in turn could result in a spread of Soviet influence to the West or even the neutralization of Western Europe. German Chancellor Kohl, whose country was most exposed to the East, unsurprisingly was also most reluctant to approve the INF treaty. Third, the Europeans judged Gorbachev more cautiously than did Ronald Reagan. They tended to see Gorbachev's rhetoric in the light of the Soviet peace propaganda of the past, as a disguise for Eastern attempts to undermine the West's defences and cohesion. From European perspectives, deeds counted more than words, and Gorbachev had yet to prove that he meant what he said.

Most of these European scepticisms dissipated during 1987. As a result, transatlantic cohesion on East–West issues improved considerably and gave rise to a general consensus. After Reykjavik, Washington made more efforts to consult the Europeans and notably heeded their opinions when preparing the INF treaty. It turned out that American and European officials shared similar concerns about Reagan's faith in Gorbachev, a fact that also favoured transatlantic dialogue. In June 1987 President Reagan visited Europe, and, standing in front of the Berlin Wall, ended his speech with the call: 'Mr Gorbachev, open this gate! Mr Gorbachev, tear down this wall!' While the German establishment clearly did not believe that these words would become reality, Reagan's gesture was nonetheless appre-ciated. More fundamentally, the Western Europeans had favoured détente and cooperation with the East since the 1960s, and their wish to reduce Cold War tensions was largely in line with US policy objectives. The American and Western European leaders also shared the general view that Gorbachev's planned reforms of the Soviet Union would be positive, if implemented.

As the authenticity of Soviet change gradually became apparent, transatlantic differences in evaluating Gorbachev lost their substance. In early 1987, the USSR released almost all its

Box 6.2 The symbolism of the Berlin Wall

The Berlin Wall (1961–1989) was the most prominent symbol of the Cold War, the drastic embodiment of a divided Europe. In the West, the Wall was often referred to as a 'wall of shame', as the symbol of bankruptcy of the communist system. Yet the meanings attributed to the wall went beyond the realm of ideology. Human rights activist Martin Luther King called it a 'dividing wall of hostility' between the peoples, and most inhabitants of Berlin perceived it as a 'prison wall'. Indeed, while many historical walls have been built to keep people out, the Berlin Wall was built to keep people in.

In East German schools, children were instructed to see the Wall as a symbol of peace and an 'anti-fascist wall of protection'. But the lie was difficult to maintain, since many East German border troops inevitably recognized the truth. Some of them reportedly said: 'If this is a wall of protection, it is built the wrong way around.' Despite increasingly sophisticated fortifications and the near-impregnability of the Wall after 1964, a large number of East Germans still tried to escape. About 200 of them were shot at the Wall, and some 60,000 East Germans were condemned to a total of 240,000 years of prison for the crime of planning to escape (*Republikflucht*). According to protocols of the 1980s, they listed their main motivations as 'no freedom of opinion', political pressure, travel restrictions and 'no future'.

In the West, by the 1980s the Wall became a trendy feature of pop culture. It fascinated and inspired artists like Pink Floyd, Iggy Pop and David Bowie, and 'wall tourists' came to admire the creative graffiti on the Western side of the Wall. The thrill for the painters and sprayers lay in the fact that the Wall was built entirely on Eastern territory, and getting caught by Eastern border troops could result in a prison sentence. American peace activist John Runnings repeatedly climbed and walked on the Wall until he was captured, under the eyes of cheering crowds and Western cameras.

The meaning of the Berlin Wall was significantly modified by the events of November 1989. While it had been a symbol of violence and oppression during the Cold War, the people's breaching of the Wall partly transformed it into a symbol of successful and peaceful revolution. For today's public opinion, the fall of the Wall has become at least as sensational as its previous existence.

political dissidents from custody, thereby giving proof that Gorbachev's promise of freedom of speech was not an empty one. In the following months, he endeavoured to increase the liberties of Soviet entrepreneurs at the expense of Communist Party leaders. In November 1987, Gorbachev's book *Perestroika: New Thinking for our Country and the World* came on the market and became a worldwide bestseller. Furthermore, Gorbachev started to consider the Western part of Europe as a potential partner in overcoming the Cold War and in 1987–1988 arranged frequent meetings with Western European leaders.

Gorbachev on these occasions promoted the ambitious concept of a 'Common European Home' comprising both the Eastern and Western parts of the continent. This concept had some similarities with former Soviet proposals designed to oust the United States from Europe, by replacing NATO and the Warsaw Pact with a pan-European security system. Still, Gorbachev convincingly made the case for a philosophy rather different from former Soviet views of class hatred and East–West confrontation. Gorbachev impressed the Western European leaders with his political vision of common European values, East–West rapprochement and economic cooperation in an interdependent world. As a result, in June 1988 the EC and its Eastern counterpart, the Council for Mutual Economic Assistance (COMECON), signed their first 'Common Declaration' and initiated formal economic cooperation. Yet the

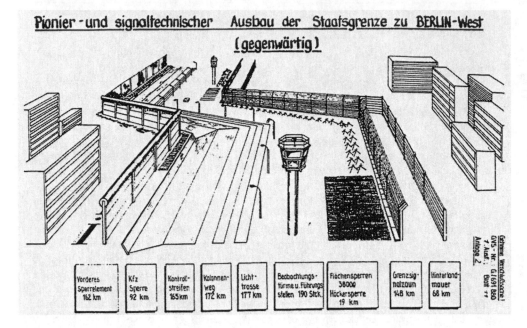

Source: Bundesarchiv DVH 32/127608 (B11)

Figure 6.1 Fortifications of the Berlin Wall (1984). After the construction of the 'first generation' brick wall in summer 1961, which could still be breached with a heavy truck, the East German government continuously strengthened the fortifications of the Berlin Wall until 1989. The drawing shows the 'fourth generation' fortifications as they were in 1984. On the left the wall towards West Berlin (the actual 'Berlin Wall'), are lorry barrages, a plainly visible control zone, lighting sets, surveillance (and shooting) towers, vehicle and person barriers, a fence with barbed wire, and a 'back-up wall' towards East Berlin.

concrete form and ultimate objective of Gorbachev's Common European Home remained ambiguous and never developed into a fully fledged plan. It appears that Gorbachev himself was somewhat unclear about what a Europe he wanted to create, and how.

While the perestroika reforms positively transformed the USSR's international image, Gorbachev's personal appearance and intelligence further added to his popularity in the West. He quickly found a common language with Reagan, Thatcher, Mitterrand, then also with Kohl. The public perceived Gorbachev's thinking as almost Western. In 1988, the American *Time* magazine named him 'Man of the Year', and in Western Europe enthusiasm spread to the point that the media coined the term 'Gorbi-mania'. So far (and until early 1990), Gorbachev also enjoyed a considerable popularity in the Soviet Union.

The USSR's political relations with West Germany improved most strikingly. After a fitful start with Gorbachev, the West German government endeavoured to mend its fences by sending President Richard von Weizsäcker to Moscow in July 1987. Subsequently, the Soviet Union encouraged closer contacts by hinting at the 'historic partnership' of the two countries. When in October 1988 Chancellor Kohl finally visited Gorbachev, both men detected compatibilities and surprising affinities. Gorbachev's return visit to Kohl in June 1989 confirmed the development of a special bond, on political and personal levels.

As in the early 1970s, again in 1988 German–Soviet rapprochement sounded alarm bells in the other Western European capitals. Because of their latent wish for reunification, the Germans were considered the only European people with a national interest in breaking out of the international structures. Margaret Thatcher clearly was worried about developments. In view of later events leading up to the Maastricht Treaty of 1992, the French reaction of accelerating the European unification process was most significant. Besides corresponding to French national interests, this move was meant to strengthen the Western framework and to prevent the eventuality of Germany drifting eastward, and it was against this background that Kohl and Mitterrand launched the project of (West) European monetary union in June 1988.

1989: the rise of the people

The Eastern European events of 1989 had not been foreseen by any Western leader and came as a complete surprise. In early 1989 it was inconceivable that the communist camp was about to disintegrate, or that German reunification would be on the international agenda at any time in the foreseeable future. The decisive factor in Europe's metamorphosis was the rise of the Eastern European peoples, and their gradual emancipation from Soviet dominance and communism. Hence in 1989 the Eastern European peoples were spearheading the change. Significantly, this rise of the people happened at a time when the top leaders in East and West deliberately stepped back and refrained from shaping the events.

George H. W. Bush became the new US president in January 1989. Although he had been Reagan's vice president for eight years, he hesitated to continue his predecessor's foreign policy. Bush and his completely new team of advisers and ministers shared the general view that Reagan had moved too fast and had gone too far in his cooperation with Gorbachev. Members of the Bush administration openly discussed the possibility that the new thinking in the Soviet Union might ultimately fail. In February 1989, Bush's call for a thorough review of US foreign policy presaged a nine-month period of American restraint in East–West issues. Negotiations on arms control were put on hold. The emerging West German enthusiasm for disarmament in East and West, and Helmut Kohl's attempt to postpone the modernization of Western missiles, were received critically. 'For me, and particularly for Margaret Thatcher, these were matters on which the Germans were heading in the wrong direction and on which compromise could be dangerous', Bush later explained in his memoirs.[9] Until Bush finally met with Gorbachev in December 1989, Washington adopted a cautious attitude of wait-and-see. This applied not only to relations with the USSR, but to all Eastern European countries as well.

The Western Europeans had traditionally been inclined to respect the Soviet sphere of influence and not to interfere with politics behind the Iron Curtain. In 1989 this basic attitude was furthered by the manifest restraint of the United States, and by Mikhail Gorbachev's repeated demand to the West not to become embroiled in Eastern Europe's transformation. The Western European leaders all agreed that the change brought about by Gorbachev merited support, and, anxious not to jeopardize the Eastern reforms, heeded his advice. Overall, in 1989 the Western powers were fairly content with their roles as (incredulous) onlookers of the Eastern happenings – at least until the fall of the Berlin Wall on 9 November 1989. After this landmark event, it was no longer possible to pretend that the influence and responsibilities of the Atlantic community ended at the Iron Curtain.

The Soviet restraint towards Eastern Europe was most significant. The year 1989 turned into a test of Gorbachev's promise not to use force in foreign policy, since the Eastern

European peoples now started to challenge their communist regimes. The Soviet troops in 1989 remained physically capable of repressing any revolution in Eastern Europe, yet they were ordered to stand down, and indeed did not fire a single shot. Remarkably, the Soviet leadership of the time did not even consider military intervention as an option to prevent a possible collapse of communist structures in Eastern Europe. As Gorbachev's foreign minister Eduard Shevardnadze put it in July 1989: 'If we were compelled to use force, that would be the end of perestroika. We would have failed.'[10]

The people of Poland and Hungary were the first to seize the opportunity and to explore the freedom of choice Gorbachev had promised in his speech at the United Nations in December 1988. The transformation of both countries began with the implementation of perestroika-style reforms, which (initially, at least) did not threaten the leading roles of the national communist parties.

The Polish opposition movement Solidarity, declared illegal in 1982, after 1986 regained some importance due to Gorbachev's perestroika and the release of political prisoners in Poland. By February 1989, President Wojciech Jaruzelski agreed to open 'round-table negotiations' with Solidarity in an attempt to introduce democratic elements into Polish politics. An agreement signed in April 1989 legalized Solidarity and stipulated new election rules. Non-communist parties were now allowed to compete for 35 per cent of the seats in the Polish Diet, yet the formula ensured that Jaruzelski would retain the power of decision. In the elections of June 1989, Solidarity won 160 of the 161 seats available, while many voters crossed out the names of the communists eligible for the other seats as a sign of protest. Thus pressured by an increasingly self-confident opposition, in August 1989 Jaruzelski accepted the Solidarity candidate, Tadeusz Mazowiecki, as his new prime minister. But not even Mazowiecki dared question Poland's loyalty to the Warsaw Pact and the Soviet Union at this point.

The events in Poland encouraged reformers in other parts of Eastern Europe, notably in Hungary. The Hungarian Communist Party had already promoted economic reforms before the advent of Gorbachev and had earned a relatively wide political acceptance among the population. By June 1989, after a struggle between moderate and radical reformers within the Hungarian Communist Party, the more radical wing prevailed. Completely free elections were announced for the following year. Yet all opinion polls predicted that the communists would come out of these elections as the dominant political force, and Hungary would remain a 'socialist state' by constitution. While these changes went beyond the intended perestroika reforms in the Soviet Union, essentially the Hungarian scenario was still in line with Gorbachev's objective of reforming socialism. On the other hand, when in September 1989 the Hungarian government opened the border to Austria, far-reaching consequences ensued. East German citizens were now able to travel to the West via Hungary, thus building up enormous pressure on the die-hard leaders of East Germany.

The East German regime viewed Gorbachev's reforms sceptically, if not with open hostility. As Erich Honecker had been heading the German Democratic Republic since 1971, admitting the need for change would have meant admitting his own mistakes. Unlike Gorbachev, Honecker could not blame his predecessors for his country's political and economic failures. The East German communists were also aware that the implementation of Gorbachev's programme would mean the end of Honecker's regime, the authority of which depended entirely on the military force of the Red Army. But the more Honecker criticized Gorbachev's reforms, the more popular they became among East German citizens. Impressed by the successes of the Polish and Hungarian people, the East Germans started to demand reforms and organized manifestations, notably in Leipzig, Dresden and East Berlin.

The evidence suggests that Honecker ordered the gunning down of a massive demonstration in Leipzig, on 9 October 1989. But the order was not executed. Egon Krenz, Honecker's designated successor, chose instead to follow Gorbachev's example of not using force, and formally replaced Honecker ten days later. The peaceful demonstrations in East Germany nevertheless continued, and swelled to enormous dimensions. Hundreds of thousands of people gathered in the streets and chanted 'Gorbi, Gorbi', and 'We are the people'. Every week more people joined in the protests, while the East German leadership gradually lost control over the situation. Gorbachev signalled that he would leave German affairs to the Germans, and that the Soviet troops would not intervene.

In this atmosphere of political turmoil, on 9 November 1989 a seemingly minor press conference caused the official order to break down. While the top leaders discussed the news of East Germany's bankruptcy in a secluded meeting, second-rank Günter Schabowski was assigned to meet with Western journalists. At the end of an otherwise dull press conference, Schabowski rather incoherently presented a new travel regulation

---

Box 6.3 Debating the end of the Cold War in Europe

The causes for the end of the European Cold War in the late 1980s have been a key object of scholarly debate ever since the early 1990s, and are likely to be so in the future. As is often the case, American authors and academics were the first to offer explanations; hence, most publications of the 1990s emphasized the argument that the United States won the Cold War. This explanation includes several elements: by means of a coherent strategy since the early Cold War the US successfully contained and ultimately rolled back the Soviet influence; in an increasingly globalized world, the US had become the only credible leader; Ronald Reagan decisively confronted and ultimately exhausted the Soviet Union. In recent years, many American scholars have argued that Reagan's role in ending the Cold War was not his hard-line policy of the early 1980s, but his later policy of engaging Gorbachev in a series of discussions.

A major part of the debate has focused on the question of whether the collapse of the Soviet empire in Eastern Europe was due to external or internal causes. With regard to internal causes, it is often argued that Mikhail Gorbachev ended the Cold War; his new ideas and leadership, his backing of reforms and his lenient policy towards Eastern Europe, were the key elements bringing about the fundamental changes of the late 1980s. Other scholars have focused on the dismal economic reality within the Soviet bloc, the corrupt communist system, and the lack of legitimacy of Eastern regimes. Many authors also point out the crucial role played by resistance among the people: the rebellious East Germans and Hungarians in 1953 and 1956, the Czechoslovak reformers of 1968, the Polish supporters of Solidarity in the early 1980s, the millions of protesters in 1989, and the countless number of nameless people who were killed or deported because of their alleged opposition to communist ideas ever since the Russian revolution of 1917.

From another perspective, the question is not only why the Cold War ended but also why it ended so peacefully. Especially in this context, academic research has increasingly focused on the West European role in ending the Cold War. Arguably, the groundwork laid by German *Ostpolitik* and the persistent European initiatives in favour of détente were decisive in bringing about Gorbachev's new policy of understanding with the West. The EC's economic and social model of success attracted the Eastern European people, and their revolts drew inspiration from the largely European-sponsored extension of human rights norms to the East in accordance with this line of thought.

for East German citizens. He thereby emphasized the East Germans' rights to freely cross national borders (already part of the official parlance), but hardly mentioned that many exceptions still applied 'for reasons of national security'. Some of the journalists rushed out of the press conference and excitedly reported that the border between East and West Berlin was being fully opened for the first time since 1961. The population of East Berlin saw the news on Western television, and, believing that the Wall had fallen, flocked to the East–West border crossings in huge numbers. The border guards tried in vain to disperse the crowds, who kept growing and in unison demanded 'open the gate, open the gate!'[11] Faced with a choice between mass violence and opening the barriers, an individual police officer decided to open the border crossing under his authority. The other checkpoint commanders followed his example and opened the barriers to the West. The Berlin Wall had fallen.

Conclusion

From 1984 until the fall of the Berlin Wall in November 1989, transatlantic relations revolved primarily around the increasingly dramatic transformation of the East–West conflict. In early 1984, President Reagan announced a significant change in American foreign policy and henceforth promoted cooperation with the USSR instead of confrontation. Even more fundamental shifts were introduced into Soviet policy upon Mikhail Gorbachev's accession to power in March 1985. He set out to reform socialism at home, to abandon the use of force abroad, and to establish positive relations with the West. After the first Reagan–Gorbachev meeting in late 1985, the two leaders developed a sense of mutual trust and within a couple of years came to agree on their common objective to end the Cold War era.

Western Europe welcomed the de-escalation of the East–West conflict, yet initially reacted with some scepticism. The Europeans doubted whether the Soviet Union could change overnight, and worried about being excluded from superpower discussions pertaining to their own security. As the authenticity of the Soviet transformation began to manifest in 1987, and Washington made more efforts to consult the Europeans, transatlantic differences lost much of their substance and gave way to a general consensus on East–West issues. By 1988, the Western world unanimously applauded the reforms initiated by the Eastern camp, and agreed that Gorbachev's foreign policy merited support. Between 1983 and 1988, the seemingly deep-rooted antagonism in American and European dealings with the Soviets had completely disappeared, and transatlantic relations had improved significantly in the process. Even the economic rise of the EC now appeared beneficial to American policymakers, as a strong Western framework in times of dynamic Eastern change.

In 1989, when the Eastern European peoples started to rise up and challenge their communist regimes, the surprised Western powers remained mere spectators. After Poland and Hungary introduced democratic reforms, the conservative East German regime gradually lost control over the masses of demonstrating people. The breaching of the Berlin Wall on 9 November 1989 sent out a strong signal, eastward and westward. It caused the implosion of the East German government, which had lost any remaining authority, and prompted the more thorough eradication of communist structures in other parts of Eastern Europe.

The Atlantic community now faced a completely new situation. The border between East and West was disappearing, and Gorbachev's Soviet Union, which had indeed refrained from using force, no longer qualified as the enemy of the West. Neither the

Americans nor the Western Europeans had foreseen such a course of events, and Western policymakers woke up empty-handed after the fall of the Berlin Wall. But important questions needed to be answered quickly, and possibly new frameworks created. The most fundamental issue was: did the Atlantic community still make sense in the face of the new situation, or did the end of the Cold War require some completely new form of international cooperation?

Suggested further reading

Bozo, Frédéric, Marie-Pierre Rey and Leopoldo Nuti (eds) (2009) *Europe and the End of the Cold War: A Reappraisal*. London: Routledge.

Dockrill, Saki Ruth (2005) *The End of the Cold War Era: The Transformation of the Global Security Order*. London: Hodder Arnold.

Fischer, Beth A. (2010) 'US foreign policy under Reagan and Bush', in Melvyn P. Leffler and Odd Arne Westad (eds), *The Cambridge History of the Cold War*, vol. 3. pp. 198–218. Cambridge, UK: Cambridge University Press.

Ludlow, N. Piers (2006) 'From deadlock to dynamism: the European Community in the 1980s', in Desmond Dinan (ed.), *Origins and Evolution of the European Union*, pp. 218–32. Oxford: Oxford University Press.

Njølstad, Olav (ed.) (2004) *The Last Decade of the Cold War: From Conflict Escalation to Conflict Transformation*. London: Routledge.

Sarotte, Mary E. (2009) *1989: The Struggle to Create Post-Cold War Europe*. Princeton: Princeton University Press.

Young, John W. (2010) 'Western Europe and the end of the Cold War', in Melvyn P. Leffler and Odd Arne Westad (eds), *The Cambridge History of the Cold War*, vol. 3. pp. 289–310. Cambridge, UK: Cambridge University Press.

7   Transitions and uncertainties, 1989–1995

New world order?

Less than halfway into his first term, George H. W. Bush had encountered more challenges than most of his predecessors. In 1989, the first year of his presidency, the Iron Curtain had been lifted, the Chinese People's Liberation Army had crushed demonstrations on Tiananmen Square and the Berlin Wall had come down. In the second year, the process of German unification had gained unstoppable momentum, the Communist Party of the Soviet Union renounced its monopoly on power and Iraq invaded and occupied Kuwait. Speaking to the Joint Session of the US Congress in March 1991, Bush made clear that his was going to be a historic presidency, a time when a 'new world order' would be crafted. Six months later he would characterize this new era as one 'where United Nations, freed from Cold War stalemate, is poised to fulfil the historic vision of its founders. A world in which freedom and respect for human rights find a home among all nations.'[1]

No doubt there would be a new kind of international system. But it was hardly the type of utopia that Bush's larger-than-life rhetoric implied. The United Nations, for one, would not emerge as a supranational overseer of international security. In the 1990s that role, for better or worse, seemed to be taken over by the remaining superpower, the United States, which took the leading role in Operation Desert Storm, the military initiative that ended Iraq's occupation of Kuwait. To be sure, freedom – if understood as the right to vote in free elections – made inroads in one part of the world: what became dubbed the former Soviet bloc. But one can hardly speak of a global explosion of democracy in the early 1990s. As for respect for human rights, in the Middle East, Africa and many parts of Asia that remained a distant goal. The world had changed. But only in part.

The changes that did take place in the early 1990s, however, had a bearing on the transatlantic relationship. The fall of the Iron Curtain, the unification of Germany, the dissolution of the Soviet Union, the end of the Warsaw Pact and the breakdown of the former Yugoslavia dramatically changed Europe. Most importantly, these changes opened the possibility of wider and deeper continental integration, economic and political. But these events – if only because of their unnervingly unpredictable and potentially dangerous nature – also served to promote the strengthening of transatlantic ties and dependencies, particularly in the security field. Paradoxically, the uncertainties of transition and the emergence of a new international system would enhance a desire for continuity in transatlantic relations.

Unification of Germany

In principle, German reunification had been an alliance goal throughout the Cold War. Yet once the reality of the prospect suddenly appeared, differences among NATO members became evident. The old notion of 'keeping Germany down' that had been one of the three proverbial purposes of NATO's founding – the others being 'keeping Russians out and Americans in' – was not easily reconciled with the existence of a strong united Germany. Even without the Eastern part, the Federal Republic had emerged as the economic power-house of the continent. Indeed, while celebrations of the collapse of the Berlin Wall abounded, the memories of the two world wars resurfaced among Germany's old adversaries.

In the aftermath of the collapse of the Wall, however, nothing could stop the momentum. On 28 November 1989 West German Chancellor Helmut Kohl unveiled his ten-point plan for reunification. Reactions within the country were overwhelmingly positive as most East Germans made clear their desire to be part of the Federal Republic. In the first – and only – free elections held in the German Democratic Republic, on 18 March 1990, the pro-unification Alliance for Germany (Allianz für Deutschland), which had been formed only a little over a month earlier, garnered almost half of the votes. Together with the Social Democrats and Free Democrats (which accounted for another 27% of the votes), the Alliance formed an East German government openly pushing for reunification as rapidly as possible. They did not have to wait for long. FRG Chancellor Helmut Kohl (of the Christian Democratic Union) and Foreign Minister Hans-Dietrich Genscher (Free Democratic Party) commenced negotiations leading up to a rapid unification. In May 1990 the FRG and GDR signed a treaty agreeing on monetary, economic and social union that came into force on 1 July 1990, when the FRG's Deutschmark replaced its East German counterpart as the official currency. The following month the two states signed the treaty of reunification, approved by large majorities in the Bundestag in West Germany as well as its East German counter-part on 20 September 1990. The process culminated on 3 October 1990, less than a year after the collapse of the Berlin Wall.

Within Germany the reunification (or unification, as many preferred to call it) process produced both winners and losers. To Helmut Kohl, the German chancellor, and his foreign minister, Genscher, this was an opportunity to play a truly historical role that translated into increasing popularity within the newly reunited nation. The Christian Democrat–Free Democrat coalition, headed by 'unification chancellor' Kohl, was the big winner in the first all-German elections held on 2 December 1990. In the midst of national euphoria the opposing coalition of Social Democrats and Greens garnered less than 40 per cent of the nationwide vote. But the euphoria of the 'unifiers' was soon dampened as unified Germany faced serious economic and social problems brought about by markedly different political cultures and extreme disparities in wealth between East and West. Currency unification, for example, prompted inflation: price levels rose between 3.7 and 6.6 per cent in 1991. Industrial production in the former East Germany was down by 50 per cent at the time of reunification and unemployment exceeded 20 per cent. With poor infrastructure in the East, most companies preferred to enlarge their operations in the West, resulting in a corresponding transfer of workers from East to West.

Indeed, in the early 1990s large-scale public transfers from West to East Germany were unavoidable lest the Kohl government was to face popular disillusionment and social unrest. In 1991 alone, such transfers amounted to 73 per cent of the former East Germany's gross domestic product (GDP). When one adds to this structural challenge such other problems as the more than 2 million claims on properties in the territory of the former GDR were filed by the end of 1992, it is no wonder that the reunified Germany's economy hit a wall of sorts in the early 1990s. Europe's largest economy experienced a negative GDP growth rate in 1993. Although the economy started to improve in the mid-1990s, the initial price of reunification was high.

In the context of transatlantic relations, however, German reunification was a central part – probably the most significant one – of the overhaul that was linked to the collapse of the Cold War order. An era that had started with the four-power occupation and division of Germany in the late 1940s had been punctuated by the many crises that prompted the construction of the Berlin Wall in the early 1960s, came to an end in a surprisingly non-violent manner. But it also prompted frantic speculation and feverish diplomacy regarding the place of the new Germany in the post-Cold War international order. Ultimately, German reunification produced the context for the birth of a new transatlantic alliance structure.

Unified Germany and transatlantic divisions

For allies and adversaries alike, German reunification was not an unequivocally positive goal. Many saw it as a harbinger of international insecurity. British Prime Minister Margaret Thatcher, for example, had told Soviet leader Mikhail Gorbachev in 1989 that Britain and its allies had no interest in the potential destabilization of Eastern Europe or the collapse of the East German regime. Whether this was a deliberate effort to convince the Soviets that there was no Western 'conspiracy' afoot to undermine the integrity of the Soviet bloc or not, the USSR also maintained its distance from the events unfolding in East Germany in the autumn of 1989. Although Moscow's attitude towards reunification hardened in early 1990, the Soviet leadership may have been further reassured by Thatcher's insistence that unification was neither desirable nor a realistic prospect in the short term. Indeed, FRG's European allies were surprisingly close to the Soviet Union's negative view on the prospects and process of unification. President Mitterrand of France reportedly said in the spring of 1990 that he would 'fly off to Mars' if Germany was reunited.[2] In the end, he stayed in office rather than live up to this promise of an extraterrestrial voyage.

The Americans had a different outlook from their European allies. Although outwardly cautious, the general thrust of the Bush administration was in favour of German unification and, importantly, a conviction that the new Germany should be an integral member of NATO. Bush later explained that he tried to do 'all we could to facilitate the peaceful unification of Germany'.[3] Casting aside French and British concerns about the rise of a new German Reich, the Americans' key diplomatic challenge was to convince the Soviets to accept the integration of an enlarged Federal Republic into the Western Alliance. For their part, the Soviets seem to have worked with two scenarios. Ideally, with the support of the French and the British, they would be able to prevent unification completely. As this possibility rapidly proved untenable, the Soviets took up a back-up solution: to accept a united Germany as long as it did not translate into NATO enlargement. In other words, the new Germany should be neutralized. Indeed, as early as 21 November 1989 the Soviet Union informed the Kohl government that it was removing nuclear weapons from East Germany. But while the Soviets may have seen this as a way of pushing Germany out of NATO and towards neutrality – a long-term Soviet goal going back to the early 1950s – Kohl and others interpreted it as a de facto Soviet acceptance of unification. In fact, the chancellor announced his ten-point unification plan only a week after the Soviet démarche.

At this point, the Soviets attempted to reassert their influence. They called a meeting of the four occupying powers in Berlin, impressing upon the British, French and Americans that unification was not feasible or desirable. Americans fired back immediately. On 11 December 1989 – the same day as the ambassadorial meeting – US Secretary of State James Baker, also in Berlin, publicly expressed support for Chancellor Kohl's ten-point plan, which was in line with what the administration had labelled a new architecture for a new era in Europe. By January, the Soviets relented to the inevitability of unification, but still pushed for neutrality. After a meeting with Gorbachev in Moscow, Hans Modrow, who had become the prime minister of East Germany in November 1989, presented his Declaration on the Way to German Unity. The step-by-step plan envisaged a gradual merging of the two German states within a federation that would distance itself from the two military alliances. After the German elections in March, however, Modrow resigned (he would later serve both in the European Parliament and the all-German Bundestag). His declaration was soon forgotten.

Unified Germany in NATO

In the end, the Americans got what they wished for: a united Germany integrated into the existing NATO structure. The Bush administration had limited sympathy with the French and British (as well as Italian, Dutch and others') concern about Germany's potential ambitions to dominate continental Europe, and even less for the Soviet desire to push for neutralization. Instead, Bush and his major advisers – Secretary of State James Baker, NSC Advisor Brent Scowcroft and others – used America's diplomatic clout to support Kohl's unification project. In February the Americans agreed with Kohl to the so-called 2+4 formula: that the international aspects of unification should be discussed between the two Germanies and the four occupying powers (rather than the all-European CSCE). Bush also stressed to Kohl the importance of united Germany's continued NATO membership without special conditions. 'One France in the alliance, with its special arrangements, is enough', the president argued during their talks at Camp David.

Inevitably, the 2+4 negotiations on Germany's international position ultimately focused on NATO membership. While the French remained less concerned over this point – given their special status – the British supported Germany's integration as a way of countering the rise of an independent German security policy. But the Soviet Union was another matter. Moscow's starting point for negotiations was that a unified Germany had two possibilities: neutrality or dual membership in NATO and the Warsaw Pact. The Soviets also insisted on linking Germany to the development of an all-European security framework; an enhanced CSCE that would entirely replace the military alliances. At the first high-level 2+4 meeting in Bonn in May 1990, Soviet foreign minister (and future Georgian president) Eduard Shevardnadze went further, proposing that unified Germany be put under a probationary period before it was granted full sovereignty.

Several high-level meetings and pledges, public and private, followed. In late May and early June, Gorbachev and Bush met at Camp David to conclude a bargain of sorts. In return for his acknowledgement that the Germans had the right to decide their alliance membership, Gorbachev was offered a trade agreement and expedited arms control negotiations (the Strategic Arms Reduction Talks). In early July, NATO's London Declaration offered inter-alliance consultation to the Warsaw Pact and proposed a joint declaration affirming that military aggression was unthinkable. Finally, in mid-July, Kohl and Genscher met Gorbachev and his advisers in the Soviet Union. The Soviet leader surprised his German counterparts by acknowledging that a united Germany would be fully sovereign and thus able to decide its alliance loyalties without outside interference; the rights of the occupying powers would end at the moment of unification. But Gorbachev still insisted that there should be no NATO presence in what would soon be former East German territory, suggested that a separate treaty should be concluded on the eventual removal of Soviet troops (by 1994) and probed for reduction in the size of the German army (Bundeswehr). In 'payment' for Soviet concessions, Kohl offered economic aid, a lump sum that would help pay for the presence of Soviet troops and an interest-free loan of 3 billion Deutschmarks. In essence, Gorbachev had given in to Western demands because of his country's weakened economic and international position. A unified Germany in NATO – effectively the first NATO enlargement into Soviet bloc territory – was to become a reality. Meanwhile, the Warsaw Pact had, in effect, become defunct. It would formally be dissolved in July 1991.

While the process of unification – its internal and international aspects – thus proceeded rapidly and peacefully, it also exemplified the power shifts that had taken place. On the Western side, the Americans and Germans were in the driver's seat. The Bush and Kohl administrations' interests were not identical, but they both saw German unification within NATO as the only acceptable solution. For the US this was significant as a way of assuring that its determinant role in the transatlantic alliance was not to be challenged. For the FRG unification was the primary goal; since the Americans were the only NATO ally willing to accept it without reservations, Kohl and Genscher found themselves coordinating policy with Washington in a manner resembling that of the Adenauer government during the early Cold War years. Meanwhile, British and French reservations were ultimately countered by the promise of further integration. In the British case, this meant Germany's continued membership in NATO; for the French President Mitterand, Kohl's assurance of deepening European integration was the necessary guarantee against anxieties of a revived 'German Threat'. To both the British and (perhaps reluctantly) the French, the continued US presence in Europe acted as a further reassurance that the Germans – according to that old NATO rationale – would be kept 'down'. Ultimately, German reunification reinforced the logic behind transatlantic cooperation.

The events that unfolded after the collapse of the Berlin Wall were dramatic and unexpected. Yet the irony of the German unification process – and the end of the Cold War division that it symbolized – was that by the time it was finalized in early October 1990, international attention had already shifted elsewhere.

The Persian Gulf War

On 2 August 1990 Iraqi forces moved in to occupy neighbouring Kuwait, a small but immensely wealthy oil-producing Gulf state. Although it claimed that Kuwait was historically an Iraqi province administered from Basra (as it indeed had been during the days of the Ottoman Empire), Saddam Hussein's regime was not primarily driven by a need to right a historic wrong. Instead, the primary causes for the invasion of Kuwait can be found in the legacy of the 1980–1988 Iran–Iraq War, Saddam Hussein's need for domestic legitimacy and stability, and Iraq's quest for regional hegemony. Kuwait's vulnerability – it had no significant military capacity – and the belief that Iraqi moves, while not condoned, would ultimately be tolerated in a period of systemic transition were additional factors weighing into the pre-invasion calculations in Baghdad.

In particular, from the Iraqi perspective, the invasion of Kuwait promised a cure to both the economic and military legacy of the Iran–Iraq War. Kuwait's oil wealth would enable the Iraqi regime to reconstruct the state and to pay its non-Arab creditors. It would keep the army busy and far away from the capital. The contestable claims of victory over Iran would be replaced with a real victory over Kuwait. The invasion was also seen as a way to project Iraqi hegemony not just over Kuwait but also over the Gulf as a whole. This would allow Iraq to dictate oil prices and quotas to serve its own interests, as it would control 21 per cent of OPEC's total production. And, ultimately, the extension of military and economic power would enable Iraq to claim the mantle of pan-Arab leadership as the region's most powerful country. This was particularly the case as Iraq was the only country that had never even signed an armistice with Israel and the only Arab state left to embrace the PLO wholeheartedly.

The decision to invade was made easier by the belief that both Arab and Western states would not intervene. Saddam Hussein interpreted a meeting he had with US Ambassador April Glaspie on 25 July 1990 as signalling that the United States would not intervene should Iraq invade Kuwait, as Washington did not wish to get involved in inter-Arab disputes. Accordingly, Saddam calculated there would ultimately be acquiescence as long as the oil flow was not disrupted. After all, no action had been taken to dislodge Israeli forces from the West Bank, Gaza and Golan since 1967, nor to force the exit of Syrian troops from Lebanon since 1976. Thus Saddam Hussein discounted the likelihood of military action against his forces, the possibility of an Arab front emerging against Iraq, and arguably even the implementation of economic sanctions by the UN.

Operation Desert Storm

In the months following an easy occupation of Kuwait, Iraq's calculations were proved dramatically erroneous. Iraq was isolated. Not only the United States and Britain but such former allies as the Soviet Union and a number of Arab countries either joined in or failed to protest as a broad coalition to evict Iraqi forces from Kuwait was assembled. On 16 January 1991, following a series of UN Security Council resolutions, diplomatic moves, the freezing of Iraq's and Kuwait's assets, and the imposition of sanctions aimed at compelling Iraq to withdraw voluntarily, an American-led multinational coalition launched Operation Desert Storm to liberate Kuwait militarily. While the coalition relentlessly bombed Iraqi targets in Kuwait, Saddam attempted to split the coalition by creating a linkage with the Israeli–Palestinian conflict by firing Scud missiles at Israel. But the latter did not retaliate militarily. American assurances and the speedy delivery of Patriot missiles assured the Israeli leadership that their interests were better served by waiting for the outcome of Desert Storm. Nevertheless, a linkage had been created, as became evident in the efforts to push for a comprehensive Middle East peace process to resolve the Arab–Israeli conflict only a couple of months later.

On 27 February 1991, 43 days after launching Desert Storm, a ceasefire was declared. By that point an estimated 120,000 sorties had been flown by coalition air forces and some 84,000 tonnes of ordnance had been dropped, including 7400 tonnes of 'smart' bombs. Iraq's adventure in Kuwait had been stopped by the use of overwhelming air power, a strategy later emulated in attempts to resolve other post-Cold War conflicts (such as Kosovo in 1999). However, while Iraqi forces had been pushed out of Kuwait, the Iraqi regime emerged relatively unscathed. Unwilling to risk large numbers of casualties or commit to a long-term occupation, the Bush administration decided – despite some hawkish advice to the contrary – not to intervene in Iraq proper. Had Americans pushed all the way to Baghdad and exceeded the terms of the UN Security Council mandate, the hard-won diplomatic unity behind Desert Storm would also have been damaged. The Arab coalition partners, France and the Soviet Union would certainly not have supported such action.

In 1991, the restoration of Kuwait to the Sabah royal family by an international coalition of 34 countries led by the United States was read as a brilliant victory for the West. The Bush administration in particular heralded the notion that the demonstration of American power in support of collective security had ushered in a 'new world order'. Together with the unification of Germany and the end of Soviet hegemony in Eastern Europe, the Gulf War signalled the end of the Cold War international system. In the emerging post-Cold War era the United States was in a uniquely powerful position. Bipolarity had been replaced, however temporarily, by unipolarity.

In the realm of security policy, the Gulf War and the demonstration of America's massive military prowess was a defining moment in transatlantic relations. On the one hand, this was extraordinary – an unprecedented moment of transatlantic cooperation in an 'out-of-area' question. France, Great Britain, Italy, Spain and a number of other NATO members participated – in varying degrees – in the massive coalition force, while a number of other countries, in particular Germany (with US$6 billion), made a significant financial contribution to the war effort. On the other hand, by highlighting the merely supporting role of Europeans, Desert Storm made it clear that America's NATO partners depended heavily on the United States in the area of security. Consequently, even before the subsequent drama related to the break-up of Yugoslavia (see below), calls for the dissolution of NATO became increasingly muted on the European side.

The Gulf War thus helped to strengthen transatlantic unity. Although the Cold War and the common security threat that had prompted the creation of NATO was fading away, calls for the dissolution of the transatlantic security structures were muted by the military spectacle in the Persian Gulf. America was at the apex, the Soviet Union seemed almost irrelevant, and Europeans were searching for their place in the emerging new world order.

New beginnings

The end of the 'evil empire'

By the time Saddam Hussein's troops withdrew from Kuwait, socialist rule in Eastern Europe had virtually evaporated. In the late 1980s, tired of economic deprivation and political oppression, a number of dissident leaders had been encouraged by Gorbachev's rhetoric to become more vocal. His repeated assurances convinced many reformist leaders that the Soviet Union under Gorbachev would not act, as the Soviets had done before, to defeat their political demands. Even before the collapse of the Berlin Wall and the reunification of Germany, in August 1989 – after partially free elections – Polish President General Jaruzelski had appointed Tadeusz Mazowiecki as the first non-communist prime minister in Eastern Europe since the 1940s. In the summer of 1989, roundtable negotiations produced a new government in Hungary. Having been promised a West German loan of half a billion US dollars, the Hungarians decided to open their borders with the West in September. This, in part, produced the chain reaction that led to the large demonstrations on the Berlin Wall two months later.

After the Wall came down and Germans started their reunification process, the collapse of Eastern European socialism continued. In Czechoslovakia, Communist Party leaders, fearful of having to face the consequences of their actions in 1968, at first tried using force to stop the demonstrators. After street battles in Prague on 17 November 1989, the opposition responded by calling strikes and boycotts, and the journalists took over control of most of the mass media, supporting the protesters. By the end of the month, the party leaders had resigned and in December the veteran dissident writer Vaclav Havel was elected president and Alexander Dubcek, the leader overturned by the Soviets in 1968, was made Chairman of the Federal Assembly. In Bulgaria, the Communist Party gave up power in a relatively orderly transformation with the first free elections held in June 1990. Only in Romania were the changes accompanied by widespread violence in December 1989. Ultimately, the Communist dictator Nicolae Ceaușescu and his wife were captured and, following a brief mock-trial, executed on Christmas Day, 1989.

While the events in Eastern Europe were unfolding, Gorbachev insisted on absolute Soviet non-intervention (the so-called 'Frank Sinatra Doctrine'). As he repeatedly explained to his Politburo, the Soviet Union could not afford to intervene, for the financial costs and potential damage to the relationship with the West would be too high. The only occasions when he did condone the use of force were when demands for independence threatened the break-up of the Soviet Union itself. Thus, in January 1991 Soviet troops were active in Latvia and Lithuania. By then, however, even the military could not prevent the dissolution of the Soviet Union.

In fact, rather than giving the USSR a new lease of life, Gorbachev's moderation probably helped to bring about an end to the once-mighty superpower. In February 1990, Gorbachev pressed the Soviet Communist Party to relinquish its monopoly on power. In subsequent weeks, the 15 republics that constituted the USSR each held their first free elections, in which nationalists and reformists were triumphant. The Baltic states as well as Armenia, Georgia and Moldova moved towards independence. In June, Boris Yeltsin, an open critic of Gorbachev, was elected the first president of the largest republic, Russia. Gorbachev, meanwhile, pushed through a new union treaty that dispersed most of the central government's powers to the various republics. The Union of Soviet Socialist Republics was to become a confederation called the Union of Sovereign States on 21 August 1991.

Two days before the treaty was set to enter into force there was a last-ditch effort to reverse the course of reform. On 19 August 1991, Gorbachev's Vice President Gennadi Yanayev, Prime Minister Valentin Pavlov, Defence Minister Dmitriy Yazov, KGB Chief Vladimir Kruychkov and other hardliners formed the General Committee on the State Emergency. They placed the vacationing Gorbachev under house arrest, and issued an emergency decree suspending political activity and banning most newspapers. In a televised broadcast the coup leaders – some of them visibly under the influence of alcohol – claimed that they were saving the state from a catastrophe. Many in the West feared that the promise of change and reform had come to a sudden halt.

But the coup attempt was short-lived and only served to accelerate the dissolution of the Soviet Union. In Moscow, Boris Yeltsin escaped arrest and became the focal point of opposition to the coup. On 21 August Gorbachev returned to government and the hard-line leaders were arrested the following day. But power in Russia shifted rapidly into Yeltsin's hands. Gorbachev himself resigned as General Secretary of the Communist Party of the Soviet Union (CPSU) on 24 August and the party's property was nationalized soon thereafter. In November all the activities of the CPSU in Russia were terminated. Meanwhile, the various Soviet republics – from Azerbaijan and Moldova to Lithuania and Estonia – declared independence. With the exception of the Baltic states, all joined to form the Commonwealth of Independent States (CIS) in December. Finally, on Christmas Day 1991, Mikhail Gorbachev resigned from his now-defunct post as president of the Soviet Union. The USSR ceased to exist. Most of its territory, as well as its seat at the UN Security Council, passed on to Russia.

The sudden and largely non-violent end of the Soviet Union came as a surprise to most observers. But its significance was clear. President Bush, as well as European leaders, praised Gorbachev's personal role in bringing about the historic and revolutionary transformation of a totalitarian dictatorship. And indeed, the end of the Soviet Union and the creation of the CIS seemed to have given an extra boost to the European integration process under way since the 1950s.

Maastricht Treaty

The end of the Cold War opened up new possibilities for both widening and deepening of European integration. At the time that the Berlin Wall came down both the German Chancellor, Helmut Kohl, and the French president, François Mitterrand, had been committed to the cause of integration. Both supported the idea of a single European currency, albeit Kohl less enthusiastically, given the strength of the Deutschmark. To be sure, bargaining and self-interest played crucial roles. Kohl needed French support to bring about the unification of Germany; Mitterrand – much like Robert Schuman through the creation of the ECSC in the early 1950s – wished to further anchor an enlarged Germany into an integrated Europe by way of a common currency.

In a broader sense, the core countries of the earlier integration process needed to respond to the structural challenge prompted by the sudden and largely unexpected end of Soviet hegemony in the eastern half of the continent. Fears of rising nationalism, further prompted by the disastrous events that soon unfolded in Yugoslavia, added urgency to the cause of creating a wider, more deeply integrated Europe.

By creating a unique entity, the European Union (EU), the 1992 Maastricht Treaty (or the Treaty on European Union, TEU) laid to rest most concerns about the revival of old national rivalries. Signed in February 1992, the TEU was divided into three so-called pillars: first, the European Communities; second, Common Foreign and Security Policy; and, third, police and judicial cooperation in criminal matters. Among the most significant outcomes was the harmonization of monetary matters: the TEU provided for the creation of a common currency (the first euro coins and notes would be in circulation ten years after the Maastricht Treaty) and the European Central Bank (ECB). The Maastricht Treaty also enhanced the power of various supranational European institutions (particularly the EP) and introduced a social chapter. To reflect the increasing scope of European integration, the most significant of the European communities, the EEC (the other two were the ECSC and Euratom), was renamed the European Community (EC).

Like any treaty related to European integration, the TEU was a compromise and it left few of those involved in negotiations satisfied. The British, even after the staunchly anti-integrationist Prime Minister Margaret Thatcher had left the premiership in 1990, remained deeply sceptical. Her successor, John Major, insisted that Britain would not join the common currency, and during the tough negotiations his continental counterparts eventually accepted this decision (Denmark joined Britain by also refusing to join the euro). In the end the treaty was ratified by all twelve member states. But the Danes had to hold a second referendum to reach that point, while French voters gave the treaty only a slim majority. In Britain, politicians did not dare to ask the public's view. Ratification was rammed through the House of Commons (the final vote in May 1993 was 292–112 in favour). In other key countries, such as Germany, there was little opposition in the legislature but much scepticism in the press. Yet, with the ratification process complete, what would hence be known as the European Union (EU) – embracing the EC, the ECSC and Euratom – had been formed.

Box 7.1 Document extract: The three pillars of the European Union[4]

The 1992 Maastricht Treaty, or the Treaty on European Union, consists of three pillars:

1 The European Communities: the European Community, the European Coal and Steel Community (ECSC) and Euratom are the domains in which the Member States share their sovereignty via the Community institutions.
2 Common Foreign and Security Policy (CFSP), enshrined in Title V of the Treaty on European Union. Member States can take joint action in the field of foreign policy via an intergovernmental decision-making process, which largely relies on unanimity.
3 Justice and Home Affairs (JHA), provided for in Title VI of the Treaty on European Union. The Union is expected to undertake joint action so as to offer European citizens a high level of protection in the area of freedom, security and justice. The decision-making is also intergovernmental.

The EU and transatlantic relations

Across the Atlantic the historic move towards further European integration was hardly a major headline. The Bush administration issued a lukewarm message of support to the process, with the president maintaining that 'European unity was good for Europe, good for the Atlantic partnership, and good for the world … a strong united Europe is very much in America's interest.'[5] Indeed, to the Americans, further steps to the direction of European unity seemed to represent no challenge to its pre-eminent position in the context of the transatlantic relationship. As Under Secretary of State Lawrence Eagleburger had stated in 1989, the deepening and widening of European integration would not change the reality that the United States was the unchallenged leader of the 'West' and that the American president 'will remain the preeminent spokesman for the free world in the decade ahead.'[6] This seemed undisputable.

Yet things had changed. When the ratification process was completed, the TEU went into force in November 1993. Economically, the new European Union was a formidable entity. Its combined population was roughly 350 million – or 15 per cent higher than that of the United States. The combined GDP of the EU was approximately US$5.7 trillion – about US$1 trillion less than that of the United States. Although this basically meant that the average per capita income was somewhat higher in the US compared with the EU, such comparisons were often considered false as they did not take into account the generally wider income gaps in the United States, as well as the relatively generous social welfare programmes of the old continent. In fact, the birth of the European Union inevitably brought to focus a continuous debate about the differences – positive and negative – of the two continents' economic and (perhaps more importantly) social, models.

Indeed, although the American media failed to get excited about it and American policymakers had a tendency to yawn when discussing the maze-like process of European integration, the Maastricht Treaty was, in a number of ways, a significant landmark for the transatlantic relationship. There was no question that, given the size of its economy, the power of its military and the demise of the Soviet Union, the United States was the most effective and influential global player in the early 1990s. But while the extreme juxtaposition of capitalism and socialism was becoming a thing of the past, a new and potentially more powerful Europe was gradually emerging.

The globalization president

The formal creation of the European Union coincided with the election and first year in office of Bill Clinton, the first baby-boomer to occupy the White House. Somewhat surprisingly, the Democratic former governor of Arkansas defeated George H. W. Bush's hopes for a second term. Clinton's most famous campaign slogan – 'It's the economy, stupid' – captured the focus of the American electorate in the year that followed the global turmoil that had characterized the Bush presidency. In 1992 America – like much of the globe – was in a recession. Bush's decision to approve a tax increase despite his much publicized 1988 vow not to do so ('Read my lips: no new taxes!') also caused the incumbent to lose some of his conservative base, which gravitated towards an independent candidate, the Texas billionaire businessman, Ross Perot. Nor did Bush's unwavering support for the North American Free Trade Agreement (NAFTA) – viewed by many as inevitably resulting in a rapid transfer of manufacturing jobs from the high-wage countries (the United States and Canada) to a low-wage nation (Mexico) – help his chances. Indeed, another memorable phrase of the election campaign was Perot's graphic description for this predicted transfer of jobs: 'the giant sucking sound'.

An underlying reason for Bush's defeat was the simple fact that in 1992 no foreign policy issue figured high on the American electorate's agenda. The Cold War was over, the Gulf War had been successfully concluded, and no serious external threat appeared on the horizon. Bush's presidency had been a foreign policy presidency from the start, and his approval rating had soared in 1990–1991, reaching a peak at approximately 90 per cent in the early months of 1991. Such popularity had caused many leading Democrats to stay out of the presidential race. By early 1992, however, Bush's approval figures were down to about 50 per cent, dipping below 30 per cent at the end of July. Only Richard Nixon (amid the Watergate scandal) and Harry Truman (two years into the Korean War), two other presidents much admired for their foreign policy achievements, had polled lower while in office. In 1992 the Americans were clearly uninterested in foreign policy challenges or new world orders. Clinton's campaign successfully reflected this mood.

Bill Clinton may have hoped to focus his energies on domestic issues. But he was never going to be able to ignore the challenges and responsibilities the United States faced in the post-Cold War international arena. In years to come his focus would shift between various crisis areas – from Somalia and Haiti to Iraq and Rwanda – and the formidable security challenges that followed from the break-up of the Soviet Union. He was the first American president who would need to deal seriously with the economic rise of the People's Republic of China. Despite election-time criticism, the new president would push ahead with NAFTA. And Clinton would try to forge ahead with the Middle East peace process, hosting the Camp David meeting between Israeli Prime Minister Yitzhak Rabin and Palestinian leader Yasser Arafat.

Indeed, while critics would later indicate otherwise, there was no 'holiday from history' during the Clinton presidency. Taking over at a time when the United States was in a historically unique position – what many referred to as the unipolar moment – the new administration was faced with massive international expectations and a plethora of often unexpected challenges. From the perspective of transatlantic relations, the events in the Balkans provided a tragic example of the dangers that lurked ahead in the post-Cold War world.

Box 7.2 Americanization and the cultural exception

In the 1990s American popular culture was an ever-present force in the world. This was particularly the case in Europe. American music, American movies and TV shows, American fast food, and other aspects of the American way of life dominated airwaves, theatres and television. The easily recognizable symbols of American-based companies – Coca-Cola, McDonald's and others – were easily recognizable in most European cities. To the discontent of many continental Europeans, the English language had become the lingua franca of the world. With the collapse of the alternative way of life in 1989–1991, America seemed to have triumphed not only politically and economically but culturally as well.

In Europe, resistance to Americanization had been a potent force throughout the Cold War. In the early 1990s such concerns were once again high on the agenda, particularly in France. In 1993, the French government introduced the notion of cultural exception (*l'exception culturelle*) during the GATT negotiations. The argument was that free trade principles should not apply equally on cultural goods and services because they might undermine national or regional cultures and value systems. The cultural exception clause ultimately allowed the French to maintain high tariffs in order to protect its domestic market from a flood of American films and television series.

The cultural exception was an example of one of the pervasive phenomena of the late 20th and early 21st centuries: the perceived threat to national cultures and values in an era of globalization. Its practical impact, however, has been relatively limited. For example, 65 per cent of films shown in France were of American origin, compared with 90 per cent throughout the EU. But it exemplified broader concerns about cultural autonomy in an era of globalization.

Old nightmares revived: conflict in the Balkans

The end of the Cold War may have been greeted with high hopes of a new era in which democracy, liberal economic principles and international law were about to triumph. But the rupture of the post-war international system also unleashed forces of nationalism in various parts of post-communist Europe. While most countries remained intact, others were split along ethnic or linguistic lines. In Czechoslovakia these forces led to the emergence of two separate nations in 1993 with the creation of the Czech and Slovak Republics. Remarkably, the transition was peaceful and the two new countries would gradually join both NATO and the EU.

The fate of the entity known as the Socialist Federal Republic of Yugoslavia – a non-aligned nation throughout the Cold War – was dramatically different. Between 1991 and 1995 a series of clashes resulted in the deaths of approximately 140,000 people, making the Yugoslav wars the costliest military conflict in Europe since World War II. Ultimately, only a reluctant US intervention (military and diplomatic) brought about an end to the conflict.

In retrospect, the disintegration of Yugoslavia should have come as no surprise. Even in the 1970s, there was a trend towards growing autonomy for the six republics and two autonomous provinces that comprised Yugoslavia after World War II. Following the death of Tito in 1980, the economic problems and ethnic divisions continued to deepen, and finally, in the early 1990s, Yugoslavia violently splintered along ethnic lines. After a failed attempt by Serbia (headed by the former communist leader, Slobodan Milošević) to impose its authority on the rest of the country, Slovenia and Croatia declared their independence from Yugoslavia on 25 June 1991. The federal army responded with a brief, abortive intervention in Slovenia and a more serious effort to support the Serb minority in Croatia.

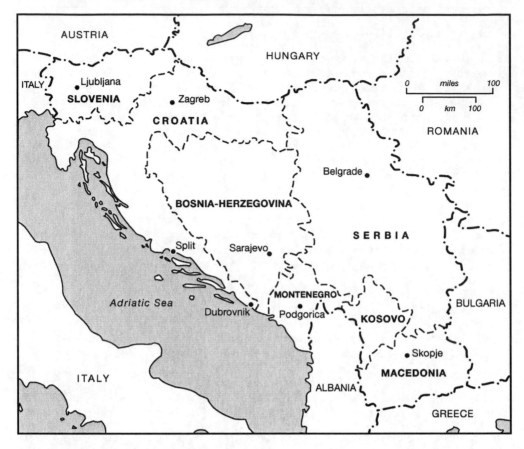

Source: adapted from Lindeman et al. (1993)

Figure 7.1 Map of the dissolution of Yugoslavia

However, once the genie of independence was out of the bottle, its influence soon spread. In September 1991, Macedonia declared its independence, and in October the citizens of Bosnia-Herzegovina voted for independence. Pressure from the international community helped initially to contain the crisis. In early 1992, a ceasefire was negotiated in Croatia, to be supervised by a 14,000-strong UN peacekeeping force.

But the Balkan wars of the 1990s were far from over. The Bosnian Serbs, with about 30 per cent of the population, seized most of Bosnia's territory and proclaimed the Serbian Republic of Bosnia and Herzegovina. The Bosnian Croats, in turn, seized about half the remainder of the land and proclaimed the Croatian Community of Herzeg-Bosnia, leaving the poorly armed Muslims (or Bosniaks), who comprised more than 40 per cent of the population, to hold the rest (15–20 per cent) of the republic's territory. A brutal three-way war ensued until early 1994 when the Washington Agreements transformed it into a two-way war by ending the hostilities between Croats and Bosniaks. But the fighting between Bosnian Serbs, supported by the Serbian government, on the one hand, and the now-allied Bosniaks and Croats, on the other hand, would continue until the Dayton Accords of December 1995.

Genocide in Bosnia

The Bosnian War was characterized by the worst violence seen in Europe since the end of World War II. Campaigns of 'ethnic cleansing', carried out mostly by the Bosnian Serbs, resulted in thousands of Muslims killed, and many more who fled the country or were placed in Serb detention camps. Bosnia's capital city, Sarajevo, was under prolonged siege and suffered extensive shelling for several years starting in the late spring of 1992. In May 1992, the UN imposed economic sanctions on Serbia and Montenegro and called for an immediate ceasefire in Bosnia. It was to no avail. Nor were the UN peacekeepers, mainly from European countries, able to carry out their humanitarian mission successfully. Repeatedly ignored or humiliated by the warring parties, the worst moment for UN peacekeepers came in July 1995 when Serb troops captured the area around the town of Srebrenica, a UN 'safe haven' (sanctuary for non-combatants) for the preceding two years. In subsequent days, the Serbs killed 8000 Bosniaks, mostly men and boys. It was the worst massacre in Europe since 1945.

The chaotic situation in Yugoslavia caused different external actors to adopt conflicting policies. While the EU and the UN stressed the necessity of political neutrality and an arms embargo vis-à-vis all belligerents, they worked together to provide the peacekeepers for Bosnia and pressed the Serbs with economic sanctions. In the United States, however, there was much support in favour of the so-called 'lift and strike' policy. This translated into the selective lifting of the arms embargo to even out the odds on the ground – the Bosniaks were far more poorly equipped than the Serbs or Croats – accompanied by the notion of selective air strikes against the Serbs to stop them from exploiting their military advantage any further. In fact, Bill Clinton had adopted 'lift and strike' as part of his 1992 electoral platform. In office he dispatched Secretary of State Warren Christopher for a tour of Europe in the spring of 1993. But John Major, François Mitterrand and other European leaders were against a policy they saw as leading to the inevitable escalation of fighting Bosnia. While Christopher returned home empty-handed, the American military leadership, Chairman of the Joint Chiefs of Staff Colin Powell foremost among them, were steadfastly against the idea, floated by some, of American-led military intervention. While public pressure to do something to stop growing violence and genocide in Bosnia increased, the US administration was stuck with a set of poor options.

Gradually, the United States pushed NATO towards action through a series of UN Security Council resolutions. In April 1993 NATO started enforcing a no-fly zone over Bosnia (Operation Deny Flight) to provide support for UN forces. In February 1994 NATO planes for the first time shot down a Serbian aircraft over Bosnia. But it took news of the Srebrenica massacre in July 1995 and enhanced mortar shelling of Sarajevo by Serbian forces before an aggressive NATO air campaign was launched.

For three weeks starting on 30 August 1995, allied planes attacked 338 Serbian targets in what was the largest military action in NATO's history. Although American planes conducted most of the 3500 sorties, Operation Deliberate Force – the code-name for the campaign – was distinctive in that the German Luftwaffe was in action for the first time since 1945. After the campaign ended, the Serbian government eventually agreed to participate in peace talks that reached an agreement in Dayton, Ohio in November. The final signing of the peace accord between Bosnia, Croatia and Serbia occurred in Paris on 14 December 1995. Bosnia remained one country, with the Croat–Muslim and Serb parts enjoying a large degree of autonomy. All was to be initially overseen by a 60,000 NATO-led Implementation Force (IFOR).

The turmoil in the former Yugoslavia, particularly the massacres of civilians in Bosnia, rekindled memories of the darkest chapters in Europe's 20th-century history. As such, it augured ill for the post-Cold War era in Europe, where nationalism appeared to be on the ascendant. The virtual paralysis of the newly formed European Union throughout the conflict gave little comfort to those hoping for a new era of peace and democracy. Indeed, within a few years another part of former Yugoslavia, the province of Kosovo (ethnically mostly Albanian) would emerge as another focal of violent conflict, prompting yet another American-led NATO bombing campaign and occupation.

From the perspective of transatlantic relations, the fighting and ethnic cleansing in the Balkans confirmed what the Gulf War had already implied: when the need for military action arose, American leadership was essential. This was true in Europe as well as in the Persian Gulf. But the Clinton administration was evidently reluctant to commit American troops; a hesitation made more acute after 1993, when US soldiers, cooperating with a UN mission, were killed in the Somali capital of Mogadishu. Nevertheless, the diplomatic pressure and capital that the administration invested in order to have a NATO 'blessing' for the bombing of Serb targets indicated that Washington considered that its interests directly linked to these events in the Balkans and also that such interests were best served by assertive American leadership. The idea that some form of assertive multilateralism would characterize the post-Cold War era – let alone George Bush's vision of a world order in which the United Nations played its intended role as the guarantor of international security – were rapidly evaporating.

As before, in the security field the Americans led, while the Europeans (complaining of American unilateralism in varying ways) followed. The Bosnian War had clearly driven home this particular dependency.

Conclusion

In a period of such dramatic changes as the early 1990s, a re-evaluation of the transatlantic relationship was to be expected. Yet it seems understandable that, with the collapse of the Soviet Union and its hold on Eastern Europe, with the spectacle of German reunification, with the launching of the European Union, with the largest joint military operation since World War II in the Persian Gulf, and with the violence that erupted in the former Yugoslavia, most political leaders yearned for some form of stability and predictability. In transatlantic relations this meant a certain reluctance to change the pattern of cooperation that had been in place for decades. Continuity was preferable to risking major institutional or structural change.

Such continuity was evident in the security field as the challenges of the post-Cold War world presented themselves with alarming rapidity. With the dissolution of the Soviet Union and the Warsaw Pact, NATO's original mission suddenly disappeared. But there was little push, on either side of the Atlantic, for ending NATO. Europeans, accustomed to an American security guarantee – and perhaps hoping that a continued US involvement would cut back the potential ambitions of a unified Germany – made no serious effort towards establishing a security identity of their own. A Common Foreign and Security Policy may have been part of the Maastricht Treaty. But it remained an aspiration. The prolonged crises in the former Yugoslavia clearly drove home this point.

Nor did the creation of the European Union – although establishing an integrated market that was much larger than the United States – seriously alter the economic interdependency between two sides of the Atlantic. Transatlantic trade remained significant, while large-scale investment (by American firms in Europe and European ones in the United States) continued. Moreover, although the creation of the EU increased the reality of political integration among the member states, the new entity was no real super-state. Its political decision-making process was still incoherent and its executive powers remained decentralized. In fact, for years to come the EU's major challenge would consist of an effort to get its own 'house' in order, trying to somehow create a unified entity out of the cacophonous collective of 12 countries. The first enlargement of 1995 – when Austria, Finland and Sweden joined – was economically relatively painless. But it did little to increase political unity of the EU. Henry Kissinger's famous statement from the 1970s appeared equally true in the 1990s: Europeans still lacked 'a phone number' that an American president or secretary of state could call in order to speak with 'Europe'. Consequently, when it came to important political or security matters, Washington continued to bypass Brussels and preferred to negotiate with the most important national governments (the UK, France, Germany and, at times, Italy).

Therefore, somewhat paradoxically, one of the most eventful periods of change in recent European and international history produced relatively little change in transatlantic relations. To illustrate this, one need only glance at a document signed by US President Bill Clinton, President of the European Commission Jacques Santer, and President of the Council of the EU (and Spanish Prime Minister) Felipe Gonzalez. The New Transatlantic Agenda (NTA) of December 1995 was agreed only a month after the Dayton Accords that ended the Bosnian War. When the NTA spoke of 'the promotion of peace, stability and democracy and development around the world', it duly reaffirmed not only the 'indivisibility of transatlantic security' but also the 'centrality' of NATO in this regard. There was a European pillar, to be sure. But it was firmly locked within the reality of a US-led defence alliance. Other parts of the NTA were equally reassuring and bland, such as the need to respond jointly to 'global challenges', to contribute to 'the expansion of world trade and closer economic relations', or to build 'bridges among our business, civic and academic communities on both sides of the Atlantic'.

While scepticism is healthy, one should perhaps not judge such banalities too harshly. The NTA made boring reading and had little practical impact. Yet it was also a rather accurate statement of a relationship that, when all was said and done, was a success. As far as transatlantic relations were concerned, the transition from the Cold War to a new era had been relatively smooth. Yet, as is often the case, new challenges lurked around the corner.

Suggested further reading

Dumbrell, John (2009) *Clinton's Foreign Policy: Between the Bushes, 1992–2000*. Abingdon, UK: Routledge.

Haftendorn, Helga, et al. (eds) (2006) *The Strategic Triangle: France, Germany, and the United States in the Shaping of the New Europe*. Washington, DC: Woodrow Wilson Center Press.

Lundestad, Geir (1998) *'Empire' by Integration: The United States and European Integration, 1945–1997*. Oxford: Oxford University Press.

Nye, Joseph (1991) *Bound to Lead: The Changing Nature of American Power*. New York: Basic Books.

Pells, Richard (1997) *Not Like Us: How Europeans have Loved, Hated and Transformed American Culture since World War II*. New York: Basic Books.

Rieff, David (1996) *Slaughterhouse: Bosnia and the Failure of the West*. New York: Touchstone.

Young, John W. (2010) 'Western Europe and the end of the Cold War', in Melvyn P. Leffler and Odd Arne Westad (eds) *Cambridge History of the Cold War*, vol. 3, pp. 289–310. Cambridge, UK: Cambridge University Press.

8 Enlargement, integration, and globalization, 1995–2001

Enlargement euphoria

Enlargement was a popular phrase in the mid-1990s. In Europe, the European Union saw its first post-Maastricht enlargement when the former Cold War neutrals Austria, Finland and Sweden all joined the new club in 1995. Soon thereafter discussions about the further enlargement of the EU were well under way. By the dawn of the new millennium others, including several former members of the Soviet bloc, were busy negotiating terms of membership. Meanwhile, NATO was given a new lease of life with the first post-Cold War enlargement, which incorporated Hungary, Poland and the Czech Republic into the alliance in the spring of 1999.

The late 1990s witnessed an enlargement on an even broader scale. Globalization was the 'hot' term that everyone – rarely defining it – used. It was a term particularly apt, or so it seemed, to countries like Great Britain and the United States, which benefited greatly from the economic opportunities offered with the opening of new markets and the emergence of new economies with the rapid expansion of the internet. Despite globalization and the gradual rise of emerging powers like China, however, the significance of the transatlantic relationship appeared secure.

Amid such enlargement euphoria and globalization, the closing years of the 20th century promised a bright future. On both sides of the Atlantic there seemed to be plenty of cause for optimism. America was the only global superpower experiencing its longest post-1945 economic boom. The EU was emerging as a civilian superpower ready to absorb former totalitarian states into a continental empire by integration. Even NATO's largest ever military operation – in the troubled former Yugoslavian province of Kosovo in 1999 – seemed to proceed without causing major tension across the Atlantic. The late 1990s appear, in retrospect, as a brief period of high hopes and bright prospects succeeded by the troubles that would characterize the transatlantic relationship of the early 21st century.

The transatlantic marketplace

In the late 1990s, North America and Western Europe were home to the most prosperous countries and peoples on the globe. In 1996, measured in terms of GDP, the only countries in the 'top ten' that came from outside the transatlantic area were Japan, China and Brazil. Other income rankings were even more slanted. Among the 25 countries with highest per capita incomes, for example, Japan, Singapore and Hong Kong (still technically a British colony until 1997) competed with Europe and America for global dominance; all fifteen EU nations were found in the top 40 of this global comparison. Americans and Europeans – those that belonged either to the EU or NATO (or both), or were otherwise closely linked to the trans-atlantic marketplace (such as Switzerland) – remained at the cockpit of the world economy.

By the dawn of the new millennium, such comparative statistics remained largely unchanged. Yet several trends were emerging. For one, America's dominant position in the world economy – with GDP more than double that of Japan – had become even more pronounced. China had moved into the number six position, while both Brazil and Mexico were now in the 'top ten.' Other emerging markets – India first and foremost – were moving up in this particular league table and some countries in the former Soviet Bloc (such as Poland, Hungary and the Czech Republic) were experiencing high rates of growth. In terms of per capita income and, hence, standards of living, however, Western Europe and North America still enjoyed a substantial lead over any other parts of the world. In this regard, even the gap between Western and Eastern Europe remained wide ten years after the collapse of communism; the Czech Republic's per capita income was less than a third of the average in the EU-15.

The dominant position of North America and the EU-15 in the global economy was matched by well-established transatlantic links. Trade and investment figures testify to the existence of a massively prosperous and relatively stable economic space, perhaps unrivalled in history. Bilateral trade in the transatlantic area accounted for 38 per cent of global bilateral trade (up from 32% a decade earlier). In 1996 the EU as a whole was the United States' largest trading partner (while Canada was the single country trading most with its southern neighbour), with roughly 19 per cent of each side's total trade in goods and services. Equally if not more significant, the EU–US investment relationship was thriving in the late 1990s. In 1996, for example, EU companies accounted for almost 60 per cent of the total foreign direct investment (FDI) in the United States. The total of US FDI in the EU amounted to $348 billion, while EU FDI in the United States was roughly US$370 billion. Proportionately, these figures remained stable throughout the rest of the millennium, with the United States and Great Britain as the most active nations (both in terms of inflows and outflows).

Moreover, the United States and the EU countries were eager to publicize their continued interest in furthering the integration of the transatlantic marketplace. The Clinton administration's New Transatlantic Agenda of 1995 was matched by the European Council's March 1998 call for the EU to promote a New Transatlantic Marketplace, to work towards the further reduction of tariffs and other impediments to free trade in goods and services. The Council set 2010 as the goal for eliminating all industrial tariffs between the United States and the EU.

Lingering transatlantic disputes

While that goal would not be achieved, the transatlantic marketplace was thriving in the 1990s. Yet, there were complications. The creation of the North American Free Trade Agreement (NAFTA) in 1994 – combining Canada, the United States and Mexico into one single market – raised the spectre of regionalism. And indeed, while the end of the Cold War had helped bring down a number of trade barriers, transatlantic trade disputes proliferated in the mid-1990s. There was growing tension, for example, over agricultural subsidies and the sale of genetically modified crops. Many such disputes ended up being referred to the newly created World Trade Organization (WTO) that in 1995 had taken over from GATT as the international organization devoted to overseeing global trade rules. Between 1995 and 2001, the WTO ruled over 32 such transatlantic disputes (for example over intellectual property, and the import regime for bananas and selected computer products).

Box 8.1   The anti-globalization movement

The 1990s saw the onset of rapid globalization, essentially the rapid reduction and removal of barriers between national borders that facilitated the flow of goods, capital, services and labour. Assisted immeasurably by the introduction of new information technologies (such as the internet), globalization was not new as a phenomenon; but the rapid pace of globalization was noticeable to most observers. To many, whether they viewed globalization as a positive or negative phenomenon, it was seen as related to the 'victory of the West' and liberal capitalism in the Cold War. North America and Western Europe appeared among the major beneficiaries of globalization.

Globalization sparked a transnational counterculture. The anti-globalization (or counter-globalization) movement targeted, in particular, multinational corporations that were seen as the true 'rulers' in the post-Cold War world. Intellectuals such as Benjamin Barber and Susan Strange coined phrases like 'McWorld' and 'casino capitalism', which were often cited by members of the anti-globalization movement.

Beyond heated debates, however, the anti-globalization movement organized protests around the major meetings of what were seen as the major drivers behind globalizations, institutions like the WTO, the IMF, the World Bank or the G7 group of countries. Sometimes violence erupted. In November 1999, for example, protesters blocked the entry of WTO delegates to their meeting in Seattle; subsequent clashes between riot police and protesters led to the arrests of 600 protesters, while several thousand were reportedly injured.

The anti-globalization movement never developed into a single, well-organized, transnational political force. Nevertheless, it can be seen as having sparked institutionalized forms of resistance to the spread of neo-liberal ideas in the aftermath of the Cold War, such as the World Social Forum that was first held in 2001. Among its major targets were the liberal trading rules championed by countries on both sides of the Atlantic.

In the area of international trade, for example, the United States took issue with the preferential treatment that Europeans tended to accord to their former colonies. Most famously, there were the banana wars of the 1990s: the United States complained to the WTO that by offering preferential trade terms to banana imports from former European colonies in Africa, the Caribbean and the Pacific, the EU countries were infracting on basic rules of free trade (and on the economic interests of American companies operating in Latin America). The Clinton administration even 'retaliated' by imposing high tariffs on European luxury imports, from French cognac to Scottish cashmere. Eventually, the banana wars were settled in 2001.

That most of these disputes were settled by the WTO and that such settlements were respected on both sides of the Atlantic is, actually, a good indication of the strong stakes that all members of the transatlantic marketplace saw in the strengthening of a strong, rules-based, international trade system. Even as eleven EU countries harmonized their exchange rates in early 1999 (as part of the process that led to the adoption of the single currency three years later), the American administration did not launch a significant protest despite the fact that the new European currency unit (ECU) was pegged relatively low vis-à-vis the US dollar and hence hurt American exports to Europe.

Despite 'good numbers' on transatlantic trade and the submission of conflictual issues to the WTO, public perceptions of transatlantic relations remained surprisingly negative in the late 1990s. Less surprising in a historical context was the fact that politicians on both sides of the Atlantic were quite eager to use the reservoir of anti-Americanism or (admittedly less prevalent) anti-Europeanism to their domestic advantage. Indeed, leading politicians in the United States and in a number of EU countries were quite keen to emphasize transatlantic differences in economic and social policies and traditions. While Americans – from President Bill Clinton down – would point to the high unemployment and social costs in continental Europe as evidence of the superiority of a more dynamic American model, European leaders such as the French President Jacques Chirac often took advantage of opportunities to pick a fight with the Americans because being tough with Washington tended to boost their popularity at home. To many Europeans the latest buzzword of the 1990s, globalization, was nothing other than the latest phase in an Americanization process that had begun in the aftermath of World War II. In December 1999, the Centre for European Reform – a UK-based think tank – described the EU–US relationship as 'unusually strained'.[1]

Strains were, though, relative and hardly detrimental. Notwithstanding trade disputes and persistent criticism of each other's social systems, the transatlantic security relationship also saw an evolution that strengthened, rather than weakened, pre-existing patterns of cooperation.

NATO's enlargement euphoria

In the mid-1990s many analysts, particularly in the United States, were writing NATO's obituary. '[T]he days of allies are over', wrote Ronald Steel in an article in the journal *Atlantic Monthly* in June 1995, adding that '[i]n a world without a single menacing enemy, alliances are deprived of meaning'.[2] Other prominent international relations theorists, such as John Mearsheimer, were equally sceptical of a continued US commitment to NATO in the post-Cold War world.

To such voices were added the gravitas of George Kennan, the man credited with fathering the policy of containment. Kennan had never been enthusiastic about NATO, seeing its creation as one of the causes of the militarization of the Cold War. In the 1990s Kennan, then in his nineties, saw NATO as the chief obstacle to the integration of post-Soviet Russia into the international community and incessantly warned against those calling for the enlargement of the Alliance. Indeed, writing in 1996, Kennan considered any 'discussion of the military interrelationships between Russia and her Eastern European neighbours, and of all of them with NATO, to be unreal, unnecessary, and in the highest degree deplorable'.[3]

Policymakers in the United States and Europe saw matters differently. Already in 1990–1991 NATO had proposed new cooperative initiatives with countries in Eastern Europe; the new Strategic Concept adopted in November 1991 emphatically stated that 'the opportunities for achieving Alliance objectives through political means are greater than ever before'. Accordingly, political consultation and confidence-building measures were emphasized over traditional military tasks. The North Atlantic Cooperation Council (NACC) was created in December 1991 to pursue these tasks. The Partnership for Peace (PfP) programme of bilateral cooperation with new partner countries was launched in 1994; virtually all former Warsaw Pact countries, including Russia, joined in (as did such non-NATO countries as Austria, Finland, Ireland, Sweden and Switzerland). PfP countries became linked to NATO's military activities by providing troops and other assistance to various NATO peacekeeping missions, most notably in Bosnia-Herzegovina, starting in 1996.

Simultaneously, the topic of extending membership eastwards was firmly planted on the transatlantic security agenda. As early as January 1994, Bill Clinton had announced in a speech at Prague that enlarging NATO eastwards was only a question of time. In 1996 the NATO ministerial meeting recommended that NATO invite 'one or more' countries to submit applications for memberships and that NATO begin accession negotiations the following year. The culmination of the process coincided with NATO's 50th anniversary in April 1999, when the Czech Republic, Hungary and Poland joined the alliance. Moreover, at the Washington Summit during which these countries formally joined NATO, it was announced that talks regarding membership were to begin with many other countries: Albania, Bulgaria, Estonia, Latvia, Lithuania, Macedonia, Romania, Slovakia and Slovenia.

The success of those pushing for the enlargement of NATO was symbolic of the overall international situation in the 1990s. The United States, the key 'Western' advocate of enlargement, was at the apex of its power; in security terms the 'traditional' NATO members of Western Europe remained dependent on America for security guarantees. Meanwhile, post-Soviet Russia, while vocally objecting to the enlargement, had limited diplomatic, economic or other types of leverage to push its position effectively. And the invitees themselves – all former members of the Warsaw Pact – saw NATO membership as key to integration with the West and, conversely, a guarantee against a return of Russian dominance in the future.

The consequences of NATO enlargement were many. The casting aside of Russian sensitivities and repeated warnings from the Kremlin were symbolic of the low esteem accorded to the Russian Federation as the Alliance moved eastwards. Warnings about the provocative nature of such an enlargement were ignored as such proponents as the American Secretary of State Madeleine Albright called NATO 'an instrument of peace' that was about to bring stability and security to an ever-expanding ring of democratic nations. Russia was down and NATO – not just the United States – was not ashamed to give it another kick. In years

---

Box 8.2 'Indispensability' of American power for Europe in the post-Cold War era

The United States emerged from the Cold War as the lone superpower, a nation without rival. Even in 1990 such books as Joseph Nye's *Bound to Lead* underscored the notion that the United States had all the power resources that it needed to sustain a leading position in world politics. While many worried about the imbalance of power, the reality was that the United States of the 1990s enjoyed a wide lead over other countries in terms of its economic, military and cultural might. In the late 1990s, French Foreign Minister Hubert Védrine repeatedly (if not without irony) called the United States a hyperpower (*hyperpuissance*).

In Europe, the continued reliance and dependency on American power was indeed an uncomfortable fact in the 1990s. This was particularly evident in the security field as Europeans were eager for a continued US role on the continent, accepting America's leadership role in the wars of former Yugoslavia and supporting the enlargement of NATO.

The enhanced American dominance in global politics did, however, spark an ongoing debate in Europe about how the EU could become a true international actor in its own right. For while there was no doubt that the EU was an economic giant (outclassing the US in terms of both population and GDP size), it remained a political and military pygmy. This state of affairs seemed to result from the very nature of European integration that had created an entity that was not a nation state like the United States due to the continued reluctance, on the part of most EU nations, to abandon the vestiges of their sovereignty.

The debate and its implications have continued to shape transatlantic relations into the 21st century. At the heart of this lies the basic dilemma of European integration: should the EU become 'deeper' or continue to grow 'wider'? As long as that puzzle is not conclusively solved, it is likely that the United States will continue to be an 'indispensable' player on the European continent.

to come, however, NATO enlargement became a useful tool for those in Russia seeking to inflame a new nationalism.

NATO's pre-eminence confirmed

The decision to enlarge NATO represented not only a blow to those advocating a more accommodating stance vis-à-vis Boris Yeltsin's Russia, but also a clear tilt towards accepting NATO as the key instrument of transatlantic security policy. Other institutions – such as the Organization for Security and Co-operation in Europe, or OSCE (until 1994 the Conference on Security and Cooperation in Europe) – remained in place but were not taken seriously. This was the case despite the fact that the OSCE, with its 56 member states, was the only 'pan-European' security organization, the sole forum outside the United Nations where all of Europe was represented alongside the United States and Canada. NATO enlargement, spearheaded by the United States and supported by its Western European allies thus symbolized the fact that post-war European security depended much more on the transatlantic connection than on any inter-European arrangements.

In fact, the divergences between the United States and Europe over NATO enlargement were rather marginal; more opposition could be found among American diplomats, senators, congressmen and journalists than their counterparts in Europe. Even in countries that were traditionally sceptical or even hostile towards American influence, support for the basic idea of NATO enlargement was relatively stable. For example, the French and Italians wanted to include more countries (such as Romania and Slovenia) in the first wave of enlargement.

As a policy pursued by the Alliance, enlargement was clearly a success story. Member states were, as much as they could be expected to be, united over the principle. Russian objections notwithstanding, the positive impact seemed clear. The United States saw NATO enlargement as a means for retaining and expanding its influence in Europe while countering potential geopolitical vacuums and instability. To Western Europeans, NATO enlargement meant not only guarantees of a continued American presence but also a way for paving the path towards another enlargement process; that of the EU. Similarly, Eastern Europeans sought membership both as a guarantee against Russian domination and as a gateway for integration into the European Union. In this regard, NATO enlargement was the first truly transatlantic initiative of the post-Cold War era.

The celebrations that took place in Washington in April 1999, however, were overshadowed by a crisis in the Balkans. On 24 March, exactly a month before the opening of the Washington summit, NATO had commenced its bombing campaign against Serbia.

The Kosovo crisis

The Kosovo crisis and war was the latest eruption of an ethnic conflict within the borders of former Yugoslavia. After the 1995 Dayton Accords ended the long conflict by granting independence to Bosnia, the province of Kosovo (ethnically mainly Albanian) formally remained part of Serbia. But rebellion and secession were in the air. Many Kosovars resisted the Milošević regime's revoking of their autonomous status in 1990 and the subsequent overt effort to reduce the presence of Albanian language and culture. In defiance of Belgrade, the writer Ibrahim Rugova's Democratic League of Kosovo launched a campaign of peaceful resistance and orchestrated two referendums among Kosovo's Albanian population. The first, in September 1991, declared Kosovo independent; the second, in May 1992, elected Rugova president. Although the Serbian government refused to recognize the referendums, passive resistance continued, but remained overshadowed by the drama unfolding in other parts of former Yugoslavia.

In the spring of 1996 the period of peaceful resistance came to an end as the so-called Kosovo Liberation Army (KLA) launched its first series of attacks against police stations and government offices. The Serbian government responded violently and declared the KLA a terrorist organization; but to no avail. In 1997, after the fall of Albania's President Sali Berisha (the first non-communist head of state of that country), the KLA received significant amounts of military supplies from across Kosovo's western border. In 1998 violence continued to intensify and spread throughout Kosovo despite attempts by Russian president Boris Yeltsin, US Balkan envoy Richard Holbrooke and America's Ambassador to Macedonia Christopher Hill to mediate an end to the fighting. The arrival of an unarmed OSCE monitoring mission in October 1998 (the Kosovo Verification Mission) did nothing to calm the situation. Finally, the so-called Racak massacre of 15 January 1999 – the killing of 45 Albanians in central Kosovo by Serb forces – brought the Kosovo crisis to the centre of international attention. Most importantly, it prompted the first NATO military action.

The outside world – UN Security Council, the OSCE, humanitarian organizations, the media – quickly condemned the Racak massacre as a Serbian atrocity, reminiscent of the ethnic cleansing in Bosnia a few years earlier. Although the US State Department had listed the KLA as a terrorist organization in 1998 and the KLA side had, up to this point, been responsible for more killings than the Serb army, the images of a potential repeat of Srebrenica prompted NATO countries to decide in favour of military intervention. On 30 January 1999 NATO declared that it was prepared to launch air strikes against Serbian targets unless a political settlement was reached. The six-nation Contact Group – the United States, Russia (the only non-NATO country), France, Britain, Germany and Italy – that had been set up to lead the international effort, set down a series of non-negotiable principles that included the restoration of Kosovo's autonomy, free elections and external supervision by international organizations.

Rambouillet to Kosovo Force

Starting on 7 February, delegations representing the Contact Group, Kosovar Albanians and the Milošević government negotiated at Rambouillet, outside Paris. The end result was, in essence, an ultimatum to Belgrade. The Rambouillet Accords of 18 March 1999 called for NATO administration of Kosovo as an autonomous province within Yugoslavia. Some 30,000 NATO troops were to maintain order in Kosovo. But Milošević refused to budge, perhaps hoping that support from Russia (which also refused to sign the Accords) would help deter a NATO military intervention. He was wrong. On 24 March 1999 the NATO bombing campaign began.

Over the next ten weeks NATO aircraft, operating mainly from bases in Italy and aircraft carriers in the Adriatic, flew over 38,000 missions against Serb targets (both in Serbia and Kosovo). Far from producing the rapid abdication that many expected of a superior military force, however, the bombing campaign triggered an intensification of the ethnic cleansing campaign by Serbia. By April, over 800,000 Kosovars had fled their homes. Meanwhile, NATO bombs hit unintended targets, including the Chinese Embassy in Belgrade, prompting both international condemnation and doubts about the effectiveness of using military force.

In the end, however, a Russian–Finnish mediation team convinced Milošević to capitulate on 3 June. On 10 June the UN Security Council passed a resolution authorizing a NATO-led peacekeeping force to enter Kosovo. Finally, on 12 June, the multinational Kosovo Force

(KFOR) started its operations, while the Serb army withdrew. Over a decade later KFOR was still operational, although the initial 50,000 participants had been whittled down to about 8700 by the spring of 2011. By this point, Kosovo had declared independence (in early 2008), although its status remains contested, not surprisingly, by Serbia.

Kosovo, NATO and American pre-eminence

The Kosovo crisis was the last bloody confrontation in a series of conflicts that ensued in the aftermath of the breakup of Yugoslavia. In years to come the division of the federation into seven separate countries (Bosnia-Herzegovina, Croatia, Kosovo, Macedonia, Montenegro, Serbia and Slovenia) was confirmed. In 2004 the first of the successor states, Slovenia, would join the European Union. Yet while reconstruction replaced armed conflict, the series of wars had left deep scars. In particular, a number of the Serbian leaders from the 1990s – including Miloševcić (who died in 2006 before sentencing) – faced trial at the International Criminal Tribunal for the Former Yugoslavia.

The Kosovo conflict further affirmed certain features in the post-Cold War evolution of transatlantic relations in general, and the role of the United States and NATO in particular. Broadly speaking, the Kosovo crisis confirmed in the minds of many the significance of NATO for Europe's security in the post-Cold War era. In Eastern and Central Europe NATO membership seemed like a long-sought-after prize, a guarantee of multilateral security and almost a requisite for a place in a stable regional system. In addition to former Yugoslav states like Croatia and Slovenia, the Baltic countries and former Warsaw Pact nations would seek and be granted membership in the decade after the Kosovo conflict. Enlargement and security were inextricably linked.

Kosovo also affirmed America's leadership role in questions of European security. Certainly, the military onslaught against Serbia in 1999, like the campaign in 1995 in Bosnia, was a NATO operation. A number of European countries – Britain, France and Italy in particular – pushed for the effort as eagerly as the United States, and made significant contributions during the air campaign and subsequent peacekeeping mission in Kosovo. But the heaviest load was carried by the US air force and navy, largely because Americans had a significant technological edge when it came to precision bombing. Even more important, the decision-making process before the launching of the air campaign in March 1999 ultimately depended on the United States. Both in terms of logistical capabilities and political will, the Europeans simply could not take effective military action without Washington's approval and support. The United States remained, as the popular phrase went, Europe's 'pacifier'.

Kosovo (and Bosnia before it) made it clear that NATO was the pre-eminent security actor in Europe. The military action – much like the coinciding enlargement process – also confirmed that some legacies of the Cold War had yet to wither away. Simply put, Russia remained the perennial outsider in the emerging post-Cold War European security structure. Although brought into the fold via various agreements – after joining the Partnership for Peace it signed in 1997 the Founding Act on Mutual Relations, Cooperation and Security between Russia and NATO – Russia was hardly considered a true partner. Historical images of Soviet domination over large swathes of Eastern and Central Europe, as well as the rise of nationalism within Russia and throughout post-communist Europe (including countries vying for NATO membership), hindered the building of trust between former rivals. Although the enlargement processes did expand the scope of the transatlantic space, Russia (and such post-Soviet states as Belarus, and even the Ukraine) remained outsiders.

Probably one of the most significant consequences of the Kosovo campaign, however, was the fact that NATO had shown its willingness to take military action beyond its borders. The Kosovo war hinted that a new more operational and even assertive NATO was in the making; the Bosnian case a few years earlier had not been a one-off affair. It was as if NATO, much like the United States during the Cold War, was starting to embrace a policy of forward defence.

NATO and the EU: competition or cooperation?

The Kosovo crisis and the first NATO enlargement implied a continued American dominance in transatlantic security relations. Yet the EU was also in the process of developing a security policy and agenda of its own. Common Foreign and Security Policy (CFSP) had been one of the two new pillars added to the already existing European Communities (for economic, social and environmental matters) when the Maastricht Treaty came into force in 1993 (the other new pillar was Justice and Home Affairs, devoted mainly to cooperation in law enforcement).

The introduction of the CFSP had limited concrete impact in the 1990s. In large part this was due to the cumbersome structure of the new EU's foreign and security policy decision-making. The European Council, consisting of the heads of state of the EU, establishes broad principles of cooperation and general guidelines. The Council of Ministers – the foreign ministers of the member states – was to be the main decision-making body, meeting roughly once a month. But the principle of unanimity necessarily reduced the ability of this body to make swift and bold decisions. While there was a general agreement on the need to, for example, embark on policies that promoted respect for human rights, it was virtually impossible to reach unanimity over weightier questions of military intervention.

Indeed, during the second half of the 1990s CFSP remained largely fictional. All member states still conducted individual foreign policies. The United States, for practical reasons as well as due to a latent concern that a truly united EU foreign policy might be directed against American interests, tended to deal directly with the leadership in London, Paris and elsewhere, rather than get mired in the bureaucratic jungle of Brussels.

Throughout the 1990s, the acronym CFSP was often confused with another that it was closely linked to: the European Security and Defence Identity (ESDI). This referred to what was sometimes called the 'European pillar' within NATO. Its main embodiment was the Western European Union (WEU), founded in 1948 as a preamble to the creation of NATO.

The WEU emerged as a significant actor in the aftermath of the Cold War. In the Petersburg declaration of 1992 – named after a hotel in Berlin were the discussions were held – it had been given several new operational responsibilities: in addition to common defence, the WEU's portfolio included humanitarian and rescue tasks, peacekeeping and crisis management. Lacking any forces of its own, the WEU directed operations – mostly in the Balkans – in the 1990s that were implemented by troops from member states and received logistical support from NATO. In effect, the WEU served a dual function in the 1990s: it was the institutional European pillar of NATO, but also the defence component of the EU. In other ways the WEU was also symbolic of the hybrid configurations that hindered the emergence of a centralized CFSP. While linked to the EU, the WEU – in the labyrinthine constellation of various institutions and organizations – suffered from a certain lack of representation: only 10 countries were full members of the WEU (Belgium, France, Germany, Greece, Italy, Luxembourg, Netherlands, Portugal, Spain and the United Kingdom). Other European countries were observers, or associates, lacking full voting rights. Ultimately, the WEU was merged into the EU structure via the Amsterdam Treaty signed in 1997 (but entering into effect in 1999). In the decade and a half that followed, WEU's functions were gradually transferred to the EU as part of the slow emergence of the CFSP.

St Malo and the European Security and Defence Policy

The CFSP received a boost from an unexpected joint project between Britain and France. In December 1998 Prime Minister Tony Blair and President Jacques Chirac issued the St Malo Declaration, which called for the EU to develop a credible defence force capable of taking rapid military action. The background to the declaration had much to do with the Blair government's effort to manoeuvre Britain into a better position in future negotiations with its EU partners, and in trying to maintain the special place (the 'special relationship') that the UK traditionally held as an intermediary between the United States and continental Europe (especially France). Indeed, British imprint could be discerned from the somewhat opaque wording of the declaration. While essentially proclaiming – giving life to yet another acronym – a European Security and Defence Policy (ESDP), the St Malo Declaration also affirmed the need for continued EU cooperation with NATO.

The sheer confusion over the multiplicity of institutions explains the slow pace of establishing a true 'European' security or foreign policy. Indeed, even the agreements in the Amsterdam Treaty represented nothing like the watershed in the evolution of EU foreign policy some billed (and hoped) it to become (and others had feared it might turn into). To be sure, it introduced the office of the High Representative for EU Foreign Policy. The EU now had a common foreign minister of sorts; Henry Kissinger's demand for a single phone number that the Americans could use when wishing to discuss foreign affairs with 'Europe' seemed to have been met. The former General Secretary of NATO, Spain's Javier Solana, was named the first permanent High Representative.

While increasing EU responsibilities for peacekeeping and humanitarian work, the Amsterdam Treaty did not provide for a common defence policy. The principles of unanimity and intergovernmentality still ruled the day: the major principles of CFSP depended upon a consensus among member states, making rapid decision-making and swift responses to challenges difficult to undertake. Common external policies were implemented largely (if at all) in the context of trade negotiations and energy matters where the weight of an EU bloc provided a distinct advantage. On 'hard core' security questions, however, most countries retained a large degree of independence. Or to put it in simple terms: there still was a French foreign policy and a British foreign policy, and the executors of such policies in London and Paris rarely yielded to any EU body in Brussels. National interests still ruled the day. During the Kosovo crisis, for example, British Prime Minister Tony Blair, French President Jacques Chirac and German Chancellor Gerhard Schroeder were the key European leaders involved in decision-making. At St Malo, it had been the French and the British that took the lead (however rhetorical it all turned out to be).

The minimalist approach to developing a common EU foreign and security policy agenda meant that established patterns of cooperation retained their primary role in the context of transatlantic relations. Even as the EU 'deepened', the United States, by strengthening and enlarging NATO, exercised a significant influence on post-Cold War Europe's security agenda. The Clinton administration's preponderant role during the extended series of crises in former Yugoslavia represented a clear example of the fact that the end of the Cold War had not reduced Europe's tendency to yield to US leadership. As Secretary of State

Warren Christopher put it: 'The first principle is that NATO is and will remain the anchor of America's engagement in Europe and the core of transatlantic security.'[4]

Other considerations illustrate the fact that not only did NATO have an 'afterlife' beyond the Cold War but the United States remained firmly implanted on the continent. For example, there was the continued presence of American troops in Europe. In 2000 they still numbered 117,600, with the great majority (almost 70,000) stationed in Germany, and some 11,000 in Bosnia and Kosovo. The rest were scattered at various postings and bases, mostly in such NATO countries as Great Britain and Italy. This was a significantly reduced number from the Cold War era (in the 1950s there had been over 400,000 American troops in Europe). Yet it was highly symbolic of a continued dependency, particularly in Germany. Perhaps more significant was the continued deployment of US nuclear weapons in Europe. While accurate information is difficult to find, it is possible that at the end of the millennium American nuclear warheads were stationed in Germany, the Netherlands, Belgium, Italy, United Kingdom and Turkey. The actual number, quality and readiness of these weapons were much debated, however, with estimates ranging from 200 to just under 500.

In the end, the 1990s had confirmed the enduring significance of the transatlantic security relationship. NATO's new Strategic Concept, approved at the Washington Summit in April 1999, became the formal expression of this post-Cold War fact. While the Strategic Concept celebrated NATO's past successes, it also warned – and hence justified the Alliance's existence – of 'complex new risks to Euro-Atlantic peace and stability, including oppression, ethnic conflict, economic distress, the collapse of political order, and the proliferation of weapons of mass destruction.' The document identified a 'new security environment' in which NATO's traditional defence mission remained important, but also emphasized that in the 21st century NATO would need to be adapting to a number of significant 'political, economic, social and environmental factors'. While not specifying these factors in detail, it was implied that NATO needed to adopt a more 'holistic' approach to security and consider ways of minimizing such 'asymmetric' threats as international terrorism. Maintaining significant defence capabilities remained important for the transatlantic alliance. But NATO was to play an important role in the development of a European security identity. It would also prevent conflicts and manage crises, develop budding security partnerships with Russia and other post-Soviet states (as well as with the countries of the Mediterranean), and actively promote disarmament and non-proliferation. The door was also wide open for new members: 'No European democratic country whose admission would fulfil the objectives of the [NATO] Treaty will be excluded from consideration [for membership].'[5]

Ultimately, in the reshaping of transatlantic security structures during the 1990s there was but one clear winner: NATO. The continued enlargement of the alliance in the 2000s would bear this out. Yet this was not the same thing as to argue that transatlantic divisions were a thing of the past; far from it.

Beyond the transatlantic space

Iraq

NATO may have been successful in reinventing itself for the post-Cold War era, but many of the contentious issues plaguing transatlantic relations remained. As had traditionally been the case, the most ardent transatlantic disputes tended to concern issues beyond the immediate physical transatlantic space. For example, in addition to the difficult decision-making

Box 8.3 Document extract: The NATO Strategic Concept (24 April 1999)[6]

The Alliance embodies the transatlantic link by which the security of North America is permanently tied to the security of Europe. It is the practical expression of effective collective effort among its members in support of their common interests ...

The resulting sense of equal security among the members of the Alliance, regardless of differences in their circumstances or in their national military capabilities, contributes to stability in the Euro-Atlantic area. The Alliance does not seek these benefits for its members alone, but is committed to the creation of conditions conducive to increased partnership, cooperation, and dialogue with others who share its broad political objectives ... the Alliance performs the following fundamental security tasks:

Security: To provide one of the indispensable foundations for a stable Euro-Atlantic security environment, based on the growth of democratic institutions and commitment to the peaceful resolution of disputes, in which no country would be able to intimidate or coerce any other through the threat or use of force.

Consultation: To serve, as provided for in Article 4 of the Washington Treaty, as an essential transatlantic forum for Allied consultations on any issues that affect their vital interests, including possible developments posing risks for members' security, and for appropriate co-ordination of their efforts in fields of common concern.

Deterrence and Defence: To deter and defend against any threat of aggression against any NATO member state as provided for in Articles 5 and 6 of the Washington Treaty ...

Crisis Management: To stand ready, case-by-case and by consensus ... to contribute to effective conflict prevention and to engage actively in crisis management, including crisis response operations.

Partnership: To promote wide-ranging partnership, cooperation, and dialogue with other countries in the Euro-Atlantic area, with the aim of increasing transparency, mutual confidence and the capacity for joint action with the Alliance ...

The Alliance does not consider itself to be any country's adversary.

regarding Bosnia and Kosovo, in the 1990s the United States clashed with the French over Rwanda and the Congo. France's President Jacques Chirac even complained that in the post-Cold War context, the United States 'has the pretension to want to direct everything, it wants to rule the whole world'. Such resentment was undoubtedly fuelled by an undisguised American belief in the fact that the United States was, as President Clinton and Secretary of State Madeleine Albright put it, 'the indispensable nation'. In an interview on NBC's *Today Show*, Albright claimed that '[w]e stand tall and we see further than other countries into the future, and we see the danger here to all of us'.[7]

Albright's proud assertion was easily interpreted as arrogance by her European counterparts. But it also reflected the evident differences between Washington and many of its NATO allies about how to deal with the unresolved question of Saddam Hussein's Iraq. In the years following the Gulf War, Iraq had been subjected to economic and military sanctions, no-fly zones, and repeated air strikes. In the autumn of 1994, when 10,000 Iraqi Republican Guards amassed at the Kuwaiti border, the United States sent an aircraft carrier and 36,000 US troops to the region. In addition, the Clinton administration actively supported the work of the UN Special Commission (UNSCOM) that was charged with verifying the destruction of Iraq's weapons of mass destruction (WMD) programmes.

In the mid-1990s the inspection regime, and hence the policy of 'containing' Iraq, began to break down. In 1997, Hussein demanded the removal of American inspectors, whom he charged with working with the CIA. Soon thereafter, the Iraqi government insisted that UNSCOM suspend surprise inspections and that so-called presidential sites be considered off-limits. After an unsuccessful US effort to rally support for military strikes and a successful mediation effort by UN Secretary General Kofi Annan, tensions abated in February 1998. But when the Iraqi leader suddenly halted all UNSCOM activities in December 1998, the United States and Great Britain launched a massive four-day strike (Operation Desert Fox) against Iraqi military facilities. The Clinton administration followed with a policy labelled 'containment plus': increased US military presence in the Gulf region, regular air strikes against Iraqi radar facilities, tougher enforcement of no-fly zones and open funding of anti-Saddam Hussein opposition forces. At the end of 1999, the UN Security Council replaced UNSCOM with the UN Monitoring, Verification and Inspection Commission (UNMOVIC). Its job of ensuring the destruction of Iraqi WMDs would be virtually impossible, and was eventually cut short by the US-led invasion in 2003.

In fact, President Bill Clinton had made it clear on numerous occasions that the ultimate goal of US policy in Iraq was regime change. Claiming that Saddam Hussein represented a threat to the security of the world, Clinton suggested in February 1998 that the 'best way to end that threat once and for all is with a new Iraqi government'. Six months later, pressed on by the US Congress, the president signed into law the Iraq Liberation Act that mandated Clinton to fund anti-Saddam groups and individuals, and specifically stated that '[i]t should be the policy of the United States to support efforts to remove the regime headed by Saddam Hussein from power in Iraq and to promote the emergence of a democratic government to replace that regime'.[8] Although the Act did not authorize the use of military force to over-throw the Iraqi regime, it did call for the administration to press for the creation of an international tribunal charged with prosecuting Saddam Hussein for war crimes.

While the Clinton administration's Iraq policy was supported by Great Britain, many Europeans were far more ambiguous. For one, there was growing concern that the sanctions were hurting the people of Iraq more than its regime. In the late 1990s, France and Russia, countries with significant business interests in Iraq, indicated their readiness to promote the relaxing of economic sanctions and objected to calls for military strikes. In the aftermath of Operation Desert Fox in December 1998, France and Russia were joined by China in criticizing the bombings and in calling on the UN Security Council to relax and lift the oil embargo imposed on Iraq since the end of the Gulf War. A major transatlantic crisis over Iraq was already in the making.

Arab–Israeli conflict

Beyond Iraq, much of the Middle East – what had been called the 'Arc of Crisis' in the 1970s – remained a source of tension in transatlantic relations. The Arab–Israeli conflict and the Israeli–Palestinian peace process continued to cast a shadow over the region. To be sure, in the aftermath of the 1990–1991 Gulf War the Arab–Israeli peace process had enjoyed a period of promise. The so-called Oslo Accords of August 1993 – a result of a series of secret meetings between Israeli and Palestinian officials in Norway – had offered a road map towards a peaceful end to the Middle East's most enduring conflict. Known later as the Oslo I Accord, the Palestine Liberation Organization (PLO) promised to renounce terrorism and recognize Israel, the Israelis offered to withdraw from Jericho and the Gaza Strip, and negotiations to resolve the other issues (refugees, borders, Jerusalem, settlements) would follow.

The Clinton administration actively promoted this process, but extremists on both sides did their best to derail the Oslo Accords. Palestinian suicide bombers continued their attacks and an Israeli extremist assassinated Prime Minister Yitzhak Rabin in November 1995. Bill Clinton managed to bring the new Israeli Prime Minister Benjamin Netanyahu and Palestinian leader Yasser Arafat together for a summit in Maryland in October 1998. In 2000, Clinton came close to mediating a historic agreement between Arafat and the new Israeli Prime Minister Ehud Barak. But, despite Clinton's energetic efforts, no deal was concluded. Instead, in September 2000 – provoked in part by the political gimmicks of Ariel Sharon, leader of Israel's right-wing Likud party – a series of violent incidents and aggressive speeches prompted the Second Intifada (the first one had taken place in 1987–1993) that would claim the lives of 3500 Palestinians and 1000 Israelis by 2005.

From the perspective of transatlantic relations, these out-of-area issues – Iraq and the Arab–Israeli conflict – were a constant reminder of two prevalent themes. First, these issues had the capacity to drive a wedge between the United States and some of its European allies. The French and the Germans, for example, were critical of both sanctions and, in particular, the use of military strikes against Iraq. Traditionally, a number of European countries tended to sympathize more with the Palestinian cause than the United States (government and public opinion). Second, by default it was clear that the United States was the country that was expected to make a difference, whether it came to pressuring a 'renegade' country into compliance (i.e. Iraq) or solving the long-standing Israeli–Palestinian conflict. Despite the end of the Cold War and the prospect of an independent European CFSP, there was no united European front that would have promised a solution to the problems of Iraq. Nor was there a significant EU option on offer for the Israelis or the Palestinians. Indeed, in the late 1990s it remained an article of faith that if anyone was going to find a solution to the Arab–Israeli conflict, it was the United States. And since Washington was incapable of bringing about a significant mediation result, the conflict endured well into the 21st century.

In fact, much as in the case of the enlargement of NATO and the interventions in Bosnia and Kosovo, the Middle East provided evidence of the imbalance in transatlantic relations after the end of the Cold War. The United States was the giant Gulliver capable of moving mountains, or so many thought; 'indispensable' to the peace and stability of the world, as Albright put it. The Europeans, by contrast, were Lilliputians, lacking coherence or a common purpose save, at times, trying to tie Gulliver down so he would not abuse his power.

New millennium, 'new' issues

The seemingly irresolvable problems of the Middle East were standard fare for transatlantic dispute. Yet in the post-Cold War era many seemingly new issues were creeping on to the international agenda. In an era of globalization, evidenced by ever-growing international trade, shrinking distances, virtual economies and rapid communications, the conventional wisdom suddenly seemed to be that the nation state was about to wither away. In Europe, this belief was strengthened by the advances in European integration that, while offering an end to the violence that had often accompanied national rivalries, also raised hot debates about identity. More significantly, however, the late 1990s saw the true emergence of 'global' concerns that, quite often, tended to create transatlantic tensions. Three such issues were potentially troublesome in the transatlantic context.

International terrorism

Although international terrorism became a major global issue in the aftermath of 11 September 2001, the question of countering terrorist threats was already high on the Clinton administration's agenda prior to that. In February 1993, only a month after Clinton took office, operatives linked to the Al-Qaeda network detonated a bomb in the parking garage of the World Trade Center in New York. Five years later, despite increasing efforts to neutralize Al-Qaeda and find its leader, the Saudi-born militant Osama bin Laden, two American embassies in eastern Africa were struck simultaneously: the attacks in Nairobi (Kenya) and Dar es Salaam (Tanzania) claimed the lives of 250 people. In retaliation, Clinton ordered missile attacks on sites in Afghanistan (were bin Laden was based) and Sudan (where Al-Qaeda was suspected of developing biological weapons). However, the attacks failed to deter further terrorist strikes: in October 2000 another terrorist attack took place against USS *Cole*, a navy destroyer based in the harbour of the Yemeni port of Aden.

International terrorism was thus prominently on the American foreign policy agenda in the late 1990s. Yet while Europeans had experienced international terrorism for decades, their support for American military strikes in the aftermath of the 1998 attacks was limited to sharing intelligence. The differences between American and European approaches to counterterrorism that would become so evident in the aftermath of 11 September 2001 were already clear. While Americans favoured a combination of methods, from retaliatory strikes to pre-emptive blows with missiles and selected assassinations, the Europeans tended to focus on intelligence gathering. Given that the most spectacular terrorist strikes were (and would be) delivered against American targets, this was understandable. The differences were also related to capabilities: while the United States could deliver lethal attacks anywhere on the globe, the Europeans could not. As international terrorism came to top the American security agenda in the 2000s, these differences in methods and capabilities would produce a transatlantic crisis of major proportions (see Chapter 9).

International law

Another global issue that separated the United States and Europe was the establishment of the International Criminal Court (ICC). In the 1990s tribunals such as the International Criminal Tribunal for the former Yugoslavia and for Rwanda had been established to prosecute and punish gross violations of human rights. However, because they were established to try crimes committed only within a specific time-frame and during a specific conflict, there was general agreement that an independent, permanent criminal court was needed. Thus, in July 1998, following extensive negotiations, 120 states voted to adopt the Rome Statute, the legal basis for establishing the permanent ICC. But seven countries voted against: the United States, China, Iraq, Israel, Libya, Qatar and Yemen.

Notwithstanding the fact that it found itself in awkward company, the American opposition to the ICC was not entirely illogical. There was concern that US soldiers might find themselves dragged to The Hague and be judged in front of the newly established court. Given America's extensive military role around the globe, the Pentagon was particularly active in opposing such a diminution of its traditional jurisdiction. Moreover, the possibility that such statesmen as the former Secretary of State Henry Kissinger might find themselves harassed over, for example, his role in the overthrow of the Chilean President Salvador Allende and the subsequent murderous dictatorship of Augusto Pinochet, raised doubts in the United States about the ICC's true purposes.

Nevertheless, it was clear that the mission of the court – to prosecute those responsible for gross violations of human rights – was not something that a democratic country like the United States could object to. Thus, in his last year in office, President Clinton did sign the Rome Statute. But, in a display of creative statesmanship, he never submitted the Statute to the US Senate for formal ratification. In 2002 Clinton's successor, George W. Bush, withdrew the signature and notified the UN Secretary General that the US would not feel compelled to observe any of the specific clauses of the Rome Statute.

Environment

In the 1990s concern over global warming became a prominent issue on the international agenda. In 1992 the UN Conference on Environment and Development (UNCED) had produced the Framework Convention on Climate Change (UNFCCC), the first international environmental treaty regulating greenhouse gas emissions. Five years later the UNFCCC was updated by the much better known Kyoto Protocol, which introduced a number of specific mechanisms – such as emissions trading, clean development mechanism and joint implementation – to be used in order to meet the goal of cutting global greenhouse gas emissions by an average of 6–8 per cent by 2012. Most industrialized countries (including all EU countries and the United States) signed the Kyoto Protocol. However, the Clinton administration failed to convince the US Senate to ratify Kyoto, mainly because of concerns over the impact that forced cutbacks in emissions would have on the American economy. Within months of taking office, the Bush administration rejected the Kyoto Protocol and participated merely as an observer in the next climate change conference, held in Morocco in late 2001.

The American rejections of the Kyoto Protocol and the Rome Statute were not, strictly speaking, transatlantic issues. Nevertheless, the apparent American intransigence on these global concerns reflected a gap of perceptions. On the one side there was a superpower that, while yielding global influence, had no wish to compromise its national prerogatives. On the other side there were the Europeans, accustomed to making compromises about their national sovereignty. The different stands towards climate change and international law did not produce a major transatlantic crisis. But they did provide a context in which a deterioration of relations could be sparked.

Conclusion

In the last years of the 20th century a number of differences between American and European perceptions had emerged. The relative success of integration and the seeming disappearance of military threats after the main conflicts in former Yugoslavia had ended meant that Europeans focused increasingly on improving and enlarging the European Union. But absorbing new aspects to what was soon called the 'civilian superpower' presented a new set of challenges that concentrated European energies on the continent. Meanwhile, America's concerns remained global and, to a degree, more 'traditionally' determined. To put the matter simply, while the Europeans were entering the largely uncharted territory of supranationalism, the United States remained the world's most powerful nation state. If European leaders were concerned with finding ways of bridging the economic, cultural and even linguistic barriers that still separated the member states (as well as the candidate nations) of the EU, Americans wished to preserve their nation's leadership role in the post-Cold War era. In a very basic sense, the construction of the European Union necessitated

Table 8.1 Comparison of EU-15 and US economies in 1999

	EU-15	*US*
Population	368 million	275 million
GDP	$8024 billion	$9255 billion
GDP per capita	$21,804	$33,655
Annual growth rate	3%	4.8%

Note:
EU-15: Austria, Belgium, Denmark, Finland, France, Germany, Great Britain, Greece, Ireland, Italy, Luxembourg, the Netherlands, Portugal, Spain, Sweden.

Source: data from the 2000 CIA World Factbook (www.cia.gov) and Eurostat (http://epp.eurostat.ec.europa.eu/portal/page/portal/eurostat/home/).

that its members accepted multilateralism and diminished sovereignty as a precondition. While differences remained – with countries like the UK, Denmark and Sweden deciding to stay outside the forthcoming launch of the common currency, the euro – European attention tended to be overwhelmingly focused on managing the continental integration project.

On the other side of the Atlantic there was a sense that a new American century was about to commence, with no serious rivals on the horizon. America remained militarily dominant. In 1999 the US was responsible for roughly a third of global military spending. This was actually a higher percentage than in 1991, more than three times the amount of China and eight times that of Russia; in fact, more than the next six countries combined. Equally significantly, US economic growth had been stable throughout the Clinton years. At roughly four per cent, unemployment was at record low levels. In 2000, the Clinton administration announced the largest budget surplus (over $200 billion), which almost doubled the surplus from the year before (which in turn had been double the one of 1998). This was a remarkable contrast to the Cold War era when the US ran budget deficits on a consistent basis. Also, the United States remained by far the largest single economy in the world (40 per cent larger than the second largest economy at the time, Japan), responsible for 23.7 per cent of global domestic product (in purchasing power parity terms) in 2000. In short, under Clinton the United States had retained its position as the world's greatest economic and military power. As the president summed it up in his State of the Union Address in January 2000:

> We are fortunate to be alive at this moment in history … Never before has our nation enjoyed, at once, so much prosperity and social progress with so little internal crisis and so few external threats … the state of the union is the strongest it has ever been.[9]

Generally speaking, at the beginning of the new millennium the transatlantic relationship was in good shape. There were some disagreements – over environmental policies, over international institutions, over trade matters – and complaints. But the word 'crisis' hardly characterized the state of affairs between America and Europe. Through the enlargement of NATO and its dominant role during the Kosovo crisis, the United States had confirmed its role as a key player in European affairs, while most Europeans regarded a continued American presence a boon. There were disagreements over the fine points of various important issues, such as the role of the state in the economy, and the need to maintain a strong military capacity or to build a nuclear missile defence system. But to most observers there was no serious cause to expect a transatlantic crisis after the US presidency passed – following an acrimonious recounting drama in the state of Florida and an intervention by the US Supreme Court – from Bill Clinton to George W. Bush at the beginning of 2001.

Suggested further reading

Auersweld, Philip and John Garofano (eds) (2003) *Clinton's Foreign Policy: A Documentary Record.* New York: Kluwer Law International.

Bindi, Federiga (ed.) (2010) *The Foreign Policy of the European Union: Assessing Europe's Role in the World.* Washington, DC: Brookings.

Bozo, Frederic (2008) 'The US changing role and Europe's transatlantic dilemmas: Toward an EU strategic autonomy?', in Geir Lundestad (ed.), *Just Another Major Crisis? The United States and Europe since 2000.* New York: Oxford University Press.

Dumbrell, John (2009) *Clinton's Foreign Policy: Between the Bushes, 1992–2000.* London: Routledge.

Golgeier, James M. (1999) *Not Whether but When: The US Decision to Enlarge NATO.* Washington: Brookings.

Hyland, William G. (1999) *Clinton's World: Remaking American Foreign Policy.* Westport, CT: Praeger.

Kupchan, Charles A. (2003) *The End of the American Era: US Foreign Policy and the Geopolitics of the Twenty-First Century.* New York: Vintage.

Lundestad, Geir (2003) *The United States and Western Europe since 1945: From 'Empire' by Invitation to Transatlantic Drift.* Oxford: Oxford University Press.

9   A new order, 2001–2011

Shock to the system

On the morning of 11 September 2001, two hijacked commercial airplanes crashed into the twin towers of the World Trade Center in New York. A third plane hit the Pentagon in Washington, DC, while a fourth was brought down by resisting passengers in Pennsylvania. The attacks, quickly traced to the Al-Qaeda terrorist network headed by Osama bin Laden, triggered what the Bush administration would call the Global War on Terror (GWT). Across the board, Europeans expressed solidarity. *'Nous sommes tous Americains'* ('We are all Americans') headlined the French daily *Le Monde* on 12 September 2001.

Despite initial sympathy and willingness to cooperate, the European allies of the United States soon found themselves in opposition to some of the aspects of this 'first war of the 21st century'. Less than a year after the terrorist attacks in the United States, the American author Robert Kagan famously argued that it was 'time to stop pretending that Europeans and Americans share a common view of the world, or even that they occupy the same world [because] on major strategic and international questions today, Americans are from Mars and Europeans are from Venus'.[1] By 2003, as the United States led an invasion of Iraq, transatlantic relations appeared to be at an all-time low.

And yet, a decade after what became known as '9-11', the significance of the terrorist attacks to the evolution of international and transatlantic relations needs to be questioned. Other developments – not least the continued rise of China and the relative decline of the United States (and the 'West' more broadly) – appear equally, if not more, significant to the overall structure of the international system. Even by 2005, as George W. Bush began his second term in office, transatlantic relations were improving. While the United States and NATO continued to fight the war in Afghanistan that commenced in October 2001, the impact of the global economic and financial crisis of 2007–2008 would loom larger in the minds of policymakers and the general public on both sides of the Atlantic than the specific campaigns aimed at undermining terrorist networks. Dramatic though the impact of 9-11 and the Iraq War were, their role in the evolution of transatlantic relations would appear, in retrospect, less significant than most commentators suspected at the time.

'We are all Americans'

The outpouring of European sympathy and support for the United States in the aftermath of the attacks on the World Trade Center and Pentagon was as unprecedented as the attacks themselves. British Prime Minister Tony Blair, French President Jacques Chirac and German Chancellor Gerhard Schröder were quick to pledge their support to the United States. For the first (and so far only) time in its history, NATO invoked Article 5, declaring the attacks on the United States an attack on the entire alliance. As it became clear that the United States was going to attack Afghanistan – where Al-Qaeda had its base under the protection of the Taliban – the British and the French offered military assistance. When the UN Security Council passed a resolution calling for intensified anti-terrorist efforts, the Spanish government announced its willingness to send troops to Afghanistan.

The Bush administration eventually decided to leave NATO out of the Afghan campaign of 2001. Only the British played a meaningful role in the bombing that commenced on 7 October. The next day, when Spain, Italy, France and Germany publicly offered to send troops to Afghanistan, Bush simply said that NATO would contribute to the effort 'if we deem it necessary'. In the end, small contingents of European troops would make their way to Afghanistan, starting in November. But Washington was clearly uninterested in a multilateral campaign. Moreover, while essentially brushing aside the Europeans, America made strenuous efforts to secure bases and support from countries that were strategically important for operations in Afghanistan, such as Uzbekistan, Pakistan and Russia.

The Bush administration's decision to include only the British in the rapidly unfolding military campaign in Afghanistan made a certain amount of logistical sense. However, it did prompt a growing concern in Europe that the United States was becoming more nationalistic and unilateral. Bush's blunt rhetoric did little to dissuade such worries and opened a gap of perception soon after 11 September: while Bush usually talked about war and fashioned himself a war president, Jacques Chirac cautioned against using 'war' to describe the international situation after 9-11. When he said that the rest of the world was either 'with us or with the terrorists', his popularity soared in the United States. But across the Atlantic doubts about the wisdom of American policy began to emerge. In a basic sense, European leaders may well have wished to get involved in the Afghan campaign not simply as a show of solidarity but also as a way of having a restraining influence over the American-led effort. In Washington, those who resisted involving NATO – such as Secretary of Defense Donald Rumsfeld and Vice President Dick Cheney – were undoubtedly doing so in part to maintain maximum freedom of action for America.

Logistical issues were, in fact, an important argument against a multilateral effort. The Pentagon had been frustrated by its experience in coordinating with allies during the Kosovo campaign – indeed, when NATO began playing a more important role in Afghanistan after 2003, logistics immediately became more complicated as a number of countries placed restrictions on the specific role that their troops could play on the ground.

No matter what the reasons were behind the American decision to operate in an essentially unilateral manner in Afghanistan, the political impact on transatlantic relations was considerable. The French were particularly concerned, worrying that the Bush administration's actions indicated that Europe no longer mattered much in US strategic thinking. By November 2001, as the bombing campaign continued in Afghanistan, *Le Monde* reported that Europeans were worried about American policy, while the *New York Times* noted a growing public apprehension in Europe over the goals of Afghanistan bombings.

By early December 2001 Afghanistan was, for the most part, under the control of the United States and its Afghan allies (the most important of which was the so-called Northern Alliance). The initial phase of the war was over and the time to think about what to do with post-Taliban Afghanistan had arrived. The nation-building efforts that followed were to be a far more multilateral effort than the fighting war. In December and January 2002 two conferences held respectively in Germany and Japan focused on creating a new Afghan government and raising money for reconstruction. A UN Resolution authorized the formation of the International Security Assistance Force (ISAF) to secure the areas around Kabul and to support the interim administration – the Afghan Transitional Authority, headed by Hamid Karzai. Germany took charge of training a new police force, the British focused on battling the narcotics trade and Italy was responsible for reforming the legal system. In the autumn of 2003 NATO – under UN auspices – assumed full leadership of ISAF operations and its mission was expanded to include all of Afghanistan. The effort to stabilize the country would continue, with mixed success, for years to come.

By the time NATO stepped in to assume overall leadership of ISAF operations, Afghanistan had, however, faded as the centre-stage of the Bush administration's foreign policy, replaced by another, far more controversial, military operation.

The Bush doctrine

In the aftermath of 9-11 the Bush administration became increasingly concerned about the possibility that weapons of mass destruction (WMD) might fall into terrorist hands. Unnerved by the events of 11 September, the United States announced in December 2001 that it intended to withdraw from the 1972 Anti-Ballistic Missile (ABM) Treaty so that it could build a new missile defence system capable of protecting itself from limited nuclear strikes by so-called 'rogue states'. The Bush administration was not, however, thinking only of passive defence. In his 2002 State of the Union Address, President Bush went further, accusing Iran, Iraq and North Korea – three countries suspected of developing WMDs in secret – of constituting an 'axis of evil' that presented a clear threat to the international community. Moreover, Bush and others repeatedly argued, such threats should be pre-empted, lest another attack were to occur, possibly more deadly than 9-11. In September 2002 the Bush administration released its first National Security Strategy, which spelled out what would be dubbed the Bush Doctrine: the presumption that the United States had the right to use military force to 'pre-empt' a potential security threat.

Reserving the right to wage pre-emptive war was, of course, problematic on any number of rather significant levels. Most of all, it was seen as a violation of current international obligations and treaties, such as the UN Charter; US national security was all that counted for the world's lone superpower. Because the document did not, as one probably could not, define what amounted to a 'sufficient threat', the road was open to any number of military adventures to counter any number of real or trumped-up threats.

In the autumn of 2002, though, the Bush administration singled out Iraq as its main target. In a series of speeches and statements, representatives of the administration charged that Saddam Hussein, despite twelve years of economic sanctions, was harbouring WMDs and seeking afresh to achieve a nuclear capability. In fact, the Bush administration had been focusing on Iraq even before 11 September. In part this arose from the belief that the president's father had erred in 1991 when he had failed to push on to Baghdad and overthrow the Saddam regime. The terrorist attacks, however, made the situation even more pressing.

The removal of Saddam was now seen as a means of alleviating some of the reasons for America's unpopularity in the Middle East. So-called neo-conservatives in the United States believed that the 'liberation' of Iraq might initiate a swing towards more democratic government in the region and that, in turn, would bring more stability. Others argued that as long as Iraq remained an unpredictable pariah state, the United States had to maintain large military forces in Saudi Arabia. This was a problem because it allowed Al-Qaeda to generate support by declaring that 'infidels' were defiling the country that contained its holiest shrines (in the cities of Mecca and Medina). Further, there was a growing concern that failure to act might only lead to a worsening of the situation. The sanctions regime that had been overseen by the UN since 1990 was coming under increasing international attack for being an ineffective and immoral instrument that hurt ordinary Iraqis while doing nothing to undermine Saddam. But ending sanctions would give Iraq the space to reactivate its WMD programmes. These considerations, along with Bush's overwhelming domestic support for any action that might enhance American security, thus pushed the administration towards the decision to invade Iraq. In October 2002 Bush requested and received the permission of both the House of Representatives and the Senate to use force against Iraq.

For the Bush administration, gaining such overwhelming support inside the United States was the easy part of the Iraq War. Allies were something else. In the next months and years it became clear that the transatlantic unity that had been evident in the months immediately post 9-11 hardly translated into a blank cheque for the Bush administration to wage war with impunity. Quite the contrary: as the Iraq War unfolded despite widespread international opposition, the critics could easily charge that America was acting like the world's bully, a superpower on steroids.

A war of choice

The United States did not wish to launch the attacks on Iraq without support from the international community. Thus, Washington took its case to the United Nations. On 12 September 2002 President Bush made his initial case for the overthrow of Saddam Hussein in a speech to the UN Security Council in which he argued that Iraq, which had refused to cooperate with UN weapons inspectors since 1997, was continuing to develop WMDs. However, he failed to get UN authorization to use force because several influential countries, including France and Germany, were sceptical of the American claims. As a result, in November the UN Security Council hammered out a compromise: instead of an invasion, Security Council Resolution 1441 authorized further inspections and threatened 'serious consequences' for Iraq in case of non-compliance. Headed by the Swedish diplomat Hans Blix, the UN's new inspection team arrived in Baghdad on 18 November 2002, a week after the resolution had been passed.

Over the next four months the noose around Iraq tightened. American, British, Australian and selected other countries' troops began arriving in the Persian Gulf region; by mid-March 2003 they numbered about 200,000. In February 2003 Secretary of State Colin Powell made a strong effort to convince the UN Security Council that authorization for disarming Iraq, which was a euphemism for invasion, was necessary. Powell presented evidence, much of which was later discredited, of an ongoing Iraqi chemical and biological weapons programme. He further outlined Saddam's supposed links to Al-Qaeda and other terrorist organizations. The United States, supported by the UK and Spain, then submitted a resolution authorizing the use of force. Faced with a likely veto from France and Russia, the Americans later withdrew the resolution, but the preparations for invasion still went ahead. On 17 March Bush publicly demanded that Saddam Hussein and his two sons leave Iraq within two days. They did not. However, the remaining UN weapons inspectors took the hint and exited the country. On 20 March 2003 the American-led attack on Iraq – 'Operation Iraqi Freedom' – commenced, despite massive European (and even domestic American) scepticism over the necessity and wisdom of such an undertaking.

The military success of the invasion was unquestionable. On 9 April Baghdad was taken over by American forces and on 15 April the invasion was officially deemed to have achieved its goals. On 1 May 2003 President Bush made this clear by declaring 'mission accomplished'.

Although cheered by most Americans, Bush spoke much too soon. The Iraqi regime may have been defeated and Saddam himself – and a number of other leading figures of his regime – would soon be captured, tried and eventually executed. But Iraq was, for years to come, a chaotic and dangerous place. After the lop-sided 2003 military campaign in Iraq, Americans and the so-called coalition of the willing found themselves mired in an ongoing conflict over the future of Iraq. Terrorist attacks against occupiers, internal sectarian conflict and the flight of millions of refugees made Iraq into the most dangerous place on Earth. Elections were held in January 2005 and a new constitution approved in October of that year. But stability was long in coming, and serious doubts about American policy began to emerge within the United States. In late 2006, the Iraq Study Group (ISG), headed by former Secretary of State James Baker and former Congressman Lee Hamilton, released a report highly critical of the occupation policies.

Instead of the ISG report President Bush opted for an alternative course, recommended by a study conducted at the American Enterprise Institute, a conservative think tank. In 2007, to quell the growing tide of violence, the Bush administration commenced a new 'surge' of an additional 20,000 American troops. Although doubts remained about the effectiveness of this instalment, most observers claimed that the 'surge' had, by the summer of 2008, managed to cut back the number of violent incidents, hence offering a hope for some form of stability. Very slowly, American troops were starting to be withdrawn. After a peak of about 170,000 in late 2007, the numbers were down to about 150,000 a year later.

Throughout 2003–2008, the Iraq War remained, by and large, an American war. The Bush administration had wished to enlist as much European support as possible. Yet, for a combination of reasons, having to do with the purposes and costs of the war as well as domestic politics, Europeans were decidedly against stepping up to the plate. Only the British participated in a significant manner in the initial military campaign. But in early 2007 – coinciding with the American surge – the new Prime Minister Gordon Brown announced the gradual and full withdrawal of British troops. Other major NATO countries that had contributed to the Iraq effort after May 2003, but withdrew by 2007, included Italy, Netherlands and Spain. NATO as a whole only provided a training mission of 150 advisers that was established in 2004. Indeed, European contributions in Iraq were mainly window dressing; South Korea, for example, contributed more troops than Italy. Notable among the missing were France and Germany (although Germany provided some aid for training police officers).

The Iraq War was, in fact, the chief cause of an acrimonious political climate in transatlantic relations.

The Iraq War and transatlantic relations

The 2003 invasion and subsequent occupation of Iraq represented the height of post-Cold War American unilateralism. Throughout the build-up to the 2003 invasion, the Bush administration cast aside advice for caution and was not deterred by widespread anti-American – or anti-Bush – sentiments captured in Transatlantic Trends, an opinion survey first conducted in June 2003 by the German Marshall Fund. Among other questions, respondents from six European countries (the UK, France, Germany, Italy, the Netherlands, Poland and Portugal) were asked whether they approved of President Bush's leadership in foreign affairs. Only 30 per cent of Europeans did; with a mere 6 per cent saying that they approved 'very much'; in France over 80 per cent disapproved either 'somewhat' or 'very much'. Even in Great Britain critics of the US outnumbered supporters by 2 to 1. By 2004 the anti-Bush sentiment in Europe continued to rise, with 76 per cent of Europeans expressing disapproval of the president's handling of international politics. Yet a sufficient number of Americans felt otherwise. Bush went on to defeat his Democratic challenger, Senator John Kerry, in the November 2004 US presidential elections.

Indeed, during the months before and for several years after the occupation of Iraq there was much talk about a fundamental crisis in transatlantic relations. There were negative projections about NATO's future. Europeans – and a growing number of Americans – criticized the Bush administration's unilateralism. Critics were handed plenty of ammunition as American transgressions of international law and disrespect for basic human rights scandalized audiences around the world – prominent examples being their locking up suspected terrorists at Guantanamo Bay without granting them any access to legal representation, and torturing prisoners at Abu Ghraib in Iraq and other installations. The fact that no WMD were discovered in post-intervention Iraq led to a growing suspicion that the Bush administration – and its chief European ally, the Blair government in Britain – had deliberately misrepresented their case in the run-up to the Iraq War.

In 2003–2004 Americans did little to calm down these negative European attitudes. In addition to Bush's blunt rhetoric, other administration members scorned the countries that failed to support the Iraq War. In January 2003 Secretary of Defense Donald Rumsfeld made a separation between 'old Europe' (France, Germany and others who refused to support US policy on Iraq) and 'new Europe' (the countries that did acquiesce). France came in for special treatment. In the spring of 2003 jokes about 'cheese-eating surrender monkeys' and calls to rename french fries 'freedom fries' were legion. The Speaker of the House, Republican Dennis Hastert, even ruminated about boycotting Beaujolais wine.

Disturbing though they were to the many Atlanticists, European anti-Americanism and American anti-Europeanism were relative and passing phenomena. Following his re-election in November 2004, President Bush reshuffled his foreign policy team and set out to gradually ameliorate transatlantic relations. The departure of some of the architects of the Iraq War – such as Deputy Secretary of Defense Paul Wolfowitz in 2005 and Donald Rumsfeld a year later – was symbolically important. In February 2005 Condoleezza Rice, the former National Security Advisor who replaced Colin Powell as secretary of state in the second Bush term, toured Europe in a concerted effort to ameliorate relations. Although scepticism remained widespread, a number of observers were talking about a 'mid-winter thaw' in transatlantic relations. The 'time of insults and tough talk is over', one French newspaper commented.

The gradual decline in transatlantic tensions during Bush's second term was in part due to changes in leadership in Europe. In November 2005 Angela Merkel became the chancellor of Germany, replacing Gerhard Schröder, a persistent critic of America's intervention in Iraq. In May 2007 Jacques Chirac, another critic of US unilateralism, had been replaced as president of France by Nicolas Sarkozy, whose agenda included improving relations with the United States and taking his country fully back to NATO. While Bush remained an extremely unpopular figure in Europe, transatlantic relations were becoming increasingly cordial.

One factor that may have helped to ameliorate transatlantic tensions was a shared climate of fear. In the years following 9-11, several European countries were subjected to several terrorist attacks and plots that were associated with Al-Qaeda or other extremist Islamist movements. On 11 March 2004, only three days prior to general elections in Spain, ten bombs went off in four separate trains in Madrid, killing 191 people. On 7 July 2005 another series of bombs went off throughout London, resulting in 56 deaths. In 2006 and 2007 intended attacks were foiled by the local police in Germany. In fact, reports of various planned attacks were common within the EU, and although most acts of terrorism in Europe were the work of local groups (such as the Basque ETA), these reports played a role in increasing Islamophobia. The 2004 French ban against the use of traditional headscarves by female students, attacks against a mosque in Preston (UK) by youth gangs in 2006 and the Swiss ban on minarets in 2009 were all part of a pattern of xenophobia directed against Muslims in different parts of Europe.

Perhaps the major impact of Islamophobia in Europe and the United States has been to awaken fears, mostly unfounded, about 'Islamization'. The strength and impact of Islamophobia naturally varies from country to country. Yet it is at the same time a wide-spread transnational phenomenon and a very real problem to societies that tend to take pride in their reputation for religious freedom, free speech and tolerance.Such incidents reflected a common trend in North America and Europe. In 2006 Transatlantic Trends recorded a significant increase, on both sides of the Atlantic, in the belief that Islamic fundamentalism represented a major global threat. More than half of Americans and Europeans surveyed (56%) did not think that the values of Islam were compatible with democracy. At the same time, in the context of globalization and the so-called Global War on Terror, the concept of the 'West' appeared in danger of losing its meaning. While many in the United States and Western Europe embraced the notion of multiculturalism, others worried increasingly about the impact of large-scale immigration on 'traditional' values. In Europe, the ongoing enlargement of both NATO and, in particular, the European Union further exacerbated such concerns.

Box 9.1　Transatlantic Islamophobia

The terrorist attacks of 11 September 2001 sparked a wave of anti-Islam sentiment in the United States and Europe. In America, hate crimes directed against Muslims increased five-fold from 2000 to 2001. At least five people were killed. In Europe, reports highlighted a similar trend, with the number of anti-Muslim incidents on the increase, ranging from verbal abuse and remarks to random violent attacks. In the media, negative stereotypes were regularly aired. In short, on both sides of the Atlantic the terrorist attacks in the United States – and the subsequent bombings in London and Madrid – prompted a wave of populist Islamophobia.

There was nothing new in anti-Islam prejudice in the United States or Europe. Ever since the 1979 Iranian Revolution and the emergence of various radical Islamist groups – whether trans-national (like Al-Qaeda) or more locally oriented (like Hizh'bollah in Lebanon or Hamas in Palestine) – the 'West' had been confronted by the spectre of 'holy warriors' bent on destroying the United States and its allies (especially, of course, Israel). The rise in the number of Muslims living in North America and Europe caused various political parties to call for restrictions in immigration and for laws prohibiting the open practice of certain traditions. In 2004 the French instituted a headscarf ban in public schools. A Swiss referendum approved a ban on minarets in 2009. Norway, a founding member of the UN and NATO, as well as home to the Nobel Peace Prize, experienced perhaps the biggest shock when, in July 2011, an openly Islamophobic right-wing extremist killed 76 people in two attacks.

Further enlargements

NATO enlargement and Russia

The historically largest NATO enlargement (in terms of the number of new member countries) took place in 2004 when Bulgaria, Estonia, Latvia, Lithuania, Romania, Slovakia and Slovenia joined simultaneously. Five years later Albania and Croatia became part of the alliance that, 60 years after its formation, boasted a roster of 28 countries. Since the end of the Cold War, NATO had almost doubled its membership. In the process, the perceptions of core and periphery that had dominated the Western assessments for many decades – the geopolitics of the alliance – were profoundly transformed. The isolated southern flank (Greece and Turkey) was reunited to the core with a large land corridor through Romania and Bulgaria. The inclusion of a number of nations that had belonged to the former Yugoslavia attested to the growing stability in the Balkan region, further enhanced by the inclusion of Bosnia, Serbia and Montenegro in the Partnership for Peace (PfP) in 2006.

Potentially problematic was the fact that for the first time a region formerly possessed by the Soviet Union was taken into the organization (the three Baltic States). For Russia, NATO enlargement has always been a thorny issue but in the early 21st century Moscow's security concerns were further complicated by the Bush administration's plans to deploy parts of the missile defence system – intended to counter a potential Iranian nuclear threat – in Poland and the Czech Republic. In late 2001, the Bush administration had announced its withdrawal from the 1972 ABM Treaty as a precursor to plans for the new system. The Russian reaction had been swift: President Vladimir Putin announced that it was not bound by the 1993

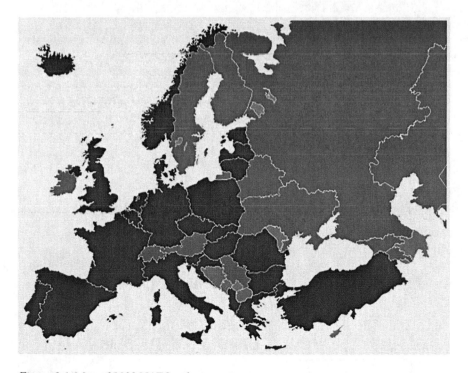

Figure 9.1 Map of 2009 NATO enlargement

Russian–American START II Treaty. To be sure, Presidents Bush and Putin signed a new treaty in May 2002 in which they agreed to 2200 deployable nuclear warheads each. But the relationship between Russia and the United States remained strained throughout the remainder of the Bush and Putin presidencies (which ended in January 2009 and May 2008 respectively).

As during the Cold War, strategic nuclear weapons remained essentially a bilateral Russian–American issue. But NATO enlargement – and the potential for further steps in this direction – made Russia increasingly wary about its influence in the so-called 'near abroad': the successor states of the former Soviet Union. In the early 2000s a number of these countries were exploring the possibility of NATO (and/or EU) membership.

The Ukrainian and Georgian crises

The November 2004 presidential elections in the Ukraine (aside from Russia, the largest successor state of the USSR), for example, witnessed a dramatic split between the pro-Russian incumbent Viktor Yanukovych and the Western-oriented challenger Viktor Yushchenko. Widespread protests against alleged electoral fraud in favour of Yanukovych – the so-called 'Orange Revolution' – resulted in a revote and a clear victory for Yushchenko (52% of the vote, compared to Yanukovych's 44%). After his inauguration in January 2005, however, Yushchenko's government ran into various problems, including an ongoing dispute about Russian energy imports (oil and natural gas), which made it increasingly difficult for him to follow up on the promises of gradually moving towards EU membership. His support base split. In 2010 Yanukovych emerged as the victor of the Ukrainian presidential election and moved to strengthen ties with Moscow.

While Ukraine's Orange Revolution dwindled, Georgia was engaged in a military confrontation with Russia. To Mikhail Saakashvili, the American-educated president since 2004 (following Georgia's 'Rose Revolution' the previous year), membership in NATO was a cornerstone of Georgia's security policy. In August 2008, a conflict over South Ossetia and Abkhazia, two separatist provinces, led to war with Russia. Moscow claimed to be acting on humanitarian grounds and referred to its troops as peacekeepers. Yet it was clear that Russian sympathies lay with the separatists. After successful mediation headed by the French government (which held the rotating EU presidency at the time), a ceasefire was reached. But while Russian forces retreated from uncontested areas of Georgia they remained in place in the two runaway regions.

At least in the short term, the unfolding of events in the Ukraine and Georgia had a significant impact on further NATO enlargement. In April 2008 NATO had approved Membership Action Plans for both Ukraine and Georgia. Eight months later, however, such plans were replaced by Annual National Programmes. This semantic twist implicitly acknowledged a sobering reality in the aftermath of Russia's military intervention in Georgia: NATO's enlargements in the next decade were extremely unlikely to incorporate any of the Soviet successor states. Russian power, even its less awesome post-Cold War form, was still an important geopolitical reality for the transatlantic alliance. NATO may well have reached its final eastern frontier.

The European Union: ever larger, somewhat deeper

Not to be outdone by NATO, the EU also continued to expand in the first decade of the 21st century. On 1 May 2004 a record number of ten countries – Cyprus, Czech Republic, Estonia, Hungary, Latvia, Lithuania, Malta, Poland, Slovakia and Slovenia – joined. They were followed only three years later by Bulgaria and Romania. Fifteen years after 12 countries formed the original EU with the signing of the Maastricht Treaty, the EU had grown to embrace 27 nations, covering virtually all of continental Europe. While a few – such as Norway and Switzerland – stubbornly resisted the idea of membership, several others – Albania, Croatia, Iceland, Macedonia, Montenegro, Serbia, Turkey – were awaiting or planning to join.

Measured by simple statistics, the 27-nation EU of the early 21st century was a formidable powerhouse. With four million square kilometres, the EU, if it had been a single country, would have ranked seventh in size, globally, in terms of area (after Australia but before India). Its combined population of almost 500 million was smaller than only those of China and India. The combined GDP of the 27 EU countries was higher than that of the United States: at US$16 trillion, it amounted to roughly a quarter of the world's GDP in 2010. For the first time in history, much of continental Europe also shared a common currency in the euro, which entered physical circulation at the beginning of 2002. Eleven countries comprised the original 'euro zone': Austria, Belgium, Finland, France, Germany, Ireland, Italy, Luxembourg, the Netherlands, Portugal and Spain. Greece joined in January 2001, just in time for the launch of the new notes and coins; later entrants have included Slovenia (2007), Cyprus (2008), Malta (2008), Slovakia (2009) and Estonia (2011). A decade after

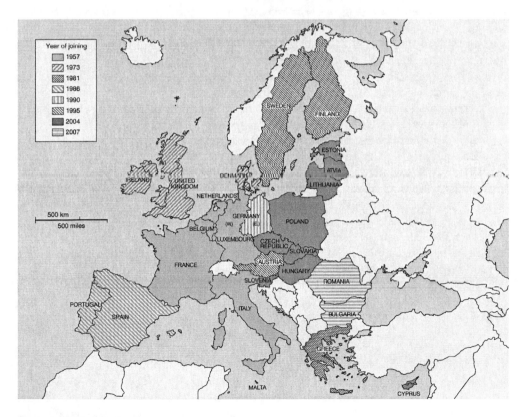

Source: adapted from www.un.org

Figure 9.2 Map of EU/EC enlargement, 1957–2007

initially replacing the traditional currencies of these countries, the euro zone (of 17 nations) had a population of around 330 million people (slightly larger than that of the United States) and a nominal GDP of some US$12.5 trillion (some 15 per cent smaller than America's and about 16 per cent of global GDP).

The growth of the EU did, however, present formidable challenges of governance and unity. The establishment of the common currency, for one, split the EU: of the original members, Great Britain, Denmark and Sweden opted out. Of the new entrants only four were economically stable enough to join; others failed to meet the financial criteria required for adopting the euro.

Beyond monetary questions, the enlarged EU was beset with a set of basic problems. How deep should and could integration of such a vast land mass be, populated with such a large population speaking in a multitude of languages and embracing a variety of cultures? How could the EU be governed in a democratic fashion? And, most importantly for transatlantic relations, would it ever be possible for the EU to embrace a common foreign and security policy? On what issues and through what institutions could the different national interests of Finland and Portugal, of Ireland and Bulgaria, be synchronized?

The EU remains, in fact, a constant work in progress. The multitude of institutions – the European Parliament, the European Council, the European Commission and others – often have overlapping competencies, a situation further complicated by the continued relevance of national prerogatives and institutions. This is not least the case in the area of foreign and security policy; the obvious differences between some of the largest members of the EU – such as Britain, Spain and Poland on the one hand, and Germany and France on the other – about the Iraq War exemplified the lack of a unified approach. Efforts to move towards a more unified structure of EU foreign policy were put in place by the creation of the office of the High Representative – essentially the chief diplomat of the EU – in 1999. A decade later, in the 2009 Treaty of Lisbon, the High Representative's powers were enhanced. Yet the current holder of the post, Britain's Catherine Ashton, has yet to emerge as a powerful diplomatic player rather than a more ceremonial spokesperson.

While 'European' foreign policy remains more an aspiration than a reality, it is difficult to talk about EU–US relations in a strict sense. In the realm of security policy, transatlantic relations are still conducted mainly within the context of NATO or in a bilateral manner. The United States sends an ambassador to the EU. But this post is not considered as important as, say, that of the chief American representative to NATO or to one of the larger European countries (Great Britain, France, Germany).

In short, the enlarged EU's sheer size and combined wealth mattered to the United States. But the inability of the 27 nations to forge a true union with a common foreign policy often made it seem as though, globally, the European Union was far less significant than the sum of its parts. The financial crisis that shook the world economy in 2007–2008 further exacerbated the divisions among EU members about the proper depth of integration in the early 21st century.

The 'Great Recession'

In 2008, terms like 'credit crunch', and 'fiscal stimulus', became part of everyday language around the industrialized world. After a series of speculative bubbles began to burst in 2007, the economies of the United States, Europe and Japan were gradually knocked into their first simultaneous recession since World War II. The financial crisis was linked to reckless lending practices by financial institutions that had produced a massive housing and equities bubble. Basically, while housing prices continued to rise in the early 2000s, mortgages were given without sufficient collateral. As housing loan losses began to pile up in 2007, other risky loans and over-inflated asset prices were exposed. The fall of one of America's most trusted financial institutions, Lehman Brothers, in September 2008, finally produced a major panic, with a rapid decline in stock and housing prices in the United States and, given the interconnected nature of the global marketplace, in Europe and Japan.

On both sides of the Atlantic the response was massive public financial assistance. In the United States, the Bush administration pushed for a $700 billion package to purchase what was termed 'troubled mortgage-related assets' (in essence, mortgages with no hope of repayment), or what became known as 'toxic assets'. The bill passed both houses of Congress in October 2008, only a month prior to the US presidential election. At the same time the British government approved an even bigger package, amounting to US$850 billion, to rescue the nation's troubled banks. Similar, if smaller, efforts were made in Germany, Netherlands, Belgium, Denmark and other countries. Overall, though, the financial crisis of 2008 appeared to have less of an impact in most parts of Europe than in the United States, resulting in uncharitable criticism about the pitfalls of the Anglo-American economic model compared to a 'continental' one.

The G20

While the initial action was spearheaded by individual countries, the so-called Great Recession of 2008 also heralded the growing significance of international cooperation beyond the 'traditional' leaders of the world economy. In particular, by late 2008, the Group of 20 Finance Ministers and Central Bank Governors (G20) was set to become a significant forum for combating the effects of the financial crisis. Founded in 1999 in response to previous economic crises, the G20 membership comprised of 19 finance ministers of the largest economies in the world (from Brazil and Argentina to Saudi Arabia, India, Russia and China) as well as a representative of the European Union. Unlike the G7, the G20 included important industrial and emerging-market countries from all regions of the world. Together, member countries represent around 90 per cent of global gross national product and 80 per cent of world trade (including EU intra-trade), as well as two-thirds of the world's population. Ideally, the G20's economic weight and broad membership gave it a high degree of legitimacy and influence over the management of the global economy and financial system. Starting in Washington in late 2008, the leaders of G20 countries have met at regular high-level summits.

It is difficult to assess the long-term impact of the Great Recession. Yet, in the context of transatlantic relations, it is safe to say that the response to the financial crisis highlighted the increasingly globalized nature of economic power. The United States, Canada, Japan and Western Europe were all represented in the G20. But the presence of a number of rising countries signalled that major economic decisions affecting the globe could no longer be taken in isolation from the parts of the world that had previously been dubbed the 'Third World'. This was even more the case as the economies of China and India continued to grow in 2008–2010 while those of North America and the European Union (with the exception of Poland) declined. The continual decline of the value of the major 'transatlantic currencies' – the US dollar, the British pound and the euro – as well as the mounting public debt that plagued most national economies on both sides of the Atlantic was further evidence of a severe economic downturn.

What might be described as a positive aspect of the Great Recession, however, was the urgent need for transatlantic cooperation that appeared a necessity for any sustainable recovery to be possible. And, for once, the timing of the American elections was opportune.

America at a crossroads

George W. Bush's presidency ended in diametrically opposite circumstances to that of his predecessor. In the early 21st century, commentators had heralded the start of the second American century and squabbled over whether the United States ruled over a global empire or simply exercised power as a liberal hegemon. By 2008 renewed talk about the decline of America was popular. To be sure, it was clear that America was a military superpower without equal. With a defence budget of $700 billion, the United States was responsible for 43 per cent of global military spending. This was six times that of China, 12 times that of Russia and, for comparison, 98 times that of Iran. All told, the United States had increased its spending dramatically both in absolute and relative terms, and now allocated more money to defence than the next 17 countries in the world combined. If military spending was a measure of security, the United States was very safe indeed.

Economically, however, the United States was in dire straits. The budget surpluses of the late Clinton years had become consistent deficits after 2001, hiking up America's national debt. In late 2008 unemployment was just over 6.5 per cent and set to rise steadily towards the 10 per cent mark in the next two years. To be sure, the United States retained its position as the largest single economy in the world, with 20.3 per cent of global domestic product in 2008. But rankings had changed: the second largest economy was China, and India had moved to the number four position, behind Japan (the EU, as a whole, still outweighed even the US). More disturbingly, US growth rates had not only stalled but turned negative in Bush's last year in office (−6% in the last quarter of 2008), while China and India boasted growth rates approaching double digits.

'Change' with Obama

Thus, it was no wonder that proposals for a new American foreign policy were abundant during the 2008 presidential race. The eventual winner, Democratic Senator Barack Obama from Illinois, promised to end the war in Iraq, embark on a diplomatic initiative with Iran without preconditions, pursue a new, comprehensive strategy vis-à-vis Russia, strengthen the transatlantic alliance, combat environmental change, stop genocide in Darfur, and fight poverty throughout Africa. This sounded impressive: if you only elect Obama, the Bush doctrine would be dead and buried. America would have a new leader who would not be driven by simple-minded ideological excesses. The 44th president would reverse course, bring back thousands of Americans from a mishandled war, and dazzle the world with his winning diplomacy. He would make America respected again, not (just) because of its military prowess but by using the irresistible appeal of the American dream of which he was such a shining example. Soft power was 'in', hard power was 'out'. Unilateralism was a thing of the past.

Certainly, in 2008 most American voters cared more about the domestic economy than foreign policy. But here, also, Obama seemed to offer a steadier hand than his Republican opponent, Senator John McCain. As the Bush administration groped to find a response to the financial crisis, Obama's campaign cast their candidate as the one who had the best programme for renewing America's fortunes. Although flirting with populist protectionism in order to court votes, Obama reassured his foreign audiences that under his watch there would be more, not less, international cooperation to combat the Great Recession.

The message and the messenger were greeted with much enthusiasm around the world, particularly in Europe. In many people's minds the election of the first African-American president showed how far the United States had progressed in its multiculturalism, while Europe – old and new – was still stuck in the ancient regime of white rule. Obama's inauguration was one of the highest-rated media events throughout Europe in early 2009, with commentators around the continent heralding the historic moment upon us all. Almost overnight, the negative view of the United States that had become commonplace during the Bush presidency was gone. It was as if the US president had been 'elected' on both sides of the Atlantic. Soon after the election Mathias Müller von Blumencron, the editor of the influential German magazine *Spiegel*, even referred to Obama as the 'world's president'.[2]

Box 9.2 Document extract: Barack Obama's speech in Strasbourg (3 April 2009)[3]

The economic crisis has proven the fact of our interdependence in the most visible way yet. Not more than a generation ago, it would have been difficult to imagine that the inability of somebody to pay for a house in Florida could contribute to the failure of the banking system in Iceland. Today what's difficult to imagine is that we did not act sooner to shape our future …

The one way forward – the only way forward – is through a common and persistent effort to combat fear and want wherever they exist. That is the challenge of our time – and we can not fail to meet it, together …

We must renew our institutions, our alliances. We must seek the solutions to the challenges of this young century. This is our generation. This is our time. And I am confident that we can meet any challenge as long as we are together.

Such an effort is never easy. It's always harder to forge true partnerships and sturdy alliances than to act alone, or to wait for the action of somebody else. It's more difficult to break down walls of division than to simply allow our differences to build and our resentments to fester. So we must be honest with ourselves. In recent years we've allowed our Alliance to drift. I know that there have been honest disagreements over policy, but we also know that there's something more that has crept into our relationship. In America, there's a failure to appreciate Europe's leading role in the world. Instead of celebrating your dynamic union and seeking to partner with you to meet common challenges, there have been times where America has shown arrogance and been dismissive, even derisive.

But in Europe, there is an anti-Americanism that is at once casual but can also be insidious. Instead of recognizing the good that America so often does in the world, there have been times where Europeans choose to blame America for much of what's bad.

On both sides of the Atlantic, these attitudes have become all too common. They are not wise. They do not represent the truth. They threaten to widen the divide across the Atlantic and leave us both more isolated. They fail to acknowledge the fundamental truth that America cannot confront the challenges of this century alone, but that Europe cannot confront them without America.

So I've come to Europe this week to renew our partnership, one in which America listens and learns from our friends and allies, but where our friends and allies bear their share of the burden. Together, we must forge common solutions to our common problems.

So let me say this as clearly as I can: America is changing, but it cannot be America alone that changes. We are confronting the greatest economic crisis since World War II. The only way to confront this unprecedented crisis is through unprecedented coordination.

Obama's popularity was evident during the president's first trip to Europe in April 2009, as he used all his persuasive powers to try and forge an international consensus behind his major foreign policy goals. The three key issues that he focused upon – the economic and financial crisis, Afghanistan, and nuclear proliferation (and nuclear strategy more broadly) – set the stage for the transatlantic relations for the remainder of the year. Indeed, it was clear that throughout this whirlwind tour of Europe (with additional stops in Istanbul, Ankara and Iraq), Obama managed to earn, not unexpectedly, the adulation of crowds and public praise from European leaders. According to Transatlantic Trends, Obama enjoyed 77 per cent approval ratings within the EU and Turkey for his handling of international affairs. And he earned the trust of the Norwegian Nobel Committee, which awarded the American president the much-coveted Nobel Peace Prize in October 2009. As Assistant Secretary of State Philip Gordon exclaimed in an interview with the German magazine *Spiegel* in November 2009: 'there is more transatlantic unity than at almost any time in the post-World War II period'.[4] That may have been the case. But the change in American policy was relative.

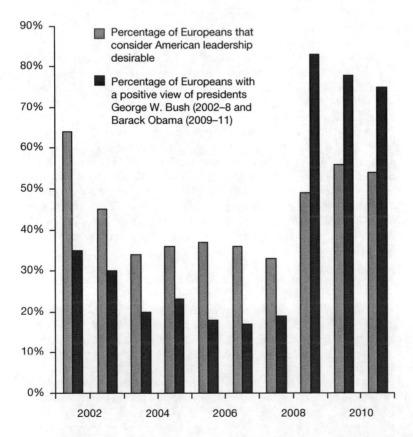

Source: Transatlantic Trends, http://trends.gmfus.org/ (last consulted: 26 September 2011)

Figure 9.3 The 'Obama bounce'

Obama's wars, NATO's wars

One of the striking things in 2009 was the amount of continuity from Bush to Obama. The new administration continued the gradual withdrawal that the Bush administration had announced in the autumn of 2008; in August 2010, the last American combat troops left Iraq. Yet a suspiciously large contingent of 50,000 American military personnel stayed behind; in the summer of 2011, 46,000 Americans were still in Iraq. Other countries had withdrawn their troops even before Obama took office. While winding down the Iraq 'war of choice', Obama escalated US commitment to the Afghan 'war of necessity' by deploying additional troops to Afghanistan, and ordering a series of deadly strikes against targets in Pakistani territory. Of course, the 2 May 2011 spectacular killing of Osama bin Laden brought some closure to many Americans (and others) who had been touched by the attacks of 11 September 2001. But the war on terror – even if no longer officially called that – went on.

Obama did, though, manage to make the war in Afghanistan into a more multilateral effort. By the summer of 2011 almost 50 countries – all NATO nations and an assortment of other European, Asian and Pacific countries – contributed to the ISAF. Yet two things had not changed. First, the United States bore the brunt of the war effort (90,000 out of a total 133,000 ISAF troops were American), with Great Britain sending the second largest contingency (9000). Second, the Americans were stationed in the most dangerous areas of the country while many other countries had sent their troops to help in the reconstruction, rather than pacification, of Afghanistan. In the end, for all his considerable charm and persuasive skills, Barack Obama found it very hard to convince his transatlantic allies that they needed to increase their contribution to the Afghan cause. Indeed, in the spring of 2009 European leaders praised the new strategy in Afghanistan. But they did so with a caveat that was neatly summed up by the French president. 'We completely support the new American strategy in Afghanistan', exhorted Nicolas Sarkozy during a press conference in April 2009.[5]

As far as most Europeans were concerned the war in Afghanistan was America's fight, not a transatlantic undertaking.

A new NATO?

If only due to the pressure of events, NATO was transforming into something that would have been hardly recognizable to its originators. At the November 2010 NATO Summit in Lisbon, the alliance unveiled its new Strategic Concept. It emphasized three basic points. First, there was the ritualistic reaffirmation of the notion of collective defence, based on Article 5 of the 1949 Treaty. Second, the Strategic Concept stressed the importance of conflict management wherever it affects transatlantic security. This was a rather broad and forward-looking concept that implied that NATO was to play a more active role in future out-of-area crises; Afghanistan was not an isolated case. Third, NATO pledged its commitment to the notion of cooperative security – towards forging partnerships (such as the Russia–NATO one) and promoting arms control, non-proliferation and disarmament.

Crucially, the alliance also stressed the need to keep its door open to new members. But the main point seemed clear: dealing with out-of-area issues was embraced as one of NATO's key missions. In a sense, the Strategic Concept implied NATO's willingness to go global if need be. Ironically, in the months following the adoption of the new Strategic Concept, NATO countries faced a series of events that could be viewed as demanding action on the part of the alliance.

Transatlantic relations and the 'Arab Spring'

The Arab Spring started in Tunisia with a series of demonstrations – some of them violent – against the 23-year rule of President Zine El Abidine Ben Ali in December 2010. On 14 January 2011, Ben Ali resigned and left for exile in Saudi Arabia. His ruling party was dissolved. Within weeks of Ben Ali's ousting, protest movements – making use of social networking media such as Facebook and Twitter – were challenging the legitimacy of other long-term rulers in North Africa and the Middle East. Most dramatically, Egypt's President Hosni Mubarak was compelled to resign in February 2011. He had been in power for three decades.

Some of the uprisings turned violent. In Libya, Muammar Gaddafi – who had ruled the country since 1968 – refused to give in to the demonstrators' demands and faced an outright civil war in February 2011. His opponents set up an interim government in the eastern city of Benghazi. As violence escalated and Gaddafi threatened his opponents with extinction, the United Nations Security Council adopted Resolution 1973, authorizing 'all necessary measures' to protect Libyan civilians. Citing humanitarian concerns, NATO countries (France, Great Britain and the United States) took the lead in enforcing a no-fly zone over Libya; in essence this amounted to the commencement of a bombing campaign against the forces that remained loyal to Gaddafi. Yet, despite initial success, the rebels failed to win a decisive victory and, by the summer of 2011, Libya was embroiled in a bloody civil war. Finally, in late August, the anti-Gaddafi forces captured the capital, effectively deposing the longest-standing dictatorship in the Arab world. On 20 October Gaddafi was killed.

Meanwhile, in Syria, the government of President Bashar al-Assad ruthlessly suppressed numerous demonstrations throughout the spring and summer of 2011. Other concurrent events in the so-called Arab Spring included protests and riots in Algeria, Bahrain, Iraq, Jordan, Morocco, Oman, Saudi Arabia and Yemen. Only in the last case did the unrest provoke the rapid exit of a long-term ruler, President Ali Abdullah Saleh.

Out-of-area dilemmas and burden-sharing

The Arab Spring provided another test of leadership and unity for the transatlantic alliance. The Libyan case, in particular, galvanized support behind a humanitarian intervention that could easily have led to the presence of land forces with a subsequent occupation and arduous nation-building effort. But with the lessons of Iraq and the ongoing conflict in Afghanistan fresh in the minds of politicians and the general public alike, Americans and Europeans relied on the use of air power. As of September 2011 this policy – more akin to the allied efforts in Bosnia and Kosovo in the 1990s than to the ones in the aftermath of 9-11 – appeared to have been relatively successful.

NATO's participation in the Libyan war also rekindled debates about burden-sharing and alliance unity. Only 8 out of 28 NATO members actively participated in the war. Some of them even ran out of ammunition, and Italy withdrew its aircraft carrier in the middle of the conflict because the Berlusconi government needed to cut expenses. The Americans' frustration with European performance boiled over in June 2011, when the then-Secretary of Defense Robert Gates warned that NATO faced a 'dim and dismal' future.

Given the high degree of transatlantic cooperation in Libya, many Europeans were offended by such remarks. In particular, the Libyan case saw Europeans – for the first time – showing a willingness to assume more responsibility for security challenges in their neighbourhood. In contrast with the early 1990s, when Europeans essentially shrank from action in the Balkans until it was too late and the Americans stepped in to 'save the day', NATO's European members both pushed for the military response to the Libyan crisis and took, when authorized to do so, decisive military action. The United States, already overstretched in Afghanistan and still maintaining a sizeable presence in Iraq, could take a back seat while the Europeans absorbed most of the risks and costs of the ultimately successful war. In the case of Libya, the Obama administration had managed to elicit more burden-sharing from Europeans than virtually any of its predecessors. In practice, Americans played a central role in the initial bombings but gradually turned most of them to the allies.

The Arab Spring and, in particular, the Libyan campaign may well have triggered a significant change in transatlantic security cooperation. Most significantly, 2011 saw the first large-scale NATO military operation not dominated by the United States (aside from the first few weeks of the campaign). To be sure, not all Europeans were eager to engage in Libya, the most notable bystander being Germany. Yet, particularly in an era of austerity and the growing reluctance of the United States to embark on costly military adventures, the evidence of an increased European role in the security field in its 'near abroad' heralded a potentially significant shift. In Libya, citing humanitarian concerns, European governments acted swiftly, and helped the rebels win the war. In fact, Leon Panetta, the new US secretary of defence, struck a very different note from his predecessor by praising NATO's Libyan operation as an example of international cooperation. To Americans, the eventual success in Tripoli seemed to herald the beginning of a new era when European leaders were willing to assume greater responsibility for the security in their own neighbourhood. While the long-term significance of the Libyan campaign remains uncertain, transatlantic security relations were experiencing an unprecedented 'multilateral moment' in 2011.

Conclusion

The decade since the dramatic events of 11 September 2001 saw turbulence in all major areas of transatlantic relations. In the security field, the Bush administration's aggressive response framed the agenda and raised doubts about the durability of the transatlantic alliance. Most NATO allies stood firm as the Americans initiated military action in Afghanistan. Yet the resistance of the United States to accept its allies' invocation of Article 5 and, more importantly, the series of decisions that ultimately led to the toppling of Saddam Hussein called into question the multilateral concept that was supposedly at the foundation of NATO. As Americans occupied Iraq, only the British offered significant support. Others, particularly the French and the Germans, were openly critical of what they saw as American unilateralism. The political crisis that ensued was the most acrimonious of the post-Cold War era.

But the crisis, like so many others before it, did not endure. By 2005 the United States was making an effort to repair its relations with Europe. Although Iraq remained an American preoccupation, as NATO celebrated its sixtieth birthday in 2009, the alliance was playing an increasingly significant role in the ongoing conflict in Afghanistan. Most Europeans took heart from the fact that the new US president, Barack Obama, was saying all the right things about the need for renewing transatlantic cooperation. By 2011 NATO leaders celebrated the heavily European effort in the Libyan campaign. In retrospect, the post-9-11 tensions appeared to have been yet another aberration, rather than a harbinger of a more distant, if not openly confrontational, transatlantic relationship.

Ten years after 9-11, however, another crisis casts a large shadow over the future of the transatlantic community. Economically, the prospects for the United States and Europe look bleak. While still home to the most prosperous populations on Earth, the transatlantic economic space was beset by debt crises and high unemployment. Meanwhile, other parts of the world – for example, China, India and Brazil – still boomed. There was nothing new about the warnings of decline that became increasingly voluminous among observers on both sides of the Atlantic. But the possibility that the global pre-eminence of the United States and the remarkable construction of the European Union were under threat signalled a potentially far more significant shift in the global constellation of power than the successes or failures in dealing with terrorism.

In the end, the evolution of transatlantic relations in the first decade of the 21st century exemplified the dual nature that has been characteristic of *pax transatlantica* since the end of World War II. As throughout the Cold War era and in the 1990s, Americans and Europeans did not see eye-to-eye on a number of issues, clashing in a supposedly unprecedented (and many thought virtually irreparable) manner over questions related to security. Americans continued acting unilaterally when they deemed it necessary, prompting, quite predictably, a series of complaints from their European counterparts. Yet while conflict remained a constant feature of the transatlantic relationship, the underlying bonds remained in place. Despite widespread gloom, there was never serious anxiety that NATO would disintegrate. In fact, it did the opposite and enlarged. While the economic crisis raised the

---

Box 9.3 Just another crisis? Change and continuity in transatlantic disagreements

The crisis in transatlantic relations in the early 21st century sparked a wave of speculation about the end of the transatlantic alliance. In 2003 the US-led and British-supported invasion of Iraq had created a seemingly irreparable breach between Washington and London, on the one hand, and much of continental Europe on the other. While the Bush administration celebrated the 'coalition of the willing' that quickly destroyed Saddam Hussein's regime, anti-war protesters in European capitals admonished American unilateralism. As anti-Americanism hit new heights in Europe, there were calls in the United States to rename french fries 'freedom fries' and ban the import of French red wine.

After 2005, however, with George W. Bush installed in the White House for another term, calm began to return to transatlantic relations. New European leaders – particularly Angela Merkel in Germany and Nicolas Sarkozy in France – made an effort to repair the rift caused by Iraq. The second Bush administration did the same, acknowledging its need for a continued partnership with the old continent. To some, it appeared that the bust-up had been, as Geir Lundestad's 2008 book title suggested, *Just Another Major Crisis*.

Only time will tell. On the one hand, it is clear that there have been many 'unprecedented' and 'major' crises before. Whether over out-of-area questions (for example, Suez and Vietnam), economic issues (tariff rules in particular) or cultural concerns (about 'Americanization'), Europeans and Americans have found themselves in continual disagreements since 1945. But the partnership has continued, and the transatlantic community has survived.

On the other hand, the context in which transatlantic relations operate in the 21st century has significantly changed. Europe no longer depends on America economically (although it still seems to do so in the security realm). Other nations and regions are increasingly challenging the transatlantic dominance of the global economy. Indeed, the relatively new and uncomfortable shared reality for countries sharing the transatlantic economic space is that their relative power is in decline. The big question for the future is whether this will prove to be a uniting factor or yet another cause for future 'major' crises.

spectre of protectionism, it actually produced closer transatlantic consultation. As on so many occasions in the past, the passions of the day had a tendency to wither away and give way to reasoned arguments about the need to preserve the transatlantic community.

There is no guarantee that this historical pattern that has characterized the evolution of transatlantic relations will continue indefinitely. A different global economic structure or the emergence of a dramatically altered security environment might well cause Americans and Europeans to rethink their respective allegiances. The record of the past six decades does, however, suggest that the transatlantic community is not in danger of imminent disintegration.

Suggested further reading

Bindi, Federiga (ed.) (2010) *The Foreign Policy of the European Union: Assessing Europe's Role in the World*. Washington, DC: Brookings.

Calleo, David (2009) *Follies of Power: America's Unipolar Fantasy*. New York: Cambridge University Press.

Daalder, Ivo and James Lindsay (2003) *America Unbound: The Bush Revolution in Foreign Policy*. Washington, DC: Brookings.

Hanhimäki, Jussi M. (2010) 'The Obama administration and transatlantic security: problems and prospects', in Jussi Hanhimäki, Georges-Henri Soutou and Basil Germond (eds), *The Routledge Handbook of Transatlantic Security*. London: Routledge.

Kagan, Robert (2003) *Of Paradise and Power: America and Europe in the New World Order*. New York: Knopf.

Lundestad, Geir (ed.) (2008) *Just Another Major Crisis? The United States and Europe since 2000*. New York: Oxford University Press.

Notes

1 American commitment to Europe, 1945–1949

1 Genoud, 1961, pp. 103–9.
2 'The Sinews of Peace' (or 'Iron Curtain') speech delivered by Winston Churchill on 5 March 1946, in Fulton, Missouri. In Hanhimäki and Westad (2004, pp. 47–8).
3 Speech by James F. Byrnes, United States Secretary of State 'Restatement of US Policy on Germany' Stuttgart, 6 September 1946. http://usa.usembassy.de/etexts/ga4-460906.htm (accessed 3 October 2011).
4 President Harry S. Truman's address before a Joint Session of Congress, 12 March 1947. In Hanhimäki and Westad, 2004, pp. 116–18.
5 Speech by George Marshall US Secretary of State at Harvard University, 5 June 1947. In Hanhimäki and Westad, 2004, pp. 121–2.

2 Institutional frameworks, 1949–1957

1 'Eisenhower Doctrine', 5 January 1957. http://millercenter.org/president/speeches/detail/3360 (accessed 3 October 2011).

3 Tension and coexistence, 1957–1961

1 Declaration of the North Atlantic Council, 16 December 1958. www.nato.int/cps/en/SID-0F390516-41373721/natolive/official_texts_17646.htm (accessed 3 October 2011).
2 Dwight D. Eisenhower, 'Radio and television report to the American people: Security in the free world', 16 March 1959. Online by Gerhard Peters and John T. Woolley, *The American Presidency Project*. www.presidency.ucsb.edu/ws/?pid=11682 (accessed 3 October 2011).
3 John F. Kennedy, 'Address of Senator John F. Kennedy Accepting the Democratic Party Nomination for the Presidency of the United States – Memorial Coliseum, Los Angeles', 15 July 1960. Online by Gerhard Peters and John T. Woolley, *The American Presidency Project*. www.presidency.ucsb.edu/ws/?pid=25966 (accessed 3 October 2011).

4 Challenged America, 1961–1972

1 Quoted in Buffet, 2002, p. 74.
2 Record of NSC Meeting, 31 January 1963. *Foreign Relations of the United States* (FRUS), 1961–1963, vol. XIII, p. 163.
3 Quoted in Peyrefitte, 1994–2000, vol.1, p. 319.
4 Johnson, 1972, p. 305.
5 From www.nato.int/cps/en/natolive/official_texts_26700.htm (accessed 16 September 2011).
6 Quoted in Pascaline Winand, 1993, p. 300.
7 Quoted in Lundestad, 1998, p. 102.
8 Quoted in Niedhart,2008, p. 125.
9 Cited in Logevall, 2003, p. 7.

5 Atlantic distance, 1973–1983

1 Department of State bulletin, 14 May 1973.
2 Quoted in Möckli, 2010, pp. 201–2.
3 Cited in Schulz and Schwartz, 2010, p. 363.
4 Lord Cromer, British ambassador to the United States, cited in Noble, 2010, p. 230.
5 Quoted in Crain, 2009, p. 182.
6 Cited in Hanhimäki, 2003, p. 37.
7 Cited in Zanchetta, 2010, p. 143.
8 Citations in Fischer, 2010, pp. 269–72 and Collins, 2007, pp. 204–6.
9 Quoted in Young, 2010, p. 294.
10 Reagan, 1990, p. 547.

6 Walls come down, 1984–1989

1 Cited in Fischer, 2010, pp. 272–3.
2 Governmental declaration by Helmut Kohl, 13 October 1982.
3 Letter from Gorbachev to Reagan (November 1985), quoted in Dockrill, 2005, p. 109. Reagan's speech at Congress (November 1985), quoted in Powaski, 2000, p. 55.
4 *Official Journal of the European Communities*, 29 July 1987.
5 Quoted in Zubok, 1996, p. 94.
6 Richard Burt quoted in Wells, 2006, p. 302.
7 Quoted in Loth, 2002, p. 197.
8 Quoted in Collins, 2007, p. 225.
9 Bush and Scowcroft, 1998, p. 64.
10 Quoted in Loth, 2002, p. 205.
11 Quoted in Sarotte, 2009, p.43.

7 Transitions and uncertainties, 1989–1995

1 George H. W. Bush, 'Address Before a Joint Session of Congress', 6 March 1991. John T. Woolley and Gerhard Peters, *The American Presidency Project*. Online at www.presidency.ucsb.edu/ws/?pid=19364 (accessed May 27, 2011).
2 Cited in Sarotte, 2010, p. 132.
3 Cited in Engel, 2010, p. 33.
4 Adapted from http://eur-lex.europa.eu/en/treaties/dat/11992M/htm/11992M.html.
5 Cited in Lundestad, 2003, p. 244.
6 Cited in Lundestad, 2003, p. 243.

8 Enlargement, integration and globalization, 1995–2001

1 Grant, 1999.
2 Steel, 1995, p. 88.
3 Kennan, 1996, p. 330.
4 Cited in Lundestad, 2003, p. 259.
5 NATO Strategic Concept, 24 April 1999. www.nato.int/cps/en/natolive/official_texts_27433.htm (accessed 19 June 2011).
6 www.nato.int/cps/en/natolive/official_texts_27433.htm (accessed 22 September 2011).
7 Cited in Hanhimäki et al., 2010, p. 269.
8 'The Iraq Liberation Act of 1998', 31 October 1998. Public Law 105–338. http://frwebgate.access.gpo.gov/cgi-bin/getdoc.cgi?dbname=105_cong_public_laws&docid=f:publ338.105.pdf (accessed 14 November 2011).
9 Auersweld and Garofano, 2003, p. 84.

9 A new order, 2001–2011

1 Kagan, 2002.
2 Cited in Hanhimäki et al., 2010, p. 273.

3   www.whitehouse.gov/the_press_office/Remarks-by-President-Obama-at-Strasbourg-Town-Hall/ (accessed 25 September 2011).
4   'Obama-Vertrauter   Gordon',   *Spiegel*,   6   November   2009.   www.spiegel.de/politik/ deutschland/0,1518,659658,00.html (accessed 14 November 2011).
5   Sarkozy cited in 'Obama asks NATO for help in Afghan war', *MSNBC News*, 3 April 2009. www. msnbc.msn.com/id/30025192/ (accessed 14 November 2011).

References

Works cited

Auersweld, Philip and John Garofano (eds) (2003) *Clinton's Foreign Policy: A Documentary Record*. New York: Kluwer Law International.

Brown, J. and W. R. Louis (eds) (1999) *The Oxford History of the British Empire. Volume IV: The Twentieth Century*. Oxford: Oxford University Press.

Buffet, Cyril (2002) 'De Gaulle, the bomb and Berlin: How to use a political weapon', in John Gearson and Kori Schake (eds) *The Berlin Wall Crisis: Perspectives on Cold War Alliances*, pp. 73–95. Basingstoke, UK: Palgrave.

Bush, George and Brent Scowcroft (1998) *A World Transformed*. New York: Knopf.

Collins, Robert M. (2007) *Transforming America: Politics and Culture in the Reagan Years*. New York: Columbia UP.

Crain, Andrew Downer (2009) *The Ford Presidency: A History*. Jefferson, NC: McFarland.

Dockrill, Saki Ruth (2005) *The End of the Cold War Era: The Transformation of the Global Security Order*. London: Hodder Arnold.

Engel, Jeffrey (2010) 'A better world … but don't get carried away: The foreign policy of George H. W. Bush', *Diplomatic History* 34(1): 25–46.

Fischer, Beth (2010) 'US foreign policy under Reagan and Bush', in Melvyn P. Leffler and Odd Arne Westad, *The Cambridge History of the Cold War*, vol. 3, pp. 267–88. Cambridge, UK: Cambridge University Press.

Grant, Charles (1999) 'Transatlantic tensions', *Centre for European Reform Bulletin* 9, www.cer.org. uk/publications/archive/bulletin-article/1999/transatlantic-tensions (accessed 15 November 2011).

Hanhimäki, Jussi M. (2003) 'They can write it in Swahili: Kissinger, the Soviets, and the Helsinki accords, 1973–1975', *Journal of Transatlantic Studies* 1(1): 37–58.

Hanhimäki, Jussi and Odd Arne Westad (eds) (2004) *The Cold War: A History in Documents and Eyewitness Accounts*. Oxford: Oxford UP.

Hanhimäki, Jussi, Georges-Henri Soutou and Basil Germond (eds) (2010) *The Routledge Handbook of Transatlantic Security*. Abingdon: Routledge.

Holland, R. (1985) *European Decolonization 1918–1981: An Introductory Survey*. Basingstoke, UK: Macmillan.

Johnson, Lyndon Baines (1972) *The Vantage Point: Perspectives of the Presidency 1963–1969*. London: Weidenfeld and Nicolson.

Kagan, Robert (2002) 'Power and weakness', *Policy Review* 113, www.hoover.org/publications/ policy-review/article/7107 (accessed 15 November 2011).

Kagan, Robert (2003) *Of Paradise and Power: America and Europe in the New World Order*. New York: Knopf.

Kennan, George F. (1996) *At a Century's Ending: Reflections 1982–1995*. New York: Norton.

Lindeman, M., William Rose and Mark Malkasian (1993) *The Role of the United States in a Changing World: Choices for the 21st Century*. New York: William C. Brown.

Logevall, Fredrik (2003) 'The American effort to draw European states into the war', in Christopher Goscha and Maurice Vaïsse (eds), *La Guerre du Vietnam et l'Europe, 1963–1973*, pp. 3–16. Brussels, Belgium: Bruylant.

Loth, Wilfried (2002) *Overcoming the Cold War: A History of Détente, 1950–1991*. Basingstoke, UK: Palgrave.

Lundestad, Geir (1998) *'Empire' by Integration: The United States and European Integration, 1945–1997*. Oxford: Oxford University Press.

Lundestad, Geir (2003) *The United States and Western Europe since 1945: From 'Empire' by Invitation to Transatlantic Drift*. Oxford: Oxford University Press.

Möckli, Daniel (2010) 'Asserting Europe's distinct identity: The EC nine and Kissinger's year of Europe', in Matthias Schulz and Thomas A. Schwartz (eds), *The Strained Alliance: US–European Relations from Nixon to Carter*, pp. 195–220. Cambridge and New York: Cambridge University Press.

Niedhart, Gottfried (2008) 'Ostpolitik and its impact on the Federal Republic's relationship with the West', in Wilfried Loth and Georges-Henri Soutou (eds), *The Making of Détente: Eastern and Western Europe in the Cold War, 1965–1975*, pp. 117–32. London: Routledge.

Noble, Alastair (2010) 'Kissinger's year of Europe, Britain's year of choice', in Matthias Schulz and Thomas A. Schwartz (eds), *The Strained Alliance: US–European Relations from Nixon to Carter*, pp. 221–35. Cambridge and New York: Cambridge University Press.

Peyrefitte, Alain (1994–2000) *C'était de Gaulle*, 3 vols. Paris: Fayard.

Powaski, Ronald E. (2000) *Return to Armageddon: The United States and the Nuclear Arms Race, 1981–1999*. Oxford: Oxford University Press.

Reagan, Ronald (1990) *An American Life*. New York: Simon and Schuster.

Reynolds, David (1994) *The Origins of the Cold War in Europe*. New Haven, CT: Yale University Press.

Sarotte, Mary Elise (2009) *1989: The Struggle to Create Post-Cold War Europe*. Princeton, NJ: Princeton University Press.

Sarotte, Mary Elise (2010) 'Not one inch eastward? Bush, Baker, Kohl, Genscher, Gorbachev, and the origin of Russian resentment toward NATO enlargement in February 1990', *Diplomatic History* 34(1): 119–40.

Schulz, Matthias and Thomas A. Schwartz (eds) (2010) *The Strained Alliance: US–European Relations from Nixon to Carter*. Cambridge and New York: Cambridge University Press.

Steel, Ronald 'The domestic core of foreign policy', *Atlantic Monthly* 275(6): 84–92.

Wells, Samuel F. (2006) 'From Euromissiles to Maastricht: The Policies of Reagan–Bush and Mitterrand', in Helga Haftendorn, Georges-Henri Soutou, Stephen F. Szabo and Samuel F. Wells Jr. (eds), *The Strategic Triangle: France, Germany, and the United States in the Shaping of the New Europe*, pp. 287–307. Washington, DC: Woodrow Wilson Center Press.

Winand, Pascaline (1993) *Eisenhower, Kennedy, and the United States of Europe*. Basingstoke, UK: Macmillan.

Young, John W. (2010) 'Western Europe and the end of the Cold War', in Melvyn P. Leffler and Odd Arne Westad, *The Cambridge History of the Cold War*, vol. 3, pp. 289–310. Cambridge, UK: Cambridge University Press.

Zanchetta, Barbara (2010) 'The United States and the "loss" of Iran: Repercussions on transatlantic security', in Jussi Hanhimäki, Georges-Henri Soutou and Basil Germond (eds), *The Routledge Handbook of Transatlantic Security*, pp. 138–52. Abingdon, UK: Routledge.

Zimmermann, Hubert (2009) 'The improbable permanence of a commitment: America's troop presence in Europe during the Cold War', *Journal of Cold War Studies* 11(1): 3–27.

Zubok, Vladislav M. (1996) 'The Soviet Union and European integration from Stalin to Gorbachev', *Journal of European Integration History* 2(1): 85–98.

Suggested further reading

Aldrich, Richard J. (2001) *The Hidden Hand: Britain, America, and Cold War Secret Intelligence.* London: John Murray.

Andrews, David M. (eds) (2008) *Orderly Change: International Monetary Relations since Bretton Woods.* Ithaca, NY: Cornell University Press.

Asmus, Ronald (2004) *Opening NATO's Door: How the Alliance Remade Itself for a New Era.* New York: Columbia University Press.

Bacevich, Andrew J. (2002) *American Empire: The Realities and Consequences of US Diplomacy.* Cambridge, MA: Harvard University Press.

Ball, Desmond (1987) *Strategic Nuclear Targeting.* Ithaca, NY: Cornell University Press.

Baylis, John, James Wirtz, Eliot Cohen and Colin Gray (2002) *Strategy in the Contemporary World: An Introduction to Strategic Studies.* Oxford: Oxford University Press.

Becker, William H. and Samuel F. Wells (1984) *Economics and World Power: An Assessment of American Diplomacy since 1789.* New York: Columbia University Press.

Beschloss, Michael (1991) *The Crisis Years: Kennedy and Khrushchev 1960–1963.* New York: HarperCollins.

Beschloss, Michael and Strobe Talbott (1993) *At the Highest Levels: The Inside Story of the End of the Cold War.* Boston, MA: Little Brown.

Best, Antony, Jussi M. Hanhimäki, Joseph A. Maiolo and Kirsten E. Schulze (eds) (2008) *International History of the Twentieth Century and Beyond.* London: Routledge.

Beylerian, Onnig and Jacques Lévesque (2004) *Inauspicious Beginnings: Principal Powers and International Security Institutions after the Cold War, 1989–1999.* Montreal: McGill.

Bozo, Frédéric (2004) 'Before the Wall: French diplomacy and the last decade of the Cold War, 1979–89', in Olav Njølstad (ed), *The Last Decade of the Cold War: From Conflict Escalation to Conflict Transformation*, pp. 288–316. London: Frank Cass.

Bozo, Frédéric, Marie-Pierre Rey, N. Piers Ludlow and Leopoldo Nuti (eds) (2009) *Europe and the End of the Cold War: A Reappraisal.* London: Routledge.

Calleo, David (1982) *The German Problem reconsidered: Germany and the World Order, 1870 to the Present.* Cambridge, UK: Cambridge University Press.

Calleo, David (2001) *Rethinking Europe's Future.* Princeton, NJ: Princeton University Press.

Clark, Wesley (2003) *Winning Modern War: Iraq, Terrorism, and the American Empire.* New York: Public Affairs.

Costigliola, Frank (1987) *Awkward Dominion: American Political, Economic, and Cultural Relations with Europe, 1919–1933.* Ithaca, NY: Cornell University Press.

Costigliola, Frank (1992) *France and the United States: The Cold Alliance since World War II.* New York: Twayne.

Crockatt, Richard (1995) *The Fifty Years War: The United States and the Soviet Union in World Politics, 1941–1991.* London: Routledge.

Daalder, Ivo (2000) *Winning Ugly: NATO's War to Save Kosovo.* Washington, DC: Brookings.

Daalder, Ivo and James Lindsay (2003) *America Unbound: The Bush Revolution in Foreign Policy.* Washington, DC: Brookings.

Daalder, Ivo, Nicole Gnesotto and Philip H. Gordon (eds) (2005) *Crescent of Crisis: US–European Strategy for the Greater Middle East.* Washington, DC: Brookings.

De Grazia, Victoria (2005) *Irresistible Empire: America's Advance through Twentieth-Century Europe.* Cambridge, MA: Belknap Press.

Del Pero, Mario and Federico Romero (eds) (2007) *Le crisi transatlantiche. Continuità e trasformazioni.* Rome: Edizioni di storia e letteratura.

Dimbleby, David and David Reynolds (1988) *An Ocean Apart: The Relationship between Britain and America in the Twentieth Century.* London: Hodder and Stoughton.

Dinan, Desmond (ed.) (2006) *Origins and Evolution of the European Union.* Oxford: Oxford University Press.

Dinan, Desmond (2010) *Ever Closer Union: An Introduction to European Integration*. Boulder, CO: Lynne Rienner.

Dobson, Alan P. (1995) *Anglo-American Relations in the Twentieth Century: Of Friendship, Conflict and the Rise and Decline of Superpowers*. London: Routledge.

Dobson, Alan P. (2001) *US Foreign Policy since 1945*. London: Routledge.

Dorfman, Andrew and Kaufman, Joyce (2010) *The Future of Transatlantic Relations: Perceptions, Policy and Practice*. Palo Alto, CA: Stanford University Press.

Duchêne, François (1994) *Jean Monnet: The First Statesman of Interdependence*. New York: Norton.

Dumbrell, John and Axel R. Schäfer (ed.) (2009) *America's 'Special Relationships': Foreign and Domestic Aspects of the Politics of Alliance*. London: Routledge.

Dunne, Tim, Michael Cox and Ken Booth (1998) *The Eighty Years' Crisis: International Relations 1919–1999*. Cambridge, UK: Cambridge University Press.

Eckes, Alfred E. and Thomas W. Zeiler (2003) *Globalization and the American Century*. Cambridge, UK: Cambridge University Press.

Ferguson, Niall (2004) *Colossus: The Price of America's Empire*. New York: Penguin.

Freedman, Lawrence (1983) *The Evolution of Nuclear Strategy*. London: Macmillan.

Freedman, Lawrence (ed.) (2002) *Superterrorism: Policy Responses*. Malden, MA: Blackwell.

Gaddis, John Lewis (1992) *The United States and the End of the Cold War: Implications, Reconsiderations, Provocations*. New York: Oxford University Press.

Gaddis, John Lewis (2000) *The United States and the Origins of the Cold War, 1941–1947*. New York: Columbia University Press.

Gaddis, John Lewis (2004) *Surprise, Security, and the American Experience*. Cambridge, MA: Harvard University Press.

Gardner, Lloyd C. and Ted Gittinger (eds) (2000) *International Perspectives on Vietnam*. College Station, TX: Texas University Press.

Garton Ash, Timothy (1993) *In Europe's Name: Germany and the Divided Continent*. London: Jonathan Cape.

Garton Ash, Timothy (2004) *Free World: Why a Crisis of the West Reveals the Opportunity of our Time*. London: Allen Lane.

Gearson, John and Kori Schake (eds) (2002) *The Berlin Wall Crisis: Perspectives on Cold War Alliances*. Basingstoke, UK: Palgrave.

Gillingham, John (2004) *European Integration, 1950–2003: Superstate or New Market Economy?* Cambridge, UK: Cambridge University Press.

Goldgeier, James M. (1999) *Not Whether but When: The US Decision to Enlarge NATO*. Washington, DC: Brookings.

Gordon, Philip and Jeremy Shapiro (2004) *Allies at War: America, Europe, and the Crisis over Iraq*. New York: McGraw Hill.

Goscha, Christopher and Maurice Vaïsse (eds) (2003) *La Guerre du Vietnam et l'Europe, 1963–1973*. Brussels, Belgium: Bruylant.

Grosser, Alfred (1980) *The Western Alliance: European-American Relations since 1945*. New York: Continuum, 1980.

Haftendorn, Helga (2006) *Coming of Age: German Foreign Policy since 1945*. Lanham, MD: Rowman & Littlefield.

Haftendorn, Helga, Georges-Henri Soutou, Stephen F. Szabo and Samuel F. Wells Jr. (eds) (2006) *The Strategic Triangle: France, Germany, and the United States in the Shaping of the New Europe*. Washington, DC: Woodrow Wilson Center Press.

Hanhimäki, Jussi (1997) *Scandinavia and the United States: An Insecure Friendship*. New York: Twayne.

Hanhimäki, Jussi (2004) *The Flawed Architect: Henry Kissinger and American Foreign Policy*. New York: Oxford UP.

Hanhimäki, Jussi (2008) 'Conservative goals, revolutionary outcomes: the paradox of détente', *Cold War History* 8(4): 503–12.

Harrison, Hope M. (2003) *Driving the Soviets Up the Wall: Soviet–East German Relations, 1953–1961*, Princeton, NJ: Princeton University Press.

Hitchcock, William I. (1998) *France Restored: Cold War Diplomacy and the Quest for Leadership in Europe*. Chapel Hill, NC: University of North Carolina Press.

Hitchcock, William I. (2004) *The Struggle for Europe: The Turbulent History of a Divided Continent, 1945 to the Present*. New York: Anchor Books.

Hoffmann, Stanley and Frédéric Bozo (2004) *Gulliver Unbound: America's Imperial Temptation and the War in Iraq*. Lanham, MD: Rowman and Littlefield.

Hogan, Michael (1987) *The Marshall Plan: America, Britain, and the Reconstruction of Western Europe, 1947–1952*. Cambridge, UK: Cambridge University Press.

Hogan, Michael and Thomas G. Paterson (eds) (1991) *Explaining the History of American Foreign Relations*. Cambridge, UK: Cambridge University Press.

Hunt, Michael (1987) *Ideology and US Foreign Policy*. New Haven, CT: Yale University Press.

Hunt, Michael (1996) *Crises in US Foreign Policy: An International History Reader*. New Haven, CT: Yale University Press.

Ikenberry, John and Risse, Thomas (2008) *The End of the West? Crisis and Change in the Atlantic Order*. Ithaca, NY: Cornell University Press.

Iriye, Akira (2002) *Global Community: The Role of International Organizations in the Making of the Contemporary World*. Berkeley, CA: University of California Press.

Iriye, Akira and Bruce Mazlish (2005) *The Global History Reader*. New York: Routledge.

Johnson, Chalmers (2004) *Blowback: The Costs and Consequences of the American Empire*. London: Time Warner.

Junker, Detlef (ed.) (2004) *The United States and Germany in the Era of the Cold War: A Handbook*, 2 vols. Washington, DC: German Historical Institute.

Kaplan, Lawrence S. (1984) *NATO: The Formative Years*. Lexington, KY: University Press of Kentucky.

Kennedy, Paul (1989) *The Rise and Fall of Great Powers: Economic Change and Military Conflict from 1500 to 2000*. London: Fontana Press.

Kupchan, Charles A. (2003) *The End of the American Era: US Foreign Policy and the Geopolitics of the Twenty-First Century*. New York: Vintage.

LaFeber, Walter (1994) *The American Age: United States Foreign Policy at Home and Abroad: 1750 to the Present*. New York: Norton.

Lamberton Harper, John (1996) *American Visions of Europe: Franklin D. Roosevelt, George F. Kennan, and Dean G. Acheson*. New York: Cambridge University Press.

Lebow, Richard Ned and Geoffrey Parker (eds) (2006) *Unmaking the West: 'What-If' Scenarios that Rewrite World History*. Ann Arbor, MI: University of Michigan Press.

Lebow, Richard Ned and Janice Gross Stein (1994) *We All Lost the Cold War*. Princeton, NJ: Princeton University Press.

Leffler, Melvyn P (2010) *A Preponderance of Power: National Security, the Truman Administration, and the Cold War*. Palo Alto, CA: Stanford University Press.

Leffler, Melvyn P. and Odd Arne Westad (2010) *The Cambridge History of the Cold War*, 3 vols. Cambridge, UK: Cambridge University Press.

Lévesque, Jacques (2010) 'The East European revolutions of 1989', in Melvyn P. Leffler and Odd Arne Westad (eds), *The Cambridge History of the Cold War*, vol. 3, pp. 311–32. Cambridge, UK: Cambridge University Press.

Loth, Wilfried and Soutou, Georges-Henri (eds) (2008) *The Making of Détente: Eastern and Western Europe in the Cold War, 1965–1975*. London: Routledge.

Ludlow, N. Piers (2006) 'From deadlock to dynamism: the European Community in the 1980s', in Desmond Dinan (ed.), *The Origins and Evolution of the EU*, pp. 218–32. Oxford: Oxford University Press.

Lundestad, Geir (ed.) (2008) *Just Another Major Crisis? The United States and Europe since 2000*. New York: Oxford University Press.

Markovits, Andrei S. (2007) *Uncouth Nation: Why Europe Dislikes America*. Princeton, NJ: Princeton University Press.

Marquand, David (2011) *The End of the West: The Once and Future Europe*. Princeton, NJ: Princeton University Press.

Mastny, Vojtech (1996) *The Cold War and Soviet Insecurity: The Stalin Years*. New York: Oxford University Press.

Mastny, Vojtech and Malcolm Byrne (eds) (2005) *A Cardboard Castle? An Inside History of the Warsaw Pact,1955–1991*. New York: Central European University Press.

Mazower, Mark (2000) *Dark Continent: Europe's Twentieth Century*. New York: Vintage.

McCormick, John (2004) *The European Union: Politics and Policies*. Cambridge, MA: Westview Press.

McCormick, John (2005) *Understanding the European Union: A Concise Introduction*. Basingstoke, UK: Palgrave Macmillan.

McGuire, Steven and Michael Smith (2008) *The European Union and the United States: Competition and Convergence in the Global Arena*. Basingstoke, UK: Palgrave.

Mearsheimer, John (2001) *The Tragedy of Great Power Politics*. New York: Norton.

Milward, Alan S. (1984) *The Reconstruction of Western Europe, 1945–1951*. London: Methuen, 1984.

Milward, Alan S. (1994) *The European Rescue of the Nation State*. London: Routledge.

Moravcsik, Andrew (1999) *The Choice for Europe: Social Purpose and State Power from Messina to Maastricht*. London: UCL Press.

Newhouse, John (1997) *Europe Adrift*. New York: Pantheon.

Newhouse, John (2004) *Imperial America: The Bush Assault on the World Order*. New York: Vintage.

Ninkovich, Frank (1981) *The Diplomacy of Ideas: US Foreign Policy and Cultural Relations*. Cambridge, UK: Cambridge University Press, 1981.

Nitze, Paul H. (1989) *From Hiroshima to Glasnost: At the Center of Decision*. New York: Grove Weidenfeld.

Njølstad, Olav (ed.) (2004) *The Last Decade of the Cold War: From Conflict Escalation to Conflict Transformation*. London: Frank Cass.

Njølstad, Olav (2004) 'The Carter legacy: Entering the Second Cold War', in Olav Njølstad (ed), *The Last Decade of the Cold War: From Conflict Escalation to Conflict Transformation*, pp. 196–225. London: Frank Cass.

Nye, Joseph S. (2002) *The Paradox of American Power: Why the World's Only Superpower Can't Do it Alone*. Oxford: Oxford University Press.

Nye, Joseph S. (2004) *Soft Power: The Means to Success in World Politics*. New York: Public Affairs.

Pells, Richard (1997) *Not Like Us: How Europeans have Loved, Hated and Transformed American Culture since World War II*. New York: Basic Books.

Pond, Elizabeth (2002) *The Rebirth of Europe*. Washington, DC: Brookings.

Powaski, Ronald E. (1994) *The Entangling Alliance: The United States and European Security, 1950–1993*. Westport, CT: Greenwood.

Quandt, William (2003) *Peace Process: American Diplomacy and the Arab–Israeli Conflict since 1967*. Los Angeles, CA: University of California Press.

Renwick, Robin (1996) *Fighting with Allies: America and Britain in Peace and War*. Basingstoke, UK: Macmillan.

Rey, Marie-Pierre (2009) 'Gorbachev's new thinking and Europe, 1985–1989', in Frédéric Bozo, Marie-Pierre Rey, N. Piers Ludlow and Leopoldo Nuti (eds) *Europe and the End of the Cold War: A Reappraisal*, pp. 23–35. London: Routledge.

Risse-Kappen, Thomas, et al. (eds) (2002) *Handbook of International Relations*. London: Sage.

Rosenberg, Emily (1984) *Spreading the American Dream: American Economic and Cultural Expansion, 1890–1945*. New York: Hill and Wang.

Ryan, David (2003) *The United States and Europe in the Twentieth Century*. Harlow, UK: Pearson-Longman.

Schmidt, Gustav (ed.) (2001) *A History of NATO: The First Fifty Years*. Basingstoke, UK: Palgrave.

Schoenborn, Benedikt (2007) *La mésentente apprivoisée: De Gaulle et les Allemands, 1963–1969*. Paris: Presses Universitaires de France.

Schwartz, Thomas A. (2003) *Lyndon Johnson and Europe: In the Shadow of Vietnam*. Cambridge, MA: Harvard University Press.

Schwartz, Thomas A. (2008) 'Legacies of détente', *Cold War History* 8(4): 513–25.

Shain, Martin (ed.) (2001) *The Marshall Plan: Fifty Years After*. New York: Palgrave.

Soutou, Georges-Henri (2001) *La guerre de Cinquante Ans: Les relations East-Ouest 1943–1990*. Paris: Fayard.

Spohr Readman, Kristina (2010) 'Germany and the politics of the neutron bomb, 1975–1979', *Diplomacy and Statecraft* 21(2): 259–85.

Suri, Jeremi (2003) *Power and Protest: Global Revolution and the Rise of Détente*, Cambridge, MA: Harvard University Press.

Thomas, Daniel C. (2001) *The Helsinki Effect: International Norms, Human Rights, and the Demise of Communism*. Princeton, NJ: Princeton University Press.

Trachtenberg, Marc (1999) *A Constructed Peace: The Making of the European Settlement, 1945 1963*. Princeton, NJ: Princeton University Press.

Urwin, D. W. (1995) *The Community of Europe: A History of European Integration since 1945*. London: Longman.

Vaïsse, Maurice (ed.) (1993) *L'Europe et la crise de Cuba*. Paris: Armand Colin.

Wagnleitner, Reinhold (1994) *Coca-Colonization and the Cold War: The Cultural Mission of the United States in Austria after the Second World War*. Chapel Hill, NC: University of North Carolina Press.

Wolfrum, Edgar (2009) *Die Mauer: Geschichte einer Teilung*. Munich, Germany: Beck.

Woodward, Bob (2002) *Bush at War*. New York: Simon and Schuster.

Woodward, Bob (2006) *State of Denial*. New York: Simon and Schuster.

Young, John W. (1992) *Cold War Europe 1945–89: A Political History*. London: Arnold.

Young, John W. (1993) *Britain and European Unity, 1945–1992*. Basingstoke, UK: Macmillan.

Zubok, Vladislav and Constantine Pleshakov (2001) *Inside the Kremlin's Cold War: From Stalin to Khrushchev*. Cambridge, MA: Harvard University Press.

Index

Pages containing figures and tables are presented in *italic* type. Text within boxes is indicated by **bold** type. As the whole book concerns the United States, there are no entries under this heading. However, the individual areas and countries within Europe are listed individually.